fun with the family
North Carolina

Praise for a previous edition of *Fun with the Family North Carolina*

"The author, a lifelong explorer of our state, knows all of
North Carolina's highways and byways firsthand, and
his energetic style keeps the guide entertaining throughout."
—*Our State* magazine

Help Us Keep This Guide Up to Date

We would love to hear from you concerning your experiences with this guide and how you feel it could be improved and kept up to date. Please send your comments and suggestions to:

editorial@GlobePequot.com

Thanks for your input, and happy travels!

fun with the family
North Carolina

hundreds of ideas for day trips with the kids

Seventh Edition

James L. Hoffman

travel

Guilford, Connecticut

All the information in this guidebook is subject to change. We recommend that you call ahead to obtain current information before traveling.

Editor: Kevin Sirois
Project Editor: Heather Santiago
Layout: Joanna Beyer
Text design: Nancy Freeborn and Linda R. Loiewski
Maps: Rusty Nelson © Morris Book Publishing, LLC
Spot photography throughout © Photodisc and © RubberBall Productions

ISSN 1539-9044
ISBN 978-0-7627-7331-2

Printed in the United States of America
10 9 8 7 6 5 4 3 2

For Kaitlyn, Michaela, Jessie, Mike, Melissa, and Bonnie . . .
I love where we've been and look forward to many miles ahead.

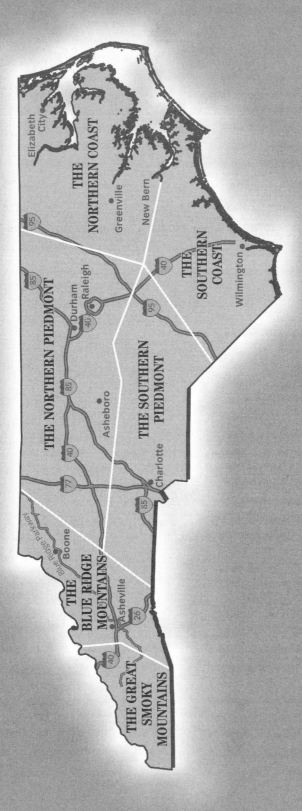

THE
NORTHERN COAST

Elizabeth
City

Greenville

New Bern

THE
SOUTHERN
COAST

Wilmington

THE NORTHERN PIEDMONT

Durham
Raleigh

Asheboro

THE SOUTHERN PIEDMONT

Charlotte

THE
BLUE RIDGE
MOUNTAINS

Boone

Blue Ridge Parkway

Asheville

THE GREAT
SMOKY
MOUNTAINS

Contents

About the Author

James L. Hoffman is a lifelong resident of North Carolina. He is a freelance writer and marketing director for Daniel Stowe Botanical Garden in Belmont. Hoffman has also been a newspaper reporter and editor and worked in marketing and public relations at Charlotte's Discovery Place science center. He is the author of *Day Trips from Raleigh-Durham* and *Day Trips from Charlotte,* also published by Globe Pequot Press. He lives in Gastonia with his wife, Bonnie. They have five children.

Acknowledgments

With this edition we continue to strive to make a more user-friendly guide with updated hours, admission information, and other helpful details. I would like to thank all the people who have helped make this book possible. Originally, this work would not have been possible without many members of my family, including my parents, K. R. and Pat Hoffman, as well as Sara Pitzer, Dana Teague, and many other people throughout the years. The previous editions of this work would not have been possible without the assistance of my family and friends across the state, who recommended numerous hotels and restaurants. I am also grateful for the North Carolina Department of Tourism and all of the travel bureaus across the state too numerous to mention here, as well as a host of park rangers, museum guides, information center staffs, hotel clerks and concierges, waiters, and many, many others.

Introduction

It seems to me that living in North Carolina is a privilege. My family and I are particularly lucky because we live in the Piedmont, where you can easily reach the mountains, the beaches, or the state's larger cities for travel and entertainment. I have many fond memories of my life here as a child, as a college student, and as an adult with my own family. We've been pretty much everywhere in the Tar Heel State, from Murphy to Manteo, as the expression goes. We've enjoyed the majesty of the mountains and the history and beauty of the coast. But one interesting thing occurred in the process of writing this book. I would ask the kids if they remembered going to the Native American village in the mountains or the loggerhead turtle that nested in front of the rental beach house, and almost every time the response would be a puzzled "no." That could be due to their young ages, or it could be a clever ploy to get me to take them back to these places. Oh well, I guess we'll have to do it all again.

Doing all that's in this book won't be much of a problem since the family has grown considerably since the first edition. Having grown children, one in elementary school, and a couple in between makes for challenging vacation planning. We've fared well so far and hope we'll continue to explore together even as the older children get jobs and start their own families.

Traveling with children, especially with a large span of ages, creates unique challenges. The ubiquitous onboard or portable DVD player certainly does make life easier, but I've always been hesitant that it would reduce our precious quality time together and dumb down the vacation. The greatest joy we've found through the years is learning things about places we haven't been before. Utilize resources in planning. Take time to learn about the area in which you'll be traveling and share that along the way. Also, plan enough time to make short side trips. There's plenty in the pages that follow that make for good stops where you can stretch your legs and let the kids sip on a juice box.

Of course, there is always a need for quiet time. For that, you might download files for your MP3 player from www.netlibrary.com. You'll find everything from Dr. Seuss to Harry Potter, so just take a look. Or even pick a book and read aloud.

Our family also creates great memories by playing silly word games, like Count the Cows, Hangman, or I-Spy. If you need to rekindle those memories or figure out some rules, check out the Ultimate Road Trip Games at www.ultimateroadtripgames.com. Still, a healthy supply of crayons, activity books, and travel games can keep the mood in the car light and fun. You can keep those activities close at hand with a handy lap tray (made by Crayola and probably others as well) with a padded bottom and pockets for crayons, coloring books, and other items. Pocketed smocks that fit over the back of the front seat for easy access by backseat passengers are also commercially available.

For **Quick Reference**

Throughout this guide you will find recommendations for places to stay. We've mostly eliminated the larger chain accommodations, assuming one of these chains has already proven its efficiency. Accommodations listed throughout this guide are ones with more local flair that you might not come across easily. We have tried to include a variety of price ranges, but in case you are set in your ways, here's how to get in touch with the larger chains that are found fairly prevalently throughout the state:

- **Best Western.** (800) 780-7234; www.bestwestern.com

- **Comfort Inn and Suites, Econolodge, Quality Inn, Clarion, and Sleep Inn.** (877) 424-6423; www.choicehotels.com

- **Days Inn.** (888) 440-2021; www.daysinn.com

- **Hampton Inns and Suites.** (800) 426-7866; www.hamptoninn.com

- **Holiday Inn and Holiday Inn Express.** (877) 424-2449; www.ichotelsgroup .com

- **La Quinta Inns and Suites.** (800) 753-3757; www.lq.com

- **Marriott (including Residence Inn).** (888) 236-2427; www.marriott.com

I've divided the state into six travel areas that roughly resemble the state's geographic regions. We begin our journey in the west in the Great Smoky Mountains and continue through the Blue Ridge Mountains, both part of the Appalachian Range. Next we go to the Northern Piedmont, traveling from west to east, and then back to the Southern Piedmont, where we again travel from west to east. Finally we move into the coastal plain, which I've divided into the Southern Coast and the Northern Coast. Traveling this route from south to north on the coast would take quite some time and require a number of ferry rides.

Each chapter is organized geographically, so you can use this guide to easily plan your itinerary or to find a nearby adventure by flipping backward or forward a page or two. In addition, you will find two indices—one general and one by type of activity—to help you select appropriate attractions and events for your family.

You will also find listed throughout the book recommended ages for attractions and events. In addition, I've included reference maps to help get you on the road. I wrote this book with the help of the map created by the North Carolina Department of Transportation, which is distributed **free** of charge. You can obtain a copy of it and more information by calling (919) 733-7600, or (800) 847-4848 if you are outside North Carolina, or by going to www.visitnc.com.

I encourage you to use the Internet as a resource as much as you are able. Websites from hotels and vacation realtors often provide peace of mind by giving you a look inside your accommodations. I've also included the web addresses for as many attractions and visitor centers as possible, but don't let that hamper your sense of adventure. I encourage you to get out, take a chance, and see what might be off the beaten path.

One more thing: Have a great time exploring the great state of North Carolina!

Lodging, Restaurants & Attractions Fees

In the "Where to Eat" and "Where to Stay" sections, dollar signs indicate general price ranges. For meals, the prices are for individual adult entrees. For lodging, the rates are for a double room, for a family of four, with no meals, unless otherwise indicated; rates for lodging may be higher during peak vacation seasons and holidays. Always inquire about family and group rates and package deals that may include amusement park tickets, discounts for area attractions, and tickets for concerts and other performing arts events.

Because admission fees change frequently, this book offers a general idea of the prices charged by each attraction.

Rates for Lodging

$	less than $100
$$	$100 to $150
$$$	$150 to $200
$$$$	more than $200

Rates for Restaurants

$	most entrees under $10
$$	$10 to $15
$$$	$15 to $20
$$$$	most more than $20

Rates for Attractions

$	less than $5
$$	$5 to $10
$$$	$10 to $20
$$$$	more than $20

Attractions Key

The following is a key to the icons found throughout the text.

SWIMMING		FOOD	
BOATING/BOAT TOUR		LODGING	
HISTORIC SITE		CAMPING	
HIKING/WALKING		MUSEUM	
FISHING		PERFORMING ARTS	
BIKING		SPORTS/ATHLETICS	
AMUSEMENT PARK		PICNICKING	
HORSEBACK RIDING		PLAYGROUND	
SKIING/WINTER SPORTS		SHOPPING	
PARK		PLANTS/GARDENS/NATURE TRAILS	
ANIMAL VIEWING		FARM	

The Great Smoky Mountains

The Great Smoky Mountains are just south of heaven. The postcard picturesque beauty of the area is unmatched as you climb to heights of more than 6,000 feet—some of the highest points in the eastern US. The region includes the most popular national park in the country as well as one of the last virgin wildernesses. The trout fishing is great, too. Hiking trails, gorgeous flowing waterfalls, and crystal-like streams are waiting around just about every corner.

Take a wild rafting adventure down one of a number of rivers, mine precious stones, ride an old-fashioned railway, or visit a theme park. The heritage of the area is as

Jim's
Top Picks in the Great Smoky Mountains

1. The Great Smoky Mountain Railway

2. Whitewater rafting on the Nantahala River

3. Oconaluftee Indian Village

4. Santa's Land Family Fun Park and Zoo

5. Tubing at Deep Creek in the Great Smoky Mountains National Park

6. Folkmoot USA

7. Mining in Franklin

8. Autumn in the mountains

9. Joyce Kilmer Memorial Forest

10. Fontana Village

THE GREAT SMOKY MOUNTAINS

important to its people as it is anywhere. Explore a Cherokee Indian reservation or learn about the Europeans who settled in the area. And don't miss all the country food and crafts the Great Smoky Mountains offer.

Travel is generally slow in this area, as it is over most of the mountains of North Carolina. Don't try to take in too much at one time, or you'll spend all your time driving and miss all the fun. US 64 runs through the southern portion of the state and is your best bet for long travel. US 74 runs from the northeast portion of the region to intersect with US 64. It combines with several other highways along the way, so don't let that confuse you. US 441 bisects the area and runs north to south.

For More Information

Smoky Mountain Host. (800) 432-4678; www.visitsmokies.org.

Murphy

Nestled in the westernmost corner of North Carolina is Cherokee County, and Murphy is where we begin our excursion. First settled by the Cherokee Indians, Murphy, in a strange twist of fate, originated as Fort Butler, where the natives were gathered before setting out on the Trail of Tears. Today the town of fewer than 2,000 offers an abundance of opportunities for outdoor activities.

Cherokee County Historical Museum (ages 5 and up)
87 Peachtree St.; (828) 837-6792; www.cherokeecounty-nc.gov. Open 9 a.m. to 5 p.m. Mon through Fri. $.

Learn about the Cherokee Indians' presence in the western North Carolina mountains and about early American life at the Cherokee County Historical Museum. The museum features an extensive collection of more than 2,000 Native American artifacts and exhibits on early mountain life. Examine tools, housewares, arrowheads, peace pipes, and games used throughout those early years of North American settlement, in addition to displays that explain the Trail of Tears—a forced westward march of more than 70,000 Native Americans following the US Congress's 1830 passage of the Indian Removal Act.

Fields of the Wood (all ages)
Highway 294, southwest of Murphy; (828) 494-7855; www.fieldsofthewoodbiblepark.com. Open daily, generally from sunrise to sunset. Free.

The county's most unique attraction is billed as a biblical theme park covering 200 acres of mountainside. No flashy rides or games are to be found at the Fields of the Wood. It

Amazing
North Carolina Facts

The US Fish and Wildlife Service and the National Park Service attempted the reintroduction of the red wolf into the Great Smoky Mountains in 1991. However, none of the 30 pups born in the wild since 1992 are known to have survived. Since then, the Western North Carolina Nature Center, the North Carolina Zoo, and the North Carolina Museum of Natural Sciences have joined forces to study, breed, and release red wolves on the Alligator River in eastern North Carolina.

features the Ten Commandments displayed in concrete on one of those mountainsides, and the world's largest cross and altar. See a depiction of Christ's tomb and displays on biblical teachings. The park's Bible, book, and gift shop are appropriate for the park's content.

Hanging Dog Recreation Area (all ages)

Located on Hiwassee Lake, just 5 miles west of Murphy on US 64. Contact Nantahala National Forest at (828) 257-4200 for more information; www.fa.usda.gov. Free admission; camping $.

Centered around a lake with 180 miles of shoreline, Hanging Dog offers a large campground, a picnic area, an opportunity for swimming, and hiking and biking trails. Only small trailers are allowed at the campground.

Where to Eat

Doyle's Cedar Hill Restaurant. 925 Andrews Rd.; (828) 837-3400. With pub-style dining and a more formal restaurant, Doyle's is an adult hangout at night, but through dinnertime the staff caters to families with chicken, seafood, and salads. $$$

New Happy Garden Chinese Restaurant. 2056 Highway 19; (828) 837-0711. This is a traditional Americanized Chinese restaurant with a buffet, so if the kids don't go for chow mein, they'll find something they like. $

Papa's Pizza To Go. 530 US 64 West; (828) 837-3335. Papa's offers eat-in and take-out pizza as well as a variety of other items from sub sandwiches to gyros. You'll find several Papa's Pizzas in the area. $

ShoeBooties Cafe. 25 Peachtree St.; (828) 837-4589; www.shoebooties.com. Clean your plate of its steak or seafood, because you'll want to check out the homemade desserts here. The cafe sometimes offers live jazz on weekend nights. $–$$

Sweet Tooth. 658 Andrews Rd.; (828) 837-8615. Soft-serve and scooped ice cream along with frozen yogurt, shakes, and smoothies make this a perfect post-dinner stop. $

Where to Stay

Appalachia Lake Wilderness Vacations.
36 Lake Point Dr.; (888) 865-2537; www
.wlvcabins.com. A handful of two- and three-
bedroom luxury cabins overlook a small lake
and vistas of the Smoky Mountains.

Cobb Creek Cabins. 106 Cobb Circle, Murphy; (828) 837-0270. Located on an alpaca
ranch, the cabins with lots of character offer
options for overnights or full-week vaca-
tions. $$

Hawkesdene House. 381 Phillips Creek
Rd., Andrews; (800) 447-9549; www.hawkbb
.com. This luxury bed-and-breakfast is more
family oriented and includes cabins. Lunch
and dinner llama trips are offered in addition
to the accommodations. $$$

For More Information

**Cherokee County Chamber of Com-
merce.** (828) 837-2242; www.cherokee
countychamber.com.

Brasstown

Brasstown, located east of Murphy just south on US 64, is not only home to one of the
country's most respected folk art schools, it also bills itself as the Opossum Capital of the
World.

John C. Campbell Folk School (all ages)

**1 Folk School Rd.; (800) 365-5724; www.folkschool.org. Craft shop and history center open
8 a.m. to 5 p.m. Mon through Sat and 1 to 6 p.m. Sun. Admission to the campus is free,
but a fee is charged for many of the special events and instructional programs.**

The 365-acre campus is home to what is recognized as the nation's only instructional folk
program. The school, founded in 1925, has become an asset to this community of only
a few hundred residents and is on the National Register of Historic Places. A variety of
special events, celebrations, and presentations are held throughout the year. The biggest, the Fall Festival, is held the first weekend in October and features crafts, music, and
more. Visit many of the campus buildings anytime and perhaps see one of the famous
Brasstown carvers at work. The small museum of crafts in the log cabin, the sawmill,
and the millhouse are also open to the public. In addition, the school offers minicourses
lasting from two days to two weeks in blacksmithing, woodworking, pottery, wood carving, weaving, basketry, mountain music, folk dancing, gardening, jewelry making, and
folklore. Most short courses are offered on weekends, and a catalog of listings is available. Children 12 years and older and parents can take weeklong classes together during
special summer programs that include everything from basket making to boat building.
Campus visitors are welcome at the Olive Dame Campbell Dining Hall, too. The ringing of
a hand-forged bell located in the middle of campus signals the serving of each meal. The
staff serves a family-style meal, much of it from the college's organic garden, and visitors
dine alongside students. Reservations are required by calling (800) 365-5724 or (828)
837-2775 by 10 a.m. ($).

Opossum **Drop**

Since 1994 they've dropped a possum in Brasstown on New Year's Eve. It's a slightly warped iteration of New York City's celebration using what in parts of North Carolina is considered a delicacy—a live, safely encased opossum. The celebration held at Clay's Corner, a local retail establishment, includes bluegrass music, church choirs, the Miss Possum Contest that permits what appear to be male entries, and other family-friendly fun.

Hayesville

Travel east on US 64 and exit to the north.

Hayesville offers opportunities aplenty to get out on the lake or simply out-of-doors. Lake Chatuge, straddling the North Carolina–Georgia state line, offers facilities for camping, fishing, swimming, and picnicking. Find hiking trails, boat rentals, and a visitor center. **Jackrabbit Mountain** recreation area, off SR 1155 (located off Highway 175), offers facilities for trailers up to 22 feet long, with a few for trailers up to 32 feet. Jackrabbit has a sandy beach area as well as fishing access along the shoreline. If the sites are full at Jackrabbit, another nice campground is less than 30 miles east. **Standing Indian Mountain,** located just off US 64, offers remarkable trout fishing, hiking trails, and scenic drives around the area. The park has become popular for mountain biking enthusiasts, and has both wilderness and developed camping sites. Jackrabbit is open May through September; Standing Indian Mountain is open April through November. Call the Tusquittee Ranger Station at (828) 837-5152 for more information.

Nearby find **Tusquittee Campground and Cabins** (9594 Tusquittee Rd.), which provides another ideal opportunity to head to the great outdoors, particularly for families with young children or those who simply refuse to camp in a tent. The park, located just east of Hayesville, provides full-service log cabins, creekside camper cabins for more rustic living, and traditional trailer and tent camping sites. The campground also has a heated bathhouse, hiking trails, a swimming hole, a swing set, and equipment for badminton, tetherball, volleyball, and horseshoes. The campground is open year-round. Call (828) 389-8520 for more information or to make reservations.

Peacock Playhouse (ages 5 and up)

301 Church St.; (828) 389-8632; www.licklogplayers.org. $$–$$$.

While you're in or near Hayesville, check out the Peacock Playhouse, where the Licklog Players present productions throughout the year. Licklog Players is a volunteer organization, but the group produces professional-quality performances ranging from drama to musicals to comedy. The theater seats about 250 people for the shows, and the annual playbill always includes some family-oriented productions.

Where to Eat

Mika's Pizza. US 64 Bypass; (828) 389-6366; www.mikaspizza.com. Standard pizza fare is offered along with sandwiches and pasta dishes. $

Rib Country Restaurant. 495 US 64 Business; (828) 389-9597; www.ribcountrybbq .com. A cafeteria-style buffet is offered here along with daily specials, steaks, snow crab legs, and, of course, succulent baby back ribs. $$

Where to Stay

Chatuge Mountain Inn. US 64 East; (828) 389-9340; www.chatugemountaininn.net. This is a nice place outside town near the lake. It offers 14 units with two doubles or king bed. Each room has a refrigerator and microwave. $$–$$$

Lakeview Cottages and Marina. Highway 175; (828) 389-6314. This facility offers 9 cottages. One- and two-bedroom cottages are fully equipped with appliances, cooking utensils and dishes, and televisions. $$–$$$

For More Information

Clay County Chamber of Commerce. (828) 389-3704; www.claycounty-nc-chamber .com.

For more information on camping in the area, contact the **Nantahala National Forest** at (828) 257-4200; www.fs.usda.gov.

Franklin

Continuing east on US 64 and heading north on Highway 28 leads to the town of Franklin, seat of Macon County, billing itself as "The Gem Capital of the World."

In addition to the logging industry, tourism has become important to the Franklin-area economy. While accommodations—cottages, cabins, chalets, and vacation homes—fill the area, its natural beauty is still undisturbed. The biggest attractions for tourists are the mines that allow families to hunt for and retrieve genuine rubies, sapphires, and other native stones. Precious stones are sometimes imported to make the hunt more interesting. Nearly a dozen mining operations are open to tourists in the area. A few require digging, while others confine your gem hunting to a flume and a single bucket. Call ahead to find out if equipment is included in the mining fee, which varies from mine to mine. Rubber gloves and plastic bags or containers as well as hats since many flumes are in the sun will come in handy wherever you go. A change of shoes and clothes might also be a good idea, as mining can be muddy work. Some operations charge per bucket, while others have an admission fee and then charge a nominal per-bucket fee. Most are open during daylight hours, and one will likely be open any day of the week. Most mines operate April through October.

Franklin-Area **Mines**

- **Cherokee Ruby and Sapphire Mine.** 41 Cherokee Mine Rd.; (828) 349-2941; www.cherokeerubymine.com

- **Cowee Mountain Ruby Mine.** 6771 Sylva Rd.; (828) 369-5271; www.cowee mtnrubymine.com

- **Gold City Gem Mine.** 9410 Sylva Rd.; (828) 369-3905; www.goldcityamuse ment.com

- **Jackson Hole Trading Post.** Located on Highway 64 near Highway 28 between Franklin and Highlands; (828) 524-5850

- **Mason Mountain Mine (The Johnson's Place).** 5315 Bryson City Rd.; (828) 524-4570; www.tjrocks.org

- **Mason's Ruby and Sapphire Mine.** 6961 Upper Burningtown Rd.; (828) 369-9742; www.masonsrubyandsapphinemine.com

- **Rose Creek Mine & Campground.** 115 Terrace Ridge; (828) 349-3774; www .rosecreekmine.com

- **Sheffield Mine.** 385 Sheffield Farms Rd.; (828) 369-8383; www.sheffield mine.com

Franklin Gem and Mineral Museum (ages 5 and up)

25 Phillips St.; (828) 369-7831; www.fgmm.org. Open noon to 4 p.m. Mon through Sat, May through Oct; Sat only Nov through Apr. **Free.**

If you don't have much luck hunting for gems on your own, stop by one of the many shops in the area or at the Franklin Gem and Mineral Museum, located in the 1850 jail. The museum, operated by the Franklin Gem and Mineral Society, features displays of all the native stones and a little bit about the history of the area's development. Step into a dark room of glowing rocks, and examine a variety of artifacts from around the world related to the gem and mineral industry.

Mountain Glides (ages 14 and up)

306 Depot St.; (828) 349-0506. $$$$.

Sightseeing tours by Segway, a high-tech, self-balancing scooter-like form of transportation, take visitors through and around town almost effortlessly. Mountain Glides offers tours alongside the Little Tennessee River on the town greenway, up Town Hill, and down Main Street. Each guest gets his or her own Segway and must be at least 14 years of age, giving the older kids in the family something fun to do. Tours start at around $50 and sell out well in advance.

Scottish Tartan Museum and Heritage Center (ages 5 and up)

86 E. Main St.; (828) 524-7472; www.scottishtartans.org. Open 10 a.m. to 5 p.m. Mon through Sat year-round except for major holidays. $.

This museum takes you to the Scotland of old. The Scottish Tartan Museum and Heritage Center, in downtown Franklin, is an extension of the Scottish Tartans Society. The museum includes displays on the tartan and Highland dress from as far back as 1700, as well as displays on the evolution of the kilt, weapons, and more. A research library also provides information about the Scottish influence on the Appalachian and Cherokee cultures. Have a bit of Scottish background? Find your roots in the library that includes a rare book collection.

Smoky Mountain Center for the Performing Arts

1028 Georgia Rd.; (828) 524-1598; www.greatmountainmusic.com.

This contemporary state-of-the-art center for music, drama, and other entertainment opened in the heart of the Smokies with the purpose of providing wholesome family entertainment. Local theater groups and regional musicians appear regularly.

Where to Eat

The Boiler Room. 1024 Georgia Rd.; (828) 349-5555; www.boilerroomsteakhouse.com. The Boiler Room at The Factory game room features upscale dining in a family atmosphere where you can enjoy steaks, seafood, pasta, and gourmet desserts. $$

The City Restaurant. 1251 E. Main St.; (828) 524-4948. You'll want to get breakfast here. The menu offers a variety of down-home selections. $$

Gazebo Creekside Cafe. 44 Heritage Hollow Dr.; (828) 524-8783; www.gazebocreek sidecafe.com. Actually located in a green and white gazebo, the cafe has a children's menu that includes popular favorites like turkey and grilled cheese sandwiches, while the rest of the menu includes treats such as ginger salad. $

The Hungry Bear Restaurant. 33 Macon Center; (828) 369-2900. Cheesesteaks are the specialty of the house, but it also offers subs, salads, and wraps. Antique bikes and other memorabilia create decor for the casual eatery. $

Sunset Drive-In Restaurant. 498 Harrison Ave.; (828) 524-4842. Drive-ins are always fun when you can find them. $

Amazing
North Carolina Facts

In 1973 the emerald was selected as North Carolina's precious stone. A 1,438-carat emerald is the largest ever found in the state.

Where to Stay

Carolina Mountaintop Homes. 150 Deer Crossing Rd.; (800) 820-1210. Located just outside Franklin on 32 acres, this company offers some pet-friendly options. $$$

Colonial Inn. 3157 Georgia Rd.; (828) 524-6600. This inn, located on Highway 441, offers 42 rooms, with basic amenities, on one level. $$

The Franklin Motel. 17 W. Palmer St.; (828) 524-4431. Children under 12 stay **free** in this downtown motel. $$

Sapphire Inn. 761 E. Main St.; (800) 401-0072; www.thesapphireinn.com. The Sapphire is a simple hotel in the middle of town. It does have a pool. $$

For More Information

Franklin Area Chamber of Commerce. (828) 524-3161 or (866) 372-5546; www.franklin-chamber.com.

Highlands

From Franklin take US 64 east to Highlands.

This region includes a particularly pleasing portion of a 61-mile scenic byway that begins to the north in Almond—a 20-mile jaunt between Franklin and Highlands, the second-highest incorporated town in the eastern US. Bring along a picnic lunch—and don't forget the camera—for this ride. It takes about 40 minutes and is truly lovely. In Highlands you'll find two of the most photographed waterfalls in the area. Heading east from Franklin, first come to **Dry Falls** about 2 miles before Highlands. From the parking lot an easy paved trail leads behind and underneath the 75-foot falls. Next, about 1 mile down the road, come to **Bridal Veil Falls.** Drive behind the 120-foot falls, which you'll first see from the highway. You should be able to tell how this thin veil of running water got its name.

On the other side of the highway, about 2 miles to the west, are a campground and a picnic area. **Cliffside Lake** and **Van Hook Glade** offer picnic, camping, swimming, fishing, and hiking facilities. Call the Highlands Ranger at (828) 526-3765 or the National Forest Office at (828) 257-4200 if you need more information or assistance while in this area.

To complete the 61-mile tour, head north out of Franklin—that's west on US 64—to SR 1310, also referred to as Wayah Road. The drive takes you along Wayah Creek, which is mostly private, to **Wayah Bald**—the county's highest peak at 5,345 feet—named for the red wolves that once lived there. From here, hike part of the Appalachian Trail, have a picnic, see wildlife, and learn about how the natural beauty has been preserved despite more than a century of development.

Take FR 69, a gravel road not on state maps, 1 mile to see the **Wilson Lick Ranger Station.** To find it, head west out of Franklin on SR 1310. Built in 1913, it was the first ranger station in Nantahala National Forest. Go 3 more miles, park, and take the paved trail to **Wayah Bald Fire Tower.** This tower, built by the Civilian Conservation Corps

North Carolina **Fishing**

If you live outside North Carolina or you don't fish much, you can get a license to fish for up to three days. Most tackle stores can sell you the license best suited for your needs. Temporary licenses cost $5 per day for residents, $10 for nonresidents. You can buy them online at www.ncwildlife.org.

in the 1930s, provides a breathtaking view of the mountains of the Carolinas, as well as those of northern Georgia and southeastern Tennessee. A picnic area and two more hiking trails are located nearby. Some trails are more difficult than others, so check in with the **Wayah Ranger District** (828-524-6441) before you head out on any of them.

Your next destination should be **Nantahala Lake,** about 6 miles west of Wayah Bald on SR 1310. With about 29 miles of shoreline, this lake offers fishing and boating (but no swimming). Picnic facilities are available on either side of the lake, accessible via SR 1310. The Nantahala River feeds the lake and provides excellent trout fishing. A license with a trout stamp is required.

SR 1310 ends at Highway 19, near Andrews. Here finish your day trip and stop for a while to watch experienced water enthusiasts rafting, canoeing, and kayaking. A walkway grants an excellent view of the brave ones traversing Nantahala Falls.

Where to Eat

Fressers Eatery at Helen's Barn. 151 Helen's Barn Ave.; (828) 526-4188; www .fresserseateryhighlands.com. While many of Highlands' restaurants are upscale, Fressers is casual enough for the kids. The food is as fine as any, but it also includes a kids' menu of peanut butter and jelly and other favorites. The main lunch and dinner menus include burgers, salads, and steaks. $$$–$$$$

On the Verandah. 1536 Franklin Rd.; (828) 526-2338; www.ontheverandah.com. Even the children's menu is upscale here. Smaller portions of beef tenderloin and grilled shrimp are offered for them, while the adults can dine on filet mignon or coconut grilled shrimp. $$–$$$

Sports Page Sandwich Shoppe. 314 Main St.; (828) 526-3555; www

.sportspagesandwichshoppe.com. Drop in here for a quick lunch or a game-time meal. $–$$

Where to Stay

Highlands Suite Hotel. 205 E. Main St.; (800) 221-5078; www.highlandssuitehotel .com. Few of the inns and B&Bs in Highlands are suitable for children, but this hotel is. It is a very nice AAA-approved suite hotel with all the amenities you would expect, including your own whirlpool and fireplace. $$$$

Whiteside Cove Cottages. Whiteside Mountain Road; (800) 805-3558; www.whitesidecovecabins.com. Five handsome log cabins are offered at the base of Whiteside Mountain between Cashiers and Highlands. The cabins are pet friendly. $$

For More Information

Highlands Chamber of Commerce Visitor's Center. (828) 526-2114; www.highlandschamber.org.

Robbinsville

Traveling northwest of Nantahala Lake to the intersection of US 129 and Highway 143 takes drivers into the town of Robbinsville.

Camping

The US Forest Service operates several campgrounds near Joyce Kilmer Memorial Forest. Contact the Nantahala National Forest office at (828) 479-6431; www.fs.usda.gov.

To camp close to the forest, head to **Horse Cove Campground,** northwest of Robbinsville near the Slickrock Wilderness Area. In addition, **Cheoah Point Campground,** located on Santeetlah Lake off US 129, offers a host of recreational activities. Campsites cost $15 per night. Make reservations at www.recreation.gov. Horse Cove is open year-round, but Cheoah Point closes between October and April. **Tsali Trail and Camping Area,** located off Highway 28, has 41 campsites and offers restrooms and showers. Here you can hike, bike, and enjoy all the fun the lake has to offer. **Cable Cove,** located just east on Highway 28, is a smaller recreation area. Tsali and Cable Cove campgrounds are open April through October.

Joyce Kilmer Memorial Forest

Call the forest ranger's office at (828) 479-6431. Free.

Robbinsville lies at the eastern edge of one of the most impressive, undisturbed wilderness areas in the country. Dedicated in 1936 to the poet who wrote "Trees," the Joyce Kilmer Memorial Forest is truly a sight to behold. Some of the trees in the forest are hundreds of years old, stand more than 100 feet high, and are 20 feet in diameter at the base. Here you will see a wide variety of trees, including yellow poplar, hemlock, sycamore, basswood, dogwood, beech, and oak, that burst into a blaze of red, yellow, and orange in early October. In spring, wildflowers, rhododendrons, mountain laurels, and azaleas take over the 3,800 acres, but you can't take the beauty with you when you go; removing any vegetation is prohibited by law. Let your camera capture your souvenirs. The forest is part of the 14,000-acre **Slickrock Wilderness Area,** which includes more than 60 miles of hiking trails running along ridges and beside cool mountain streams. A 2-mile loop is easy enough for families to navigate, and a picnic area is located on Route 416 at the entrance parking area.

Cherohala **Skyway**

Located off Highway 143 West and Santeetlah Road, the $100 million Chero-hala Skyway, though less famous and shorter than the famed Blue Ridge Parkway, is majestic in its own right. One of 20 National Scenic Byways, it climbs to elevations of 5,300 feet and runs for 50 miles through the Chero-kee and Nantahala National Forests. (Chero-hala, get it?) In North Carolina it begins in the town of Robbinsville, overlooking Snowbird, Slickrock, and Joyce Kilmer Forests until drivers get to the state line and travel into Tellico Plains, Tennessee.

Scenic overlooks and strategically placed picnic tables give travelers ample time to while away the hours. Hiking trails, which vary greatly in degrees of difficulty, lead into the forest. The Cherohala Skyway also has rest facilities but no gas stations. For more information call (800) 470-3790.

For More Information

Graham County NC Travel and Tourism Authority. (800) 470-3790; www.graham countytravel.com.

Fontana Village

Fontana Village is an expansive rustic resort located north of Robbinsville along Highway 28. For information on Fontana Village attractions, call (800) 849-2258 or log on to www .fontanavillage.com.

This is the largest established resort in the area. Built by the Tennessee Valley Author-ity (TVA) in the early 1940s to house construction workers who were building Fontana Dam, the town was turned into a family resort following World War II. Today it has main-tained its rustic, historic charm but offers everything you need for a wonderful, relaxing vacation. When visiting Fontana Village, check out **Fontana Dam,** an elaborate engineer-ing feat for the time. Not only is the dam impressive, but so is the fact that the TVA built a railroad and an entire community—including a hospital, bank, library, post office, and schools—essentially overnight. Fontana Dam is a massive concrete structure that stands 480 feet above its rock foundation, creating a 10,600-acre lake. From the visitor center at the top of the dam, take a tram or cable car into the powerhouse to explore educational displays on the production of hydroelectricity. There is no admission charge. The visitor center is open from 9 a.m. to 8 p.m. daily, May through October.

Amazing
North Carolina Facts

Fontana Dam is 480 feet high and 2,365 feet wide, and includes 2.8 million cubic yards of concrete. It cost $74 million to build in the 1940s.

Fontana Marina

Located on Highway 28 about 1.5 miles from the village on Fontana Lake; (800) 498-2211. Fees vary by activity.

This establishment offers canoe, kayak, and Jet Ski rentals and fishing trips. Fishing licenses are available here as well. To get out on the water with someone else doing the work, try one of the two cruises the marina offers during the day. Take a picnic cruise at noon ($$$) or a sightseeing cruise at 2 p.m. ($$). At 9:30 a.m. and 3 p.m., you can ride down the lake to the location where the 1994 motion picture *Nell,* starring Jodie Foster, was filmed ($$–$$$). The marina offers a sunset cruise in the evening ($$).

The Stables at Fontana Village (ages 6 and up)

On Highway 28. $$–$$$.

These stables offer easy rides for children under the age of 10 ($$). For older children and adults, rides on trails through the dense forests of the area are offered ($$$).

Where to Eat

Finding a place to eat won't be a problem at Fontana Village.

Mountview Bistro. Located in The Lodge at Fontana Village, on Woods Road. The bistro serves breakfast, lunch, and dinner that usually includes fresh-baked bread and pastries alongside home-style meals. $$

The Wildwood Grill. Located in Fontana Village on Welch Road West. The Grill offers a bit more atmosphere with dining on the patio and music inside. $$

Where to Stay

Fontana Campground. Located on Highway 28 on the Little Tennessee River near the dam; (800) 849-2258. Find something for everyone in the family at this self-contained resort, which offers tent and trailer camping sites from May through October. There are 3 swimming pools, including 1 indoor pool, and a number of hot tubs that you can enjoy year-round. The kids will certainly love the village's nearby water slide. A crafts workshop (828-498-2211), with gift shop, provides instruction in copper tooling, enameling, basketry, leather crafting, and stenciling. The kids might like the opportunity to learn the craft of shirt painting or birdhouse building. An activities center provides equipment for bike riding, archery, badminton, tennis, volleyball, shuffleboard, and horseshoes. The recreation department also plans structured activities such as softball and basketball games, pony rides, and guided hikes and bike rides. $

Fontana Village Resort. Highway 28; (800) 849-2258; www.fontanavillage.com. Fontana Village's Main Lodge offers 94 rooms, in addition to the resort's 150 cottages and cabins. The cottages, ranging from one to three bedrooms, come with all cooking and eating utensils. $$–$$$$

Bryson City

Drive east from Fontana Village to US 74/Highway 28 to find Bryson City. This is one of the region's most popular travel destinations and offers a greater variety of dining and accommodation options.

Deep Creek Campground

1090 W. Deep Creek Rd., Bryson City; (828) 488-6055.

This great campground is located on the edge of Great Smoky Mountains National Park. To get there follow the signs from the railway depot. The sites get crowded next to the creek, but you can find quieter sites on the hill in Section D. The most popular activity here is tubing. You can rent a tire inner tube with a plastic or wood seat crafted in the middle ($). The plastic seats glide better over rock.

Great Smoky Mountains National Park

Bryson City is an outdoor recreation center for the area and one of two North Carolina entrances to Great Smoky Mountains National Park. Contact the park office at (615) 436-1200 or visit www.greatsmokies.com for information on the park and its campgrounds.

Fontana Lake forms the southwestern border of Great Smoky Mountains National Park, which covers a total of 520,000 acres and is bisected by the North Carolina–Tennessee state line. This is the most-visited national park in the US, but don't worry if you're looking for space to stretch out. You'll find plenty of room to fish, hike, and camp.

The mountains of the park are among the oldest in the world and rise more than 6,000 feet. Plant and animal life is varied, with more than 140 species of trees and 200 species of wildflowers identified in the park. In the spring, the park comes alive with color as azaleas and wildflowers begin to bloom. Among the animal life that you might spot in the park are deer, wild turkey, ruffed grouse, and bear. You will also find 900 miles of horseback riding and hiking trails and 735 miles of fishing streams. Many area campgrounds have organized activities, including presentations by park rangers and by people from the Cherokee Indian Reservation.

Make sure to take a drive up **The Road to Nowhere** from Bryson City to the national park. It was meant to be a route from Bryson City to Fontana Village when construction was begun following World War II. Bits and pieces of the road were built until the 1960s to the east side of Fontana Lake. Now it's one of the prettiest drives in the park.

Great Smoky Mountain Railway (all ages)

226 Everett St.; (800) 872-4681; www.gsmr.com. Trips run Mar through Dec. $$$–$$$$; **free** for children under 2. Reservations are recommended.

One of the best ways to see the area is by taking a ride on the Great Smoky Mountain Railway. The railway offers regularly scheduled trips originating in Bryson City, Dillsboro to the south, and Andrews to the west on a train pulled by a steam locomotive or one of four conventional diesel locomotives. While the railway offers a number of different trips, the most popular is a four-hour excursion along Fontana Lake to the Nantahala Gorge and back. Beverages, snacks, and light meals are available on the trains. Ride in either a comfortable enclosed coach or an open car, which provides breathtaking views and excellent photo opportunities. Special events include a holiday Polar Express and visits from Thomas the Train, among others.

Whitewater Rafting (ages 7 and up)

Prices vary; check with individual outfitters (see "Outdoor Adventure" sidebar).

Perhaps the most popular activity in the Bryson City area is rafting, which is easily combined with the railway trip. The area has several rivers that accommodate adventure

Outdoor **Adventure**

Two of the largest rafting outfitters, **Wildwater, Ltd.** (866-319-870; www .wildwaterrafting.com) and the **Nantahala Outdoor Center** (888-905-7238; www.noc.com), offer special packages in conjunction with the railway. Other Bryson City outfitters include:

- **Adventurous Fast Rivers Rafting.** (800) 438-7238; www.white-water.com
- **Endless River Adventures.** (800) 224-7238; www.endlessriveradventures .com
- **Nantahala Rafts and Carolina Outfitters.** (800) 468-7238; www.nantahala rafts.com
- **Paddle Inn Rafting Company.** (800) 711-7238; www.paddleinnrafting.com
- **Rolling Thunder River Company.** (800) 408-7238; www.rollingthunderriver co.com
- **USA Raft.** (800) 872-7238; www.usaraft.com
- **Wildwater Adventure Center.** (877) 247-5535; www.wildwateradventure centers.com

Most offer other outdoor adventure equipment rentals and sales, too.

Going **Tubular**

Companies that provide tube rentals for tubing on Deep Creek include **J. J. Tubes** (828-488-3018), **Deep Creek Store & Tubes** (828-488-9665), **Deep Creek Lodge/Creekside Tubing** (828-488-2587), and **Deep Creek Tube Center** (828-488-6055). All are easy to find on your way to Deep Creek by vehicle and by tube as you finish your day.

seekers ready to get out on the water, but the Nantahala is by far the most popular. While some rivers may be too dangerous for a family excursion, the Nantahala is considered safe for children. Most outfitters will allow children as young as 7 (a minimum of 60 pounds) on the trips. Check with several to find a trip that suits your needs.

Where to Eat

Anthony's Italian Restaurant. 103 Depot St.; (828) 488-8898. Conveniently located on Depot Street next to the train, hand-tossed pizzas, and fresh subs and salads hit the spot after a long train ride. $

Everett Street Diner. 126 Everett St.; (828) 488-0123. Get a country breakfast as well as a variety of sandwiches, homemade soups, salads, and desserts. Local artwork is also displayed. $

Nantahala Village Restaurant. 9400 Highway 19 West; (828) 488-2826. The Village Restaurant offers a family-friendly atmosphere and a pretty good rib eye. The menu also includes trout and salmon along with children's selections. $$

Slow Joe's Cafe at Nantahala Outdoor Center. US 19/74 West; (828) 488-2176. If anyone stays behind on the rafting trip, they can grab a bite at Slow Joe's while enjoying the action on the river. $

Soda Pops. 141 Everett St.; (828) 488-5379; www.sodapopsicecream.com. This old-time soda shop serves ice cream with special toppings, fountain sodas, malts, sundaes, and shakes. $

Where to Stay

Almond Boat and RV Park. 1165 Almond Boat Park Rd.; (828) 488-6423. Almond offers RV sites as well as a dozen cottages with kitchenettes. $–$$$

Bryson View Cabin Rentals. 120 Sturken Dr.; (828) 488-6298. These cabins, located in town, accommodate up to 10 people and their pets. $$$–$$$$

The Cabins at Nantahala. 299 Dills Rd.; (888) 447-4436. These two-bedroom cabins are perfect for small families, but you have to provide your own bath towels and utilize the nearby bathhouse. $$

Carolina Mountain Vacations. 40 Greenlee St.; (828) 488-7500. This agency offers cabins, homes, and cottage rentals that are privately owned. $$$$

Creekside Cabins. 1044 W. Deep Creek; (828) 488-2235. Located on the banks of the creek, you'll find 8 rustic cabins and a country home that sleeps 8. $$–$$$

Parent's **Tip**

Bryson City, Highlands, and other mountain resort towns offer a number of country inn and bed-and-breakfast dining rooms that make for a quiet, romantic evening. Some restaurants allow you to put a tie on junior and take him along, but I recommend leaving him with an older sibling.

Euchella Sports Lodge. 9698 Highway 19 West; (800) 446-1603. The Euchella offers rooms at this site plus cabins and cottages from here to Almond. $$–$$$$

Freeman's Motel and Cottages. Highway 28 North, Almond; (828) 488-2737. Located just outside Bryson City, this relatively small operation offers a variety of accommodations. $–$$$$

Galbreath Creek Cabins. 24 Fry St.; (877) 943-8292. Twenty modern cabins with hot tubs and other amenities are tucked away just outside the national park. $$$

Lands Creek Log Cabins. 3336 Balltown Rd.; (888) 346-9793. Some of these cabins already have established places for campfires. You'll find Jacuzzis in some. $$$–$$$$

Smoky Mountain Retreat. 51 Green Valley Acres; (828) 488-6347. Amazingly elegant custom-crafted log homes are offered for rent at the foot of a mountain, just outside Bryson City. $$$$

For More Information

Swain County Chamber of Commerce. (800) 867-9246; www.greatsmokies.com.

Cherokee

Just a few miles east of Bryson City on US 19 is the town of Cherokee and the Cherokee Indian Reservation.

Cherokee combines the best of how things once were prior to European settlement of the area and good old-fashioned tourism marketing. It is the sole town located in the 56,000-acre Qualla Boundary Cherokee Indian Reservation, home to roughly 8,500 members of the Eastern Band of the Cherokee. It is nestled between Great Smoky Mountains National Park and the western end of the Blue Ridge Parkway. The town has become a burgeoning tourist attraction, also home to a reservation-run Harrah's Casino, but amid all the commercialism there's plenty of wholesome things to do and learn.

Cherokee Fun Park (all ages)

US 441; (828) 497-5877; www.cherokeefunparknc.com. Hours vary according to season and weather. Prices vary by attraction.

More modern recreation as colorful as the brightest neon is waiting at Cherokee Fun Park, located near the entrance to Great Smoky Mountains National Park. The park features 4 acres of go-karts, bumper boats, miniature golf, and a big game room. The kids will let you know where it is. Yeah, it even looks fun.

Museum of the Cherokee Indian (all ages)

Located at US 441 and Drama Road; (828) 497-3481; www.cherokeemuseum.org. Open 9 a.m. to 5 p.m. daily, with hours extended to 7 p.m. Mon through Sat in summer. $$; free for children under 6.

The best place to begin exploration of Cherokee is at the Museum of the Cherokee Indian. The museum offers a primer on Cherokee heritage, history, and culture. In front is a 20-foot California redwood statue of Sequoyah, who invented the Cherokee alphabet. In addition to a massive collection of clothes, crafts, weapons, and artifacts—some of which are more than 10,000 years old—the museum also has an art gallery and theaters that feature this culture's history through innovative audiovisual shows and computer-generated graphics combined with traditional collections. Especially interesting are special phones allowing you to hear the Cherokee language spoken and an exhibit of striking contemporary photos taken along the Trail of Tears.

Oconaluftee Indian Village (ages 5 and up)

Located just off US 441; (828) 497-2315; www.cherokee-nc.com. Open 9 a.m. to 5 p.m. daily, mid-May through late Oct. $$–$$$.

While you will see a number of people dressed in Native American attire complete with headdress and ready to be photographed throughout Cherokee's tourist activity, these are not authentically dressed Cherokee. The real way the Native Americans lived can be seen at several attractions on the reservation. One of the most enlightening places to visit in the Cherokee area is the Oconaluftee Indian Village, where the 18th-century past comes alive. The village is an authentic re-creation of an 18th-century Cherokee Indian community. Here costumed guides lead tours of the village, where local people work at the ancient arts of basket making and pottery, and demonstrate blowguns, canoe hulling, and finger weaving, an art that involves using the fingers in place of a shuttle to produce colorful belts, headbands, and other articles. Tours include a visit to the 7-sided council house—a simple wood and dirt structure—to learn how the Cherokee tribes functioned.

Oconaluftee Islands Park (all ages)

US 441, near downtown; (800) 438-1601. Free.

This is an attractive little grassy island park with a lovely river running through it, where you can get away from the tourist activity that abounds in Cherokee. Kids can wade in the creek, build a dam, or just chill under a canopy of oak and sycamore trees!

Santa's Land Family Fun Park and Zoo (all ages)

US 19 or Soco Road, 3 miles west of downtown; (828) 497-9191; www.santaslandnc.com. Open 9 a.m. to 6 p.m. daily, May through Oct, and on weekends in Nov. $$$; children 2 and under free. The admission includes all rides, entertainment, and exhibits.

Celebrate Christmas during the summer at Santa's Land Family Fun Park and Zoo. An especially good attraction for younger children, it is a few minutes' drive east of Cherokee. The kids get an early order to Santa and his elves and visit the animals in the petting zoo, where they will see dozens of domestic and exotic animals. Also found in this temperate wonderland are paddleboats, train rides, and the Rudi-Coaster.

Unto These Hills (ages 5 and up)

Located on US 441, north of downtown; (828) 497-2111; www.cherokee-nc.com. Shows presented at 7:30 p.m. Mon through Sat, mid-June through late Aug. $$–$$$.

Near the village is the Cherokees' Mountainside Theater, where *Unto These Hills* is performed during the summer. The outdoor drama, written by Kermit Hunter, is an inspirational piece that captures the history of the Cherokee Indians from the mid-1500s to the tragedy of the Trail of Tears in the late 1830s. The Cherokee people originally settled much of this land, but many were forced off it by the US government and made to march to Arkansas and Oklahoma. During these marches more than 4,000 of the 15,000 Native Americans involved died of disease or exposure. Others, whose descendants still live here, managed to escape into the mountains. The play, produced by more than 130 performers and technicians, runs about two hours.

The Great Outdoors

Don't forget about all the outdoor activities the Cherokee area has to offer. Trout fishing on the Cherokee Indian Reservation is excellent, with dozens of miles of streams and several ponds in the area. Two North Carolina trout-fishing records have been established on the reservation in recent years. A special reservation fishing license, available at local tackle shops, costs $10 per day, and children younger than 12 can fish on a parent's license.

Whether you want to stay in a luxury hotel, a cabin, or at a campground, you won't have any problem finding a place to suit your recreational needs. One of the best campgrounds nearby is **Smokemont Campground,** 6 miles north of Cherokee off US 441 in the Smokemont community. In addition to fishing streams and hiking trails, you will find great horseback riding trails and stables offering arrangements to rent horses. Smokemont Campground is open year-round, and sites cost $17 to $20. Make reservations at www.recreation.gov. **KOA Kampgrounds,** located on Star Route north of Cherokee, is the largest commercial campground in the area. It offers a wide range of sites, from tepees and primitive tent sites to paved sites with full hookups to rustic cabins on the creek, that fit any budget. You will also find a wide variety of activities at the 35-acre campground, including swimming, tennis, volleyball, a game room, and more. The campground's Fun Bus is ready to take you on a fun-filled day trip or shuttle you up the river

Bear **with Them**

Even if the kids try to feed the two dozen or so bears in downtown Chero-kee, they won't eat. These bears are fiberglass works of art. Initiated in 2005, the bears are commissioned pieces that are reflective of Cherokee history and culture and regional landscapes. The colorful life-size adult black bears include portraits of local people who have been important to the Cherokee, as well as occupations and trades that have kept the reservation thriving into the 21st century. Even a "Tourism Bear" represents for that industry.

for a 3-mile tubing trip. Call (828) 497-9711 or log on to www.cherokeekoa.com for more information.

Another popular pastime in Cherokee is a lazy ride down the Oconaluftee River. Two local retailers offer a daylong rental of an inner tube for about $10: **Cherokee Rapids Tube & Kayak Rentals** (1681 Acquoni Rd.; 828-736-3535) and **Indian Summer Gifts & Tube Rentals** (833 Tsali Blvd.; 866-317-2975).

Where to Eat

The Chestnut Tree. 37 Tsali Blvd.; (828) 497-9181. A nice prime rib buffet and salad bar offer enough options for everyone in the family. $$

Grandma's Pancake and Steak. US 441 and US 19; (828) 497-9801. Want pancakes in the middle of the day? Get 'em here. Grandma also serves country-style food. $

Granny's Kitchen. 1098 Painttown Rd.; (828) 497-5010; www.grannyskitchenchero kee.com. Roast beef, fried chicken, and other country-kitchen favorites are waiting on the buffet. $$

Where to Stay

Drama Inn. 462 Tsali Blvd.; (828) 497-3271; www.dramainn.com. The Drama Inn, on the banks of the Oconaluftee River, is within walking distance of the Museum of the Cherokee Indian and other attractions. $$

Ol' Smoky Log Cabins. (828) 497-6922; www.olsmokylogcabins.com. New but old-feeling log cabins, all on the reservation and all with porches on the river, are available for rent. $$

Pageant Inn. 739 Tsali Blvd.; (828) 497-5371; www.pageantinn.com. Located on US 441, this motel offers 42 rooms. $

Pioneer Motel and Cottages. US 441 near US 19; (828) 497-2435; www.pioneermotel .net. This motel offers rooms as well as riverside cabins. Lots of extras, such as horse-shoes and basketball courts. $$–$$$

Rivers Edge Motel. 1026 US 441; (828) 497-7995; www.riversedgecherokee.com. Hanging out over the water is this small hotel with private balconies outside all 21 rooms. $$

Riverside Motel and Campground. US 441 South; (828) 497-9311; www.riverside motelnc.com. This small motel features all riverfront rooms and a covered area with picnic tables and grill. The campground has 30 sites for a camper, RV, or tent—on the river, of course. $–$$

Smoky Mountain Cabins. US 19 North; (828) 497-0088. You can find quieter accommodations by calling Smoky Mountain Cabins. $$$$

For More Information

Cherokee Welcome Center. (800) 438-1601, (828) 497-9195, or (828) 497-5737; www.cherokee-nc.com.

Maggie Valley

Keep heading east on US 19, and the family arrives in Maggie Valley, a small town with big adventures, within about 30 minutes. Plan to spend several hours in downtown Maggie Valley, its streets lined with specialty shops, restaurants, and various amusements. The community is a popular tourist resort and gets crowded during peak vacation times, but that doesn't spoil the old-time country feel of the town. Accommodations are as varied here as they are throughout the Smoky Mountains, but the area's hotels and cottages rise above the rest with spectacular views of the surrounding landscape.

Clingman's **Dome**

In the next chapter we'll explore North Carolina's highest peak, but let's break here to include Tennessee's highest peak since it, in fact, shares the state line with North Carolina. Clingman's Dome earns its title at 6,643 feet and was named after US senator Thomas Lanier Clingman. It is the tallest mountain in Great Smoky Mountains National Park.

Clingman's Dome is accessible via a paved road, which is closed November through March, off US 441 (Newfound Gap Road) north of Cherokee. The road leads to within 300 feet of the summit, and from there visitors can walk a trail to the top. A stroller- and wheelchair-accessible tower is located at the summit, and on clear days visitors can see four states (Tennessee, North Carolina, South Carolina, and Georgia). The area is developed with picnic tables and restrooms. For more information call the Great Smoky Mountain National Park office headquartered in Gatlinburg, Tennessee, at (423) 436-1200.

The Cataloochee **Valley**

After nearly a decade, park officials are calling the introduction of elk to the Cataloochee Valley area of Great Smoky Mountains National Park a success. In 2002 the US Department of Fish and Wildlife successfully reintroduced the species that once thrived in the area but was hunted out more than 200 years ago. The massive creatures with a haunting mating call can often be seen grazing in the Cataloochee Valley, accessible from Maggie Valley, in the early morning and in the evening. Their population has grown from the 50 introduced to the area to almost three times that number.

Cataloochee Guest Ranch
(all ages; horseback riding ages 6 and up)

119 Ranch Dr.; (800) 868-1401; www.cataloochee-ranch.com. $$$$.

To get out of the crowds, give Cataloochee Ranch a try. Located just a few miles north of Maggie Valley, the resort has been operating for more than 70 years. A rugged sheep and cattle farm is set on the rolling landscape of the Smokies, but this ranch provides all the amenities of a modern vacation. The 1,000-acre ranch is one of only three private entrances to Great Smoky Mountains National Park, offering individual cabins as well as rooms at the Silverbell Lodge and at the ranch house. The vegetable garden produces a great variety of food that makes its way to the dinner table in a hearty family-style setting. In addition to meals, the only structured activity at the ranch is horseback riding ($$$$). The rest of the time is your own, as the lodge offers tennis, hiking, trout fishing, horseshoes, table tennis, badminton, and croquet. You can relax by the swimming pool, take a hayride, or walk through the ranch's glorious meadows, where wildflowers abound in spring and summer. Bonfires, complete with storytelling and roasted marshmallows, round out the day.

Cataloochee Ski Area (all ages)

1080 Ski Lodge Rd.; (800) 768-0285; www.cataloochee.com. $$–$$$$.

The guest ranch is located right next door to the Cataloochee Ski Area. With the help of snowmakers, the North Carolina ski season usually starts in early December. Cataloochee has 10 slopes and trails that range from gentle slopes for beginners to the monstrous 5,400-foot Moody Top, plus a snow-tube park. The Cataloochee Ski School offers skiing and boarding lessons; inquire about special lesson packages for children and family-special days. Hours of operation may vary according to weather.

The Stompin' Ground (ages 3 and up)

3116 Soco Rd.; (828) 926-1288. Shows begin at 8 p.m. nightly May through Oct. $$.

Get out your dancing shoes when you visit the Stompin' Ground, offering a glimpse of mountain heritage through clogging, square dancing, line dancing, and other traditional mountain dances adapted from the area's Irish and Scottish heritages. Musical acts include bluegrass, gospel, and traditional country performances. You'll be moved to stomp your feet yourself during the shows that are presented nightly.

Wheels Through Time Museum (ages 5 and up)

Soco Road; (828) 926-6266. Open 9 a.m. to 5 p.m. Thurs through Sun, May through Nov; 10 a.m. to 5 p.m. Thurs through Sun, Dec through Apr. $$–$$$; free for children 4 and under.

This museum features hundreds of commercial, police, and military motorcycles that date back as far as 1909, when motorcycles began to emerge as a reliable form of transportation. More than 60 working machines (some of which they crank up) and other memorabilia create a sort of time line through the 20th century and into the 21st. From classic Harleys to one-off production models that just didn't catch on, the museum takes guests right up to the machines that thrill today's riders.

Where to Eat

J Arthur's. 2843 Soco Rd.; (828) 926-1817; www.jarthurs.com. Steak and prime rib are the specialties of J. Arthur's house, but there's a big selection of kids' items, too. $$$$

Maggie Valley Restaurant. 2804 Soco Rd.; (828) 926-0425; www.maggievalley restaurant.net. The Carver family has run this Southern-style diner since the 1950s. They serve breakfast, lunch, and dinner 7 days a week. $$

Where to Stay

Jonathan Creek Inn and Villas. 4324 Soco Rd.; (800) 577-7812. This inn with 42 rooms plus several suites and a cottage is family oriented, with a playground and children's programs. It's appropriately located on Jonathan Creek, which runs parallel with the main road through Maggie Valley. $$–$$$

Laurel Park Inn. 257 Soco Rd.; (800) 451-4424. This is a small, very affordable inn. $–$$

Smoky Falls Lodge. 2550 Soco Rd.; (877) 926-7440. A game room and miniature golf make this 32-room facility a great place from which to explore the area. The rooms are spacious and comfortable. $$–$$$

For More Information

The Maggie Valley Area Convention and Visitors Bureau. (800) 785-8259 or (828) 926-1686; www.maggievalley.org.

Waynesville

Take US 19 east to US 23 into Waynesville, the largest NC town west of Asheville.

This quaint mountain community still has brick sidewalks in the historic downtown district. More than 100 charming shops, galleries, and restaurants line the walkable streets. Among them is one of the links in the popular **Mast General Store** chain (828-452-2101) and **Smith's Drugs** (828-456-8607), where you can get a drink from the old-fashioned soda fountain. Everything from antiques to clothes is available in the shopping district, but you might want to schedule your trip here for midsummer. Waynesville is home to North Carolina's Official International Festival, **Folkmoot USA,** a two-week celebration of the world's cultural heritage through folk music and dance. Held in late July, Folkmoot features performances by more than 300 artists representing more than a dozen countries. It also includes parades and workshops. Events demonstrate cultural heritage through colorful, authentic costumes; lively dance; music; and lots of food. For more information call (828) 452-2997 or log on to www.folkmoot.com.

Museum of North Carolina Handicrafts (ages 5 and up)

307 Shelton St.; (828) 452-1551. Open 10 a.m. to 4 p.m. Tues through Fri, May through Oct; hours vary at other times. $.

While in Waynesville, stop in at the Museum of North Carolina Handicrafts. Housed in the Shelton House, a farm home built in 1875, the museum features works by some of the state's best-known artisans. Hand-carved dulcimers, spectacular carved bowls, wooden mule-drawn wagons and sleds, and other toys capture the imagination. The Indian room features a collection of Navajo rugs, baskets, and jewelry as well as Cherokee crafts and artifacts.

Where to Eat

Nick & Nate's Pizza. 111 N. Main St.; (828) 452-0027; www.nickandnatespizza.com. Gourmet pizzas, subs, wings, and salads are served in a fun atmosphere. The kids can even get PB&J with Oreos. Mom and Dad can get a handcrafted beer. $$

O'Malley's On Main Pub & Grill. 172 N. Main St.; (828) 452-4228. The name probably gives away the fun Irish theme in a grill that's typically crowded with locals. It's still low-key enough for the kids, however. $$

Fishing **Fun**

If there isn't an experienced angler in the family but you want a successful fishing experience with the kids, try a trout farm. The farms provide rod, line, and bait, and it's not difficult to bring home a catch for dinner. They typically charge by the pound. Here is a list of area places to try your luck: **Ferguson's Trout Pond,** Clyde, (828) 627-6404; **Holland's Trout Pond,** Maggie Valley, (828) 926-0313; **Maggie Valley Trout Pond,** Maggie Valley, (828) 926-0766; **Soco Gap Trout Ponds,** Maggie Valley, (828) 926-3635; **Sorrell's Creek Trout Farm,** Canton, (828) 648-9903; and **Tusquitee Trout Ranch,** Hayesville, (828) 389-6598.

Where to Stay

Boyd Mountain Log Cabins. 445 Boyd Farm Rd.; (828) 926-1575; www.boydmountain.com. Seven hand-hewn renovated log cabins are nestled in a cove of the Smokies. Fishing ponds, cows in a meadow, and a swimming hole comprise the bucolic setting. $$$

Oak Park Inn. 314 S. Main St.; (828) 456-5328. Rooms, condos, and efficiencies are offered at this AAA-approved motel. There is also a handful of pet-friendly rooms. $$–$$$

Parkway Inn. 2093 Dellwood Rd.; (828) 926-1841. This is another AAA-approved motel that's very pleasant and affordable. $$

For More Information

Haywood County Tourism Development Authority. (800) 334-9036; www.smokymountains.net or www.waynesville.com.

Canton

Canton is a small town a few miles east of Waynesville on US 74.

Canton Area Historical Museum (ages 5 and up)

36 Park St.; (828) 646-3412; www.cantonmuseum.org. Open 9 a.m. to 4 p.m. Mon through Fri and by appointment Sat and Sun. **Free.**

The Canton Area Historical Museum, just a few miles east of Waynesville, is a small but interesting museum that also serves as the area visitor center. It offers a look at how this area, once a hunting and fishing ground for the Cherokee Indians, developed. Following European settlement, it became a popular stopping point for western ranchers moving their cattle and swine to market in the East. In addition, the Pigeon River made it an important shipping point, leading to the establishment of the Champion Paper Mill, which remains the area's biggest employer. This history is presented in displays on the mill and through area artifacts, pictures, and records that provide a glimpse into life from the late 1800s to the present.

Dillsboro

Dillsboro is located at the junction of US 23/441 and 74, southwest of Waynesville.

Maintaining the distinction of an old railway town, Dillsboro has been turned into a charming shopping and historic district. The **Dillsboro Historic District** is nestled at the edge of the Great Smoky Mountains on the Tuckasegee River. Log cabins and homes from the late 1800s provide showcases for handmade crafts and homemade treats. Get a walking map of the district by calling the **Jackson County Visitor's Center** at (800) 962-1911. Then just park your car and stroll through the village to meet friendly shopkeepers and artisans. Visitors will find more than 60 shops, restaurants, and more in a 3-block area. So if the kids aren't exactly thrilled with the thought of going shopping, point out the blown glass, pottery, candles, and other items you'll see being made before your eyes. **Nancy Tut's Christmas Shop** (800-742-7155) might catch their attention for a while, and if you promise them a sample from the **Dillsboro Chocolate Factory** (828-631-0156), a good time is a lock. You might also check out **Bradley's General Store** (828-586-3891), a "Family Tradition Since 1888" (at least that's what they say). This old-time soda fountain sells local honey, jams and jellies, antiques, gifts, T-shirts, Yankee Candles, and Amish furniture. Pottery studios, jewelry makers, and other artists occupy other spaces throughout town.

Great Smoky Mountain Railway (all ages)

119 Front St.; (800) 872-4681; www.gsmr.com. Trips run Apr through Dec. $$$–$$$$; Free for children under 2. Reservations are recommended.

Dillsboro is the "other end" of the Great Smoky Mountain Railway. You might find this location a little less crowded than the Bryson City end. The town has great charm and more than enough opportunity to soak up mountain life. This is also a good location to visit for special events conducted by the railroad such as the Santa Express, when the kids can have brunch with Santa, or "A Day Out with Thomas the Train."

Where to Eat

Dillsboro Smokehouse. 403 Haywood St.; (828) 586-9556. Locals like this barbecue restaurant as much as tourists. It has great ribs! $$

Kostas Family Restaurant. 489 E. Haywood Rd.; (828) 631-0777; www.kostasdillsboro.com. Greek and Italian are mainstays on the menu here. $$

Where to Stay

Dillsboro Inn. 146 N. River Rd.; (866) 586-3898. Riverfront suites here include balconies overlooking the waterfall. The inn also serves a continental breakfast. $$$$

Olde Towne Inn. 364 Haywood Rd.; (828) 586-3461; www.dillsboro-oldetowne.com.

Located directly across the railway, this B&B welcomes families in several of its rooms. $$$

Smoky Mountain Getaways. 12 Young Ln., Sylva; (866) 586-8058. This agency offers a wide variety of rental vacation homes in woods on the river and at the lake. $$$$

For More Information

The Dillsboro Merchants Association. www.visitdillsboro.org.

Cullowhee

To get to Cullowhee, the home of Western Carolina University, from Dillsboro, take Highway 107 South.

Other Things to See & Do
in the Great Smoky Mountains

- **Chunky Gal Stables.** Hayesville; (828) 389-4175; www.chunkygalstables.com
- **The Fun Factory.** Franklin; (828) 349-8888; www.funfactoryfranklin.com
- **Franklin Family Entertainment Center.** Franklin; (828) 524-8567
- **Great Smoky Mountain Fish Camp and Safaris.** Franklin; (828) 369-5295; www.fishcamp.biz
- **Cherokee Bear Zoo and Exotic Animals.** Cherokee; (828) 497-4525; www .cherokeebearzoo.com
- **Fantasy Golf and Gameroom.** Maggie Valley; (828) 926-8180; www.fantasy golfmaggievalley.com
- **Maggie Valley Carpet Golf.** Maggie Valley; (828) 926-3255
- **The Mini-Apolis Grand Prix.** Maggie Valley; (828) 926-1685
- **Canton Recreation Park.** Canton; (828) 646-3411
- **Old Pressley Sapphire Mine.** Canton; (828) 648-6320; www.oldpressley mine.com
- **Queen's Farm Riding Stables.** Waynesville; (828) 926-0718
- **Waynesville Recreation Park.** Waynesville; (828) 456-8577

The Mountain Heritage Center (ages 5 and up)

Robins Administration Building, Western Carolina University; (828) 227-7129; www.wcu .edu/mhc. Open 8 a.m. to 5 p.m. Mon through Fri and 10 a.m. to 5 p.m. Sat, June through Oct, except during university holidays. Free.

The Mountain Heritage Center is part of Western Carolina University in Cullowhee. The center promotes the rich tradition of the southern Appalachian Mountains through exhibits, educational programs, and demonstrations. Exhibits at the center present life in the mountains through the years. See photographs, artifacts, relics, and other displays that relate to the migration of the Scotch-Irish people who settled the area in the 18th century. The center also presents temporary exhibits on mountain crafts and works such as blacksmithing as well as programs on the natural beauty of the area. Thousands of people from across the Carolinas, Georgia, and Tennessee come to Cullowhee the last Saturday of each September for **Mountain Heritage Day,** which is sponsored in part by the Mountain Heritage Center. The usually quiet town of Cullowhee comes alive with crafts, mountain music, food, storytelling, and more during this event. Admission and events are free. For more information call the Mountain Heritage Center.

The
Blue Ridge
Mountains

Find out how much fun a waterfall can be in North Carolina's Blue Ridge Mountains. In this land of waterfalls, each one is a beautiful sight, but one waterfall stands out from the rest and promises hours of fun in the chilly water for your family. Explore western North Carolina's biggest city, including the largest private residence in the US that in recent years has provided more opportunity for great family adventure. This region also offers an opportunity to learn about some of the state's most prominent residents, or climb the tallest peak east of the Rockies.

Jim's
TopPicks in the Blue Ridge Mountains

1. Tweetsie Railroad

2. Sliding Rock and surrounding area in Pisgah National Forest

3. Chimney Rock Park in Chimney Rock

4. Grandfather Mountain

5. Biltmore Estate in Asheville

6. Linville Falls and Linville Gorge Wilderness Area

7. Ski areas

8. Canoeing on the New River

9. Pack Place in Asheville

10. Mount Mitchell State Park

THE BLUE RIDGE MOUNTAINS

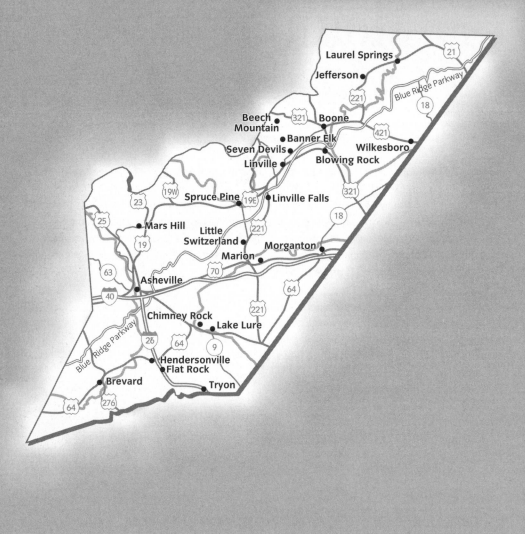

Laurel Springs
Jefferson
21
Blue Ridge Parkway
221
18
Beech
Mountain
321 Boone
Banner Elk
421
Seven Devils
Wilkesboro
Linville
Blowing Rock
19W
Spruce Pine
19E Linville Falls
321
23
25
Mars Hill
221
18
19
Little
Switzerland
Morganton
Marion
70
63
64
Asheville
40
64
221
Chimney Rock
Lake Lure
Blue Ridge Parkway
26
64
9
Hendersonville
Flat Rock
Brevard
Tryon
64
276

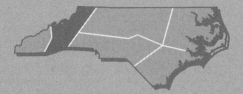

I-40 is the main route in the Blue Ridge from points east. I-26 or US 321 will get you here from the south. One of the main attractions here is the Blue Ridge Parkway, and you'll easily discover all the activities it has to offer in addition to its breathtaking views. For quick travel, however, stick to the other highways because the parkway speed limit is 45 miles per hour.

Brevard

Brevard is located on US 276 south of the Blue Ridge Parkway. It's one of the busiest sections of Pisgah National Forest with several popular attractions.

Brevard and Transylvania County are known as the land of waterfalls. The Davidson and French Broad Rivers and their tributaries in this area account for more than 250 waterfalls and 200 miles of cool mountain streams winding through the area. Make a day out of visiting some of the lovely falls in this area by heading west from Brevard on US 64, then south on Highway 281 to **Whitewater Falls,** where you can hike the short trail for a panoramic view of the falls. At 441 feet, the upper part of this two-level cascade is the highest in the eastern US. Also on Highway 281 find **Rainbow Falls,** which drops more than 200 feet. On US 64 is **Toxaway Falls,** cascading 123 feet, with the highway running across the top. For more information on some of the beautiful sites in this area, contact the Brevard/Transylvania County Visitors Center at (800) 648-4523 or check out www .visitwaterfalls.com.

Blue Ridge Corn Maze (all ages)
1605 Everett Rd.; (828) 884-4415; www.blueridgecornmaze.com. Operates midsummer through Halloween. $–$$; free for children age 5 and under.

Escaping the Blue Ridge Corn Maze is a challenge for children and adults, who are asked to figure out a riddle as they wander through the rows of corn. Special events such as concerts throughout the period the maze is open add to the fun.

White **Squirrels**

In Brevard the white squirrels have their own festival held in late May; they also have their own soapbox derby and even their own website. While white squirrels, possibly albino squirrels, populate other towns in the US and Canada, the Brevard variety are believed to be a variation of the eastern grey squirrel. Although unsubstantiated, the critters are believed to have originated here as escapees from a carnival truck more than a half century ago. Today they are a popular curiosity even in local shops where one can find all manner of white squirrel memorabilia.

Bobby N. Setzer Fish Hatchery and Pisgah Center for Wildlife Education (all ages)

1401 Fish Hatchery Rd.; (828) 877-4423; www.ncwildlife.org. Hatchery open to the public 8 a.m. to 4:45 p.m. Mon through Sat. **Free.**

Come see why the trout fishing in this area is so good when visiting the Pisgah Forest Fish Hatchery. The hatchery breeds and raises 500,000 brown, brook, and rainbow trout annually for stocking in area streams during the month of March, when no trout fishing is permitted. At the hatchery you can walk along the troughs the fish are raised in to see their various stages of growth. Displays in the center provide information on the hatchery and how the fish are raised. In addition to an exhibit hall that includes aquariums with native species, the hatchery also features a short, paved trail that provides a look at other wildlife. From the trail, visitors can see dioramas, including preserved specimens such as bear and other woodland creatures.

Cradle of Forestry (all ages)

2002 Pisgah Hwy., Pisgah Forest; (828) 877-3130; www.cradleofforestry.com. Open 9 a.m. to 5 p.m. daily, Apr through Nov. $–$$; **free** for children under age 5.

What would a national forest be if it didn't provide an opportunity to study nature? The Cradle of Forestry is a great hands-on museum that gets you on the road to discovering the wide variety of plant and animal life that inhabits this forest. Nearly 100 years ago the Cradle of Forestry was opened as the country's first school of forestry. The museum is now operated by the US Forest Service and is a National Historic Site. It's located about 14 miles north of Brevard on the main forest road (US 276). In addition to the displays of plant and animal life, the museum also displays tools and other relics that relate to the history of the area. Young children will love learning about forest conservation at the Forest Fun exhibit, where they can play with puzzles, puppets, and costumes. A touch-screen monitor lets them find more information on selected topics. Then head out on one of two nature trails that interpret more of the history of forestry and logging. On one trail you'll see an old logging locomotive. On another, occasional demonstrations of spinning, weaving, blacksmithing, and quilting are held.

Musical **Inspiration**

The Brevard Music Center over its 75-year history has become legendary in the performing arts world and has hosted the talents of Yo-Yo Ma, Joshua Bell, and Renée Flemming. But it's also a bastion of musical inspiration for young talent. Each summer 400 of the nation's most gifted musicians between the ages 14 and 29 are invited to participate in the center's summer institute and festival. For students, it's an opportunity of a lifetime. For visitors, it means more than 80 concerts in just a few weeks.

A Hoffman **Family Adventure**

Michaela was 8 when we took her on her first trip to Sliding Rock, cautioning her about how cold the water would be. She wasn't worried. She was going to slide! We watched from an observation deck overlooking the foot of the waterfall, ready to snap photos as she and her cousin stepped onto the rock and got into position. I snapped a photo as they began the 120-foot slide. I snapped another as they went airborne into the pool below. But we knew something was wrong as the girls' heads poked out of the water. Michaela was a little angry and more than a little frightened. "I didn't know I had to swim," she said. In our haste to warn her about the cold, we had neglected to tell her the pool at the bottom was over her head. It's good she is a strong swimmer. It's OK, Michaela. Dad didn't slide that day because he can't make it across the creek leading to the rock without slipping.

Sliding Rock (ages 7 and up)

Pisgah Highway, (828) 877-3265. Open 10 a.m. to 5:30 p.m. Memorial Day to Labor Day. $.

North of Brevard head into Pisgah National Forest, using US 276, also known as Pisgah Highway, which provides a wide range of camping facilities and great fishing streams. You'll find waterfalls here, too, and more adventure than one might expect. Sliding Rock was named Sliding Rock for just that reason. The 150-foot natural waterslide is a favorite of visitors to the area who aren't afraid to get wet. It's an exhilarating blast to slip down the huge rock along with the 11,000 gallons of 60-degree water that flow each minute. The ride down the rock ends in a pool, so if the kids want to make the slide, be sure they are strong swimmers. Walk smaller children down the rock and let them make a short slide. Use extreme caution: The rocks are very slippery. After your slide, stop by **Looking Glass Falls** and **Looking Glass Rock,** believed to be the largest single piece of granite in the southern Appalachians. Park at the side of the road and walk down to the bottom of the 85-foot falls. Inner tubes are also available for rent at local retailers located at the entrance to the national forest.

Where to Eat

Cardinal Old-Fashioned Drive-In. 344 S. Broad St.; (828) 884-7085; www.cardinaldrivein.com. Burgers and fries are, of course, the specialty of the house. $

The Clock of Brevard. 1015 Asheville Hwy.; (828) 884-4010. Chicken is the specialty of the house, but you can also get a pretty good burger, hot dog, and even gyros here. $

Hawg Wild Bar-b-cue. 91 Pisgah Hwy.; (828) 877-4404; www.hawgwildbar-b-cue.com. With several mountain locations, this Hawg Wild is conveniently located at the entrance of the national forest. Expect good barbecue selections here. $$

Poppie's Market and Cafe. 1 Market St.; (828) 885-5494; www.poppiesmarket.com. This farm-to-table market includes the Chef's Kitchen from which come fish tacos, burgers, salads, and other items from locally grown products. $$

Where to Stay

Ash Grove Cabins and Camping. 749 E. Fork Rd.; (828) 885-7216; www.ash-grove.com. Secluded cabins and campsites are located on a small mountaintop just outside Brevard. $

Davidson River Campground. US 276 in Pisgah National Forest; (828) 862-5960; www.recreation.gov. This is a great campground with fairly private spaces, a swimming hole, and showers, and it is conveniently located. $

Earthside Mountain Lodge. Route 1, Golden Road, Lake Toxaway; (828) 862-4207. This beautiful cedar log lodge has rock fireplaces and porches to help you kick back. It includes 10 guest rooms, all with patchwork quilts, stained glass lamps, log beds, and private baths, some with lofts that seem to come right out of *Little House on the Prairie*. Activities on-site include a challenging zip-line tour, hiking trails, scavenger hunts, and many evening entertainment events. $$$$

The Red Lion Inn. 4259 Pickens Hwy., Rosman; (828) 884-6868. This inn includes rooms by the creek as well as cabins on the mountain way behind the inn. $$–$$$$

Sunset Motel. 415 S. Broad St.; (828) 884-9106. This older motel also offers a few efficiencies. The rooms are basic but neat and clean. $$$

For More Information

Brevard/Transylvania County Tourism. (800) 648-4523; www.visitwaterfalls.com.

Hendersonville

From Brevard, head east on US 64 to the junction with Highway 25 to reach Hendersonville, a town that was once at the heart of the mountain tourism industry.

Antique Toy Museum (all ages)

154 White St., (828) 694-1480; www.hendersonvilleantiquetoymuseum.com. Open 1 to 4 p.m. Sat and Sun. $; **Free** under age 6.

Dollhouses, trains, miniatures, and old-fashioned wind-up dolls might bring back more memories for Mom and Dad than the kids, but it's an interesting diversion nonetheless. Exhibits span the late 1800s to the 1960s.

Elijah Mountain Gem Mine (ages 5 and up)
2120 Brevard Rd.; (828) 693-3123; www.elijahmountain.com. Open 10 a.m. to 6 p.m. Mon through Fri, 9 a.m. to 6 p.m. Sat and Sun. $$$–$$$$.

Covered flumes make mining for rubies, sapphires, and other gems comfortable rain or shine. Gold mining is also conducted here. A nice picnic area is located on-site near a gently rolling stream.

Hands On! (ages 1 to 10)
318 N. Main St., Ste. 2; (828) 697-8333; www.handsonwnc.org. $.

This children's gallery provides interactive educational exhibits and programs that stimulate the imaginations of young children and is especially appropriate for kids up to age 10. The attraction includes a costume theater, a nature area, and areas dedicated to mountain music, food, and art. Kids can dress up as postal workers, shop for groceries, build their own LEGO race cars, and more.

Historic Downtown Hendersonville
Henderson County Travel & Tourism Visitor Center, 201 S. Main St.; (800) 828-4244; www.historichendersonville.org.

Start off a trip to historic downtown Hendersonville at the centrally located visitor center for information about the area. A visit here won't be a tremendously wild adventure, but you'll find a little something for everyone in the family. Main Street is beautifully adorned with seasonal plantings and benches scattered along the sidewalks, providing an opportunity for a short break or to sit back and people-watch. Be sure to drop in at **Days Gone By,** 303 N. Main St. (828-693-9056), an old-fashioned drugstore that has been in town since 1882. After a drink or snack, head out to any one of the variety of stores downtown has to offer. You'll find everything from a specialty toy store to antiques to clothing stores and boutiques. Among the shops are one of five **Mast General Stores** (828-696-1883), **Dancing Bear Toys** (828-693-4500), and **Narnia Studios** (828-697-6393), a whimsical art gallery full of flowers, fairies, and other fanciful items. Although some stores are open 7 days a week, most shops are closed on Sunday.

North Carolina features a number of apple festivals, but downtown Hendersonville is the site of the "official" **North Carolina Apple Festival.** The festival is a 4-day event that is usually held in early September. Downtown and the surrounding area come alive during the festival, which features sporting events, arts and crafts, entertainment, and of course lots of apples—applesauce, apple jelly, apple cider, and more. The celebration is highlighted by the King Apple Parade. Call (800) 828-4244 for more information.

Holmes Educational State Forest (all ages)
1299 Crab Creek Rd., 8 miles southwest of Hendersonville; (828) 692-0100; www.ncesf.org. Open 9 a.m. to 5 p.m. Tues through Fri and 11 a.m. to 8 p.m. Sat and Sun, mid-Mar through mid-Nov. Free.

Dupont State **Forest**

Another location between Hendersonville and Brevard where families can explore nature is Dupont State Forest, located about 11 miles from Hendersonville off Crab Creek Road. This is the true land of waterfalls, with more dropping water per square mile than any other place in the Southeast. Among the sights families will want to see are Triple Falls and Bridal Veil Falls. The forest also has 80 serious miles of biking trails, but there are easier routes to be ridden, too.

At Holmes Educational State Forest the trees talk. Everyone in the family will get something out of a visit to the trails in the 235-acre forest. The short Talking Tree Trail features various hardwood trees that relate their origin and history on push-button tape recordings. Another trail, which is slightly longer at 3 miles, allows you to touch various forest objects in special boxes and guess what they are without seeing them. Both picnic facilities and campsites are available in the forest, and park rangers present various interpretive programs throughout the year.

North Mills River Recreation Area and Campground

Located in Pisgah National Forest off Highway 191 North, 13 miles from Hendersonville; (800) 283-2267. Open year-round.

If the hotels or inns in the area don't suit your needs, a good place to camp is the North Mills River Recreation Area and Campground. In addition to fine fishing, the area offers picnic sites with grills and campsites for tents as well as trailers up to 22 feet. It's also a good place to take a trip down the river in an inner tube. Another plus this campground has to offer is the large, grassy playing area, where the kids can run off some steam.

Where to Eat

Apple Annie's Cafe. US 64 West; (828) 685-8890. The cafe is open for breakfast and lunch 7 days a week and serves just about everything under the sun. $

Haus Heidelberg. 630 Greenville Hwy.; (828) 693-8227; www.hausheidelberg.com. This restaurant features German beer for Mom and Dad and apple strudel for the kids. There is a children's menu with German cuisine. $$

Mills River Restaurant. Highway 191; (828) 891-4039. This is another good restaurant for families, with a variety of favorites. Items on the menu range from spaghetti to steak to seafood. $

Two Guys Pizza & Ribs. 746 6th Ave. West; (828) 693-6755; www.2guyspizza.net. Two Guys is a specialty pizza shop with a range of other items on the menu. $$

Where to Stay

Cedarwood Inn. 1510 Greenville Hwy.; (800) 832-2032. A few efficiencies are offered in addition to the rooms. $$

Cranmore Cottages. 220 Millard J. Dr.; (888) 868-1779. Two- and three-bedroom cottages provide respite from a full day of sightseeing. Among the selections is an 1800s homestead cabin. $$

Echo Mountain Inn. 2849 Laurel Park Hwy.; (828) 693-9626. Rooms and apartments offer very nice views. $$–$$$$

For More Information

Henderson County Travel & Tourism. (800) 828-4244; www.historichendersonville.org.

Flat Rock

Flat Rock is south of Hendersonville on Highway 25.

Connemara (ages 5 and up)

81 Carl Sandburg Ln.; (828) 693-4178. Open 9 a.m. to 5 p.m. daily. Admission is free; guided tours are available ($; free for children 16 and younger; call ahead for schedule).

Flat Rock, one of the oldest resort towns in the state, was for more than 20 years home to poet-historian Carl Sandburg. Connemara, Carl Sandburg Home National Historic Site, is located west on Highway 25. Sandburg's works ranged widely from children's books to stark political and social commentary, and his homesite offers insight into how he lived and worked. The home was built around 1838; Sandburg moved into it in 1945 with his wife and daughters. While he wrote, his family managed to maintain a working goat farm on-site. The home has been largely preserved as it was when Sandburg died in 1967. More than 10,000 manuscripts, books, and notes are still scattered throughout. It also houses descendents of the dairy goats that Sandburg's wife kept.

Where to Eat

There are few economical/family-friendly dining options in Flat Rock, so to feed the troops make the 10 minute drive back to Hendersonville.

Where to Stay

Highland Lake Inn. 86 Lily Pad Ln.; (800) 635-5101; www.hlinn.com. Twenty-six acres, a pool, and a big private lake with canoeing and other activities make for more than enough room to roam. Suites, cabins, and cottages are available. $$–$$$$

Lakemont Cottages. 101 Lakemont Dr.; (828) 693-5174. Waterfront cottages are offered here. $$$

Tryon

From Flat Rock head south on Highway 25 and east on Highway 176 to Tryon, one of North Carolina's centers for equestrian sports. The town is also a center for fine arts and fine dining, so while there are few family accommodations and the town proper offers little family adventure, the natural landscape offers a host of activities.

Foothills Equestrian Nature Center (FENCE) (all ages)
3381 Hunting Country Rd.; (828) 859-9021; www.fence.org.

Located at the western edge of the Blue Ridge Mountains, Tryon is home to numerous equestrian events year-round. The Foothills Equestrian Nature Center is host to most of these events and also includes nature trails and interpretive nature programs. Among the most popular events are the **Tryon Horse Show,** which has been held each June since 1929, and the **Block House Steeplechase,** which is held each April. The 484-acre center also offers hiking trails and regularly scheduled programming such as bird-watching and stargazing.

Green River Float Trips (ages 5 and up)

The Green River, which runs from the center of Polk County, north of Tryon, to the county's eastern edge, provides a great opportunity to take an adventurous cruise in an inner tube or specially made kayak ($–$$). **Green River Cove Campground** (828-749-3781; www.greenrivercovetubing.com), located at 5200 Green River Cove Rd., off Highway 9 (take Highway 108 north out of Tryon to the junction with Highway 9 and continue north); **Wilderness Cove,** 193 Green River Cove Rd., Saluda (828-817-1095; www.wilderness covecampground.com); and **Green River Adventures,** 1734 Holbert Cove Rd., Saluda (800-335-1530; www.greenriveradventures.com) can set you up with all the equipment you need for a trip down the river. While the pace of the Green River is slower than the whitewater of the rivers at higher elevations, there are several series of rapids that make it fun for the younger as well as the older members of the family. The outfitters offer tube, raft, and inflatable "funyak" rentals, as well as shuttle service so you can simply float back to your car. Trips range from 3 to 6 miles. The outfits offer camping, fishing trips, and other fun, too.

Pearson's Falls (all ages)
Located 4 miles west of Tryon off Highway 176. Open 10 a.m. to dusk daily. $.

For a slow-paced but spectacular trip, head to Pearson's Falls. The falls, which cascade down a gentle 90-foot slope, are beautifully maintained by the Tryon Garden Club. The area includes several hundred acres of wildlife preserve and botanical gardens. Paths through 200 species of ferns and plants wind around the falls. Picnic facilities are available, but no fires are allowed.

Where to Stay

Orchard Lake Campground. 460 Orchard Lake Rd., Saluda; (828) 749-3901; www.orchardlakecampground.com. Fully furnished A-frame cabins here sleep up to 6 people, and their pets are welcome. Two lakes are on-site for swimming and fishing. $

Lake Lure

Located near US 74, north on Highway 9 from the Green River, Lake Lure is a tiny but popular and pretty resort town created by the flooding of the area that is now the lake.

Beach at Lake Lure (all ages)

Memorial Highway; (877) 386-4255; www.lakelure.com. Open Memorial Day through Labor Day 10 a.m. to 6 p.m., weather permitting. $$; free for children under age 4.

A sandy beach surrounded by the beauty of the Blue Ridge Mountains, almost in the shadow of Chimney Rock, provides for an incredible relaxing day. The beach-area admission also includes a small water park with slides, water cannons, and more.

Cedar Creek Stables (all ages)

542 Cedar Creek Rd.; (828) 625-2811; www.cedarcreekstables.com. Open 8 a.m. to 5 p.m. daily. $$$$.

Cedar Creek offers trail rides for ages 8 and up and pony rides for younger children. Other activities include gem mining and fishing. There is also a small petting zoo of farm animals.

Lake Lure Tours (all ages)

2930 Memorial Hwy.; (877) 386-4255; www.lakelure.com. Tours depart on the hour typically from 10 a.m. until about one hour before dusk, Mar through Nov. $$–$$$; free for children under age 4.

Get a lakeside view of this charming town by boat. Tours coast past local attractions and landmarks as the skipper tells tales of local legend and natural and cultural history. Both lunch and dinner tours are also offered.

Where to Stay

Many of the accommodations in the Lake Lure area are more suitable for adults, but you can find a place here and there that has kids in mind.

Geneva Motel. 3147 Memorial Hwy.; (828) 625-4121; www.geneverivermotel.com. Fish from the shore while Mom watches from a hammock just a few feet away. The motel has a playground, grill, and lawn games and offers cottages, cabins, and apartments in addition to rooms. $–$$$

Premier Properties Vacation Rentals.
Highway 74, #7 Arcade Building; (800) 742-9556. You can probably find a place for Fido to stay in one of the facilities offered here. $$$

Willowbrook Inn. 103 Resort Ln.; (828) 625-1010; www.willowbrookinn.com. This little inn offers small suites a short drive from Lake Lure Beach. $$$

Chimney Rock

Head north on Highway 74 from Lake Lure to find one of the state's most recognizable symbols of tourism. Main Street in Chimney Rock runs parallel to the Rocky Broad River, which will have the kids kicking off their sneakers or Rainbows in no time. Picnic tables line the bank just off the road, and shops and restaurants populate downtown on both sides of the entrance to Chimney Rock Park.

Chimney Rock State Park (all ages)

US 64 and Highway 74A; (800) 277-9611; www.chimneyrockpark.com. Open year-round except Thanksgiving, Christmas, and New Year's Day, but trails may be closed due to inclement weather. Ticket office open daily 8:30 a.m. to 4:30 p.m. or to 5:30 p.m. during daylight savings time. $$–$$$.

On a clear day you can see almost 75 miles east as you stand on top of the 500-million-year-old rock at Chimney Rock Park, which is easy to find at its location on Highway 74A north of Lake Lure. Chimney Rock became a state park in 2010, and the state launched renovation plans in 2011, but families can still plan to spend several hours climbing on the well-manicured rocks and exploring the curious caves at this great park. Safety rails guard most of the dangerous places, but you'll still want to keep a close eye on the little ones. An elevator installed in the rock will take you up the equivalent of 26 stories to the top of Chimney Rock, or explore the outside of it on a unique hiking trail. As you walk along the trail, you can take a subterranean shortcut and hike on the walkways that lead from rock to rock. A climb down the wooden stairs affords a view of a moonshiners' cave. Two other trails offer views of **Hickory Nut Falls,** which cascades down 404 feet. While at the park you'll enjoy panoramic, breathtaking views all around. Snacks are available at the top of Chimney Rock, and picnic facilities and a nature center are also on-site.

Where to Stay

Carter Lodge. 273 Main St.; (828) 625-8844. All 16 rooms at the Carter Lodge have balconies overlooking the river or a covered sitting area outside charming rooms. It's located within walking distance of Chimney Rock Village. $$–$$$$

Chimney Rock Inn. 126 Main St.; (828) 625-1429. More rustic than elegant, this inn gets the job done nicely with rocking chair balconies and a swimming pool. Cabins are also offered. $$

For More Information

Rutherford County Tourism Development Authority. (800) 849-5998; www.rutherfordtourism.com.

Asheville

Asheville is easy to find from almost any direction. It's located on I-40 and Highway 74.

If you plan a trip to Asheville, western North Carolina's biggest city, plan on being here a while: It's almost two towns in one. A burgeoning bohemian arts area has grown downtown, while the Biltmore Estate region has remained a more refined cultural district. With a population of about 67,000, it's a great place for family adventure—to escape the heat of summer, to enjoy the colors of fall and spring, or to spend a cozy weekend during the winter holidays. Asheville, nestled at the edge of the Smoky Mountains where I-26 and I-40 cross, has become a cultural and educational center for the western part of the state. Still, its mountainous beauty has been preserved through relatively well-managed growth and by the vigilance of the environmentally conscious citizens who date back to the city's most famous resident, George Vanderbilt.

Biltmore Estate (ages 5 and up)

1 Approach Rd. (on US 25 just off I-40); (800) 624-1575; www.biltmore.com. Open 8:30 a.m. to 6:30 p.m. daily. Hours for attractions, restaurants, and shops at the estate vary. $$–$$$$; free for children 9 and younger.

A trip to North Carolina's mountains, or anywhere nearby, wouldn't be complete without seeing the Biltmore Estate, the 255-room French Renaissance mansion that, although no longer occupied by the Vanderbilt family, is the largest private residence in the country. Even the approach to this 8,000-acre estate, built by George Vanderbilt in 1895, is simply dazzling. Vanderbilt, the grandson of a railroad tycoon, originally bought more than 125,000 acres of land in this area, much of which he would later sell to the federal government for a token price to develop what is now Pisgah National Forest. He is best known for having led an effort to manage forestry, instead of simply cutting down trees anytime the logging companies needed them. The home includes more than 50,000 works of art, furnishings, and antiques, which Vanderbilt spent years collecting in Europe and Asia. Among the works at the home are pieces by Renoir and Whistler, in addition to a chess table once owned by Napoleon Bonaparte.

The home was constructed over a five-year period and took a total of one million hours of labor, much of it from European designers whom Vanderbilt brought here. In addition to the 22 rooms in which the Vanderbilt family lived, the home also includes an indoor swimming pool and bowling alley. The home is especially beautiful during the evening candlelight tours during the Christmas holidays. Be sure to allow time to take a stroll around the expansive gardens, pools, and natural areas, and to visit to the winery, where sparkling, red, white, and rosé wines are produced. **Antler Hill,** the newest part of the estate, was developed in the winery area to add space for concerts, exhibits, shopping, and dining. It also includes an outdoor adventure center that is a base for carriage rides, biking, Segway tours, and even off-road Land Rover experiences. The **Inn on Biltmore Estate** provides a gracious environment and outstanding views. A carriage ride or meal in one of Biltmore's restaurants tops off a day trip nicely.

Historic Biltmore Village (all ages)
Located on US 25, adjacent to the Biltmore Estate; (828) 274-5570; www.biltmorevillage .com. Most shops are open 10 a.m. to 5:30 p.m. Mon through Sat and 1 to 5 p.m. Sun.

Adjacent to the Biltmore Estate is Historic Biltmore Village, a group of restored homes that now contain shops, restaurants, and galleries. At these shops you will find handcrafted jewelry and pottery, blown glass, fine art, children's books and games, collectible dolls, and more. In all there are more than 30 shops and most likely something for everyone in the family. Of particular interest for children are **Biltmore Village Dolls & Gifts, Claying Around, Once Upon a Time,** and **William & Grace . . . A Children's Boutique.** Also, the **Biltmore Village Historic Museum** presents photographs, maps, and artifacts on the history of the village.

Botanical Gardens at Asheville (ages 5 and up)
151 W. T. Weaver Blvd.; (828) 252-5190; www.ashevillebotanicalgardens.org. Open daily during daylight hours. Free.

More natural beauty awaits at the Botanical Gardens at Asheville, on the campus of the University of North Carolina at Asheville. Here examine hundreds of species of plants and flowers that are native to the southern Appalachian Mountains. Within these 10 acres are a large azalea garden and a charming rock garden. In addition, visit the renovated earthworks from the Battle of Asheville as well as a garden for the blind.

Grove Park Inn (all ages)
290 Macon Ave.; (800) 438-5800; www.groveparkinn.com. $$$$.

While there is a larger choice in the variety of accommodations in and around Asheville, clearly the best place to stay is the Grove Park Inn. This resort is one of the state's top hotels, first opened in 1913 and nestled in the hills of the Blue Ridge. Made of huge local granite stones, the hotel has 510 guest rooms, including 12 suites in the main building and the two wings. You can also play a round of golf on the 18-hole course, play tennis inside or out, swim inside or out, rent a mountain bike from the fitness center, or relax in the spa. Planned children's programs are also scheduled from week to week. The Inn's Cub's Adventure Camp for kids over age 3 includes activities such as nature hikes, swimming, lawn games, arts and crafts, and team competitions. Sign the kids up for a full or half day. Kid's Night Out provides a night out for parents, too. Activities include themed dinner parties, outdoor activities, games, swimming, face-painting, and movies for the kids! Even visitors who are not guests can play golf or visit the spa.

Health Adventure (all ages)

800 Brevard Road; (828) 254-6373; www.thehealthadventure.org. Open 10 a.m. to 5 p.m. Tues through Sat and 1 to 5 p.m. Sun. $–$$; free for children under age 2.

The Health Adventure is a spectacular interactive facility that has dozens of exhibits and displays about the human body. It's now located in Biltmore Square Mall after spending nearly 20 years in downtown's Pack Place. Here you can touch a 5-foot-high brain and challenge your own gray matter in a display that introduces you to a number of creativity-testing games. Next, enter the Bodyworks Gallery, where you can try to jump as high as Michael Jordan or take a journey through a giant replica of a human bloodstream. At the Miracle of Life Gallery you'll learn all about heredity and life before birth. Children younger than 8 will get a kick out of dressing up as a cowboy, pirate, or other characters at the Creative PlaySpace. Here they can also put on a puppet show or take a slide down the giant tongue.

Pack Place (all ages)

2 S. Pack Sq.; (828) 257-4500; www.packplace.org. Admission varies by activity.

After visitng downtown, the next thing families want to do while in Asheville is pay a visit to Pack Place, the city's downtown center of arts, education, and science. It includes several museums as well as space for performing arts.

Asheville Art Museum (ages 5 and up)

(828) 253-3227; www.ashevilleart.org. Open 10 a.m. to 5 p.m. Tues through Sat and 1 to 5 p.m. Sun. $$; free for children under 4. Additional fees may apply for selected exhibitions.

Modern American art makes up the biggest permanent collection at the Asheville Art Museum. The collection also features a wide range of work from Impressionists as well as contemporary abstract artists. Regular events and other programs for families are also conducted.

Colburn Earth Science Museum (ages 5 and up)

(828) 254-7162. Open 10 a.m. to 5 p.m. Tues through Sat and 1 to 5 p.m. Sun. $.

This museum is like many of the mineral museums in the mountains, with a twist or two. It has local stones as well as displays of 4,500 precious stones and other specimens, including fossils, from around the world. *Weather, Climate, and You* is a fun interactive exhibit that uncovers the science behind the weather report. It illustrates what happens when wind hits a mountain, teaches visitors about the history of weather in the region, and lets kids do their own TV weather report. The History of Mining in North Carolina exhibit takes visitors from the very earliest mining by Native Americans and early Spanish explorers through the present day. The exhibit also chronicles the major role that gold mining played in the state's history.

YMI Cultural Center (ages 5 and up)

39 Market St.; (828) 252-4614. Hours vary. $–$$.

The YMI Cultural Center is formerly the Young Men's Institute, founded by George Vander-bilt in 1893. The center houses a few permanent and temporary art exhibits related largely to the African-American heritage of the area. The center also develops programs for local residents and youths and stages various performances in its small informal theater.

Thomas Wolfe Memorial (ages 5 and up)

52 N. Market St.; (828) 253-8304; www.wolfememorial.com. Open 9 a.m. to 5 p.m. Tues through Sat and 1 to 5 p.m. Sun, Apr through Oct; 10 a.m. to 4 p.m. Tues through Sat and 1 to 4 p.m. Sun, Nov through Mar. $.

The Thomas Wolfe Memorial, located at N. Market and Woodfin Streets (the entrance is next to the Radisson Hotel), was the childhood home of the world-famous author. Although Wolfe left the home at age 15 to attend school in Chapel Hill, he wrote about it in his novel *Look Homeward, Angel,* published in 1929. The Wolfe House was the victim of arson in 1998, but historians restored it and reopened the house in 2004. Kids will also enjoy the visitor center next door, which includes a small exhibit hall, a theater, and many items from the home.

Western North Carolina Nature Center (all ages)

75 Gashes Creek Rd.; (828) 298-5600; www.wncnaturecenter.com. Open 10 a.m. to 5 p.m. daily. $–$$.

The Western North Carolina Nature Center offers an opportunity to study wildlife up close in its exhibit halls and along a hilly but manageable wooded trail. The center is a living nature museum that shows visitors how animals, the environment, and people work together to shape the world. The center's World Underground exhibit demonstrates the importance of this unique environment; look really closely to find more life than you could imagine. Other exhibits include spiders, snakes, and even the least weasel. Along the trail come face to face with coyotes, gray and red wolves, mountain lions, a huge bear, deer, and more. Kids can play alongside otters or see butterflies emerge from chrysalises in a seasonal exhibit. The petting zoo and barn gives the kids an opportunity to pet a goat or even milk a cow.

Zebulon B. Vance Birthplace (ages 5 and up)

Reems Creek Road, just off US 25, Weaverville; (828) 645-6706; www.nchistoricsites.org. Open 9 a.m. to 5 p.m. Tues through Sat. Free.

Just a few miles north of Asheville, but off the beaten path, visit the Zebulon B. Vance Birthplace. Vance, born in 1830, was a revered US senator and served as governor of North Carolina during the Civil War. His home takes the family back to the pioneer farm life of the 18th century. The 2-story pine log structure has been reconstructed around the original chimney. Some of the furnishings in the home belonged to the Vance family, and all of it is representative of the late 18th and early 19th centuries. Also visit the museum, which includes exhibits relating to Vance's life, and the 6 outbuildings that surround the house. Special living-history re-creations are presented in the spring and summer, and **free** guided tours are conducted year-round on the hour.

Where to Eat

Asheville Pizza and Brewing Company. 675 Merrimon Ave.; (828) 254-1281; www .ashevillebrewing.com. Mom and Dad can enjoy one of Asheville's many handcrafted beers at this pizza joint that has a game room and movie screen, too. $

Burgermeister's Kitchen and Tap. 697 Haywood Rd.; (828) 225-2920; www.burger meisters.com. Locals say this restaurant serves the best burgers in town. $

Corner Kitchen. 3 Boston Way; (828) 274-2439; www.thecornerkitchen.com. Located in Historic Biltmore Village, this cozy restaurant provides options for outdoor dining with a varied menu. Even the kids' menu has a little flair, with offerings like salmon and cucumber noodles. $–$$$

El Chapala. 868 Merrimon Ave.; (828) 258-0899. A Mariachi band plays occasionally at this Mexican restaurant with 6 locations in the area. $

Hunter's Lodge. 330 Weaverville Hwy.; (828) 645-8383. Inside the walls of this log cabin, staff serves everything from trout to pan-fried chicken with thick creamy gravy in a Bavarian tradition. $$$

Moose Cafe. 570 Brevard Rd.; (828) 255-0920; www.eatatthemoosecafe.com. Located next to the farmers' market, the Moose menu includes dishes made with local fresh ingre-dients. $$$

Three Brothers Restaurant. 183 Haywood St.; (828) 253-4971. This is a casual, family-style restaurant with a lot of variety in a Greek style. $

Where to Stay

Asheville is a large enough destination to support many hotels, including larger chains, so you shouldn't have much trouble finding a place to stay. Watch, however, for inns and B&Bs that are not equipped to handle chil-dren. Here are a few places in various parts of the city with local flair:

Forest Manor Inn. 866 Hendersonville Rd.; (828) 274-3531. Located near the Biltmore Estate, this inn offers a heated outdoor pool, a playground, and shuffleboard. $$$$

Haywood Park Hotel. 1 Battery Park Ave.; (828) 252-2522. Located in the heart of Ashe-ville's downtown, the Haywood Park Hotel is a luxurious, upscale inn offering rooms and suites, but still pets and kids are OK here. $$$$

The Mountaineer Inn. 155 Tunnel Rd.; (828) 254-5331. This historic landmark is located outside busy tourist areas but near the Asheville Mall. $$$

The Pines Cottages. 346 Weaverville Hwy., Asheville; (828) 645-9661. If you plan an extended stay in Asheville, you might want to try The Pines, which offers two-bedroom cot-tages. $$–$$$$

For More Information

Asheville Convention and Visitors Bureau. (800) 257-1300; www.explore asheville.com.

Blue Ridge Parkway

In the Asheville area are the most-used entrances to the Blue Ridge Parkway, which runs from Great Smoky Mountains National Park near Cherokee into Virginia at I-77. You'll find a great deal to do along the parkway's nearly 500 miles, and the section near Asheville is no exception. Keep in mind the parkway, with its overlooks, tunnels, and a 45 mph speed limit, is built more for tourists than traveling. Get recorded information on weather, road conditions, recreation, and more by calling (828) 298-0398 or check out www.blueridge parkway.org.

Clear Creek Guest Ranch (all ages)
100 Clear Creek Dr., Burnsville; (800) 651-4510; www.clearcreekranch.com. $$.

Standing in the shadow of Mount Mitchell is this family-oriented guest ranch, offering mountaintop horseback riding on hundreds of acres of Pisgah National Forest. The ranch offers lodging in cabin units with heart of pine siding set among rhododendron and other colorful mountain flora. In addition to fun family-style meals, hosts Rex and Aileen Rederick offer line dancing, karaoke, whitewater rafting on the South Toe River, fishing trips, golf outings, and more. The site also includes a swimming pool, hot tub, and old-fashioned fishing pond.

Craggy Gardens (ages 5 and up)
Blue Ridge Parkway between Mileposts 363 and 369; (828) 298-0398. Open daily, generally during daylight hours, May through Oct. Free.

The gardens are a beautifully sculptured sight when colorful rhododendron are at their peak bloom in early summer. See a wide variety of other mountain wildflowers here as well. You'll also find a visitor center, nature trails, and picnic facilities.

Mount Mitchell State Park (all ages)
Exit off Blue Ridge Parkway at Milepost 355 onto Highway 128, Burnsville; (828) 675-4611 or www.ils.unc.edu/parkproject. Open daily, generally 8 a.m. to sunset. Free.

From Craggy Gardens you are only a few minutes away from Mount Mitchell State Park. At 6,684 feet, Mount Mitchell is the tallest peak east of the Mississippi River. This extraordinary peak pokes out of the Black Mountains, which are among the oldest mountains on earth. If the clouds aren't hanging too low, an observation tower at Mount Mitchell's peak affords spectacular views of the Smoky Mountains. A small interactive museum has displays on the mountain's flora and fauna, and a restaurant is open near the peak in the summer. Enjoy a number of outdoor activities at the 1,600-acre park, including hiking, picnicking, and some camping (although camping is not recommended for families). The park is open according to weather conditions, so call ahead. Because of the elevation, it has been known to snow here as early as September and as late as May, not at all common in North Carolina.

Amazing
North Carolina Facts

Dr. Elisha Mitchell, the University of North Carolina mathematician for whom Mount Mitchell is named, died in 1857 while attempting to prove the mountain's height. He made a number of attempts to measure the mountain as early as the 1830s. Mitchell's grave is on the top of the mountain.

Southern Highlands Folk Art Center (ages 5 and up)
Blue Ridge Parkway at Milepost 382; (828) 298-7928; www.southernhighlandguild.org. Open 9 a.m. to 5 p.m. daily, Jan through Mar; 9 a.m. to 6 p.m. daily, Apr through Dec. Closed Thanksgiving, Christmas, and New Year's Day. Free.

In addition to some beautiful overlooks, the biggest parkway attraction in this area is the Folk Art Center. Opened in 1980, this is southern Appalachia's oldest and best-known crafts shop. The center is operated by the Southern Highland Craft Guild; the Appalachian Regional Commission, which operates shops here and in 4 other cities in the southern highlands; and the National Park Service. The 30,000-square-foot center is also one of the largest crafts shops you will find. A museum in the upstairs portion of the center is dedicated to displaying remarkable changing exhibits created by its members. You'll also have an opportunity to purchase quilts, toys, furniture, and stoneware made by guild member artisans. In addition, live demonstrations are held most of the time the center is open.

North Carolina Arboretum (all ages)
100 Frederick Law Olmsted Way; (828) 665-2492; www.ncaboretum.org. Generally open 8 a.m. until dark. Free; fee charged for parking.

Nature trails, an art walk, manicured gardens, and space for changing exhibits are located at the arboretum. Highlights include a curious bonsai collection and the production greenhouse. Tours are typically self-guided, but regular activities for families are scheduled throughout the year.

Mars Hill

Drive north from Asheville on US 23.

Wolf Ridge Ski Resort (all ages)
Located north of Asheville on US 23; (800) 817-4111; www.skiwolfridgenc.com. $$$–$$$$.

Before leaving the Asheville area, get in a little skiing, tubing, or snowboarding only about 40 minutes away. Wolf Ridge features 20 slopes for various skill levels and activities. In addition, the ski school there features a special program for children ages 4 through 7, offering simple lessons and instructions, as well as races, games, and other planned activities. The lodge here is nice, too. The resort has food ranging from snacks to full meals, in a restaurant that provides beautiful views of the slopes. Accommodations are available at **Wolf Ridge Lodge** as well as in vacation homes that surround the area. Snowmaking machines allow this slope to open in late November.

Spruce Pine

If you're looking for a scenic drive, make your way back from Mars Hill to the Blue Ridge Parkway by taking US 19 north to Highway 80 South, or head straight over to Spruce Pine by staying on US 19.

Along the twisting and turning route through these mountain highways are handicraft shops and galleries, where local crafters and artists are hard at work. If you want to see more, you can obtain a guidebook for a scenic drive that highlights this local work by contacting the Yancey County/Burnsville Chamber of Commerce (828-682-7413; www.yancey chamber.com).

Gem Mountain (ages 5 and up)

13780 Highway 226; (888) 817-5829; www.gemmountain.com. Open 9 a.m. to 5 p.m. Mon through Sat (until 7 p.m. during the summer), Mar through Dec. Free admission to Gem Mountain, including the museum; mining buckets start at $$$.

In addition to the local crafts, this area's biggest attraction is its mines. Gem Mountain features flumes where you can hunt for gems for a per-bucket fee. In addition, visit Gem Mountain's Sands of Time museum, have a picnic by the stream or eat at the restaurant, and enjoy an ice-cream cone.

Little Switzerland

From Spruce Pine, travel south on Highway 226.

Everything that makes the mountains of North Carolina so great—the crafts, the mines, the beautiful scenery, the lodging, the shopping, and the dining—can be found in Little Switzerland, a bit of European landscape in the heart of North Carolina's mountains.

Emerald Village (ages 5 and up)

McKinney Mine Road off Highway 226A; (828) 765-6463; www.emeraldvillage.com. Open 9 a.m. to 5 p.m. Mon through Fri and 9 a.m. to 6 p.m. Sat and Sun, Apr through Oct. Fees vary by activity.

This is probably one of the biggest and most popular public mining operations in the mountains. Dozens of different minerals, gems, and rocks have been found here, including aquamarine, emerald, garnet, and uranium. Attendants are on hand to help identify finds, as are artisans for cutting and mounting newly found stones. Also visit the **North Caro-lina Mining Museum,** located in an underground mine, where you can examine old min-ing equipment and displays on the area's mining heritage. Other **free** village attractions include the Company Store and Discovery Mill, where you'll find more displays related to mining as well as souvenirs and gifts.

Orchard at Altapass (all ages)

1025 Orchard Rd., Blue Ridge Parkway at Milepost 328.3; (828) 765-9531; www.altapass orchard.com. Hours vary by season; closed in winter. Fees charged for some activities and events.

When the Blue Ridge Parkway was built in the middle of the 20th century, it split this his-toric orchard in half and almost left it for dead. But in the mid-1990s Kit Trubey and her brother and sister-in-law, Bill and Judy Carson, bought the orchard, with turning it into something special in mind. Today the half south of the parkway thrives as an orchard, but it also includes a host of activities including mountain musical events, hayrides, storytell-ing, and a seasonal butterfly exhibit.

Where to Eat

Switzerland Cafe & General Store. High-way 226 near the Blue Ridge Parkway; (828) 765-5289; www.switzerlandcafe.com. Light items, soups, and salads are served in an old-time general-store atmosphere. $

Where to Stay

Big Lynn Lodge. Highway 226A; (800) 654-5232. This is a very nice country inn with rooms, cottages, and condos. $$$$

Skyline Motel. Highway 226; (828) 765-9394. The Skyline is located just off the park-way on a mountaintop. $$

Marion

Travel south from Little Switzerland to Highway 126 to find the town of Marion and one of the state's most impressive and beautiful lakefront properties.

Lake James State Park (all ages)

Northeast of Marion on Highway 126; (828) 652-4496; www.ncparks.gov. Open year-round, generally during daylight hours. **Free.**

At the base of Linvillle Gorge, Lake James State Park is a great place to play golf, fish, camp, swim, and hike. The lake, which is fed by two mountain streams and the Catawba River, offers 150 miles of shoreline along beautiful, crystal-clear water. A sandy beach is located near the park office. Ten golf courses are located in this area, and the park con-tains great campsites for low-impact camping. Each site has a grill, water, and a picnic

Brown Mountain **Lights**

I have never experienced the Brown Mountain Lights personally, but many North Carolinians swear they are there. The mystery purports that on certain clear evenings, small, brilliant orbs can be seen wavering, bobbing up and down, disappearing, and reappearing from several points in this area. Sometimes they are red, sometimes blue. This mystery has attracted thousands of curiosity seekers, who have set up camp here since 1771. Extensive scientific research by the US Geologic Survey has failed to explain the phenomenon. There are several vantage points along Highway 181 and from Wiseman's View on the Kistler Memorial Highway (SR 138) near Linville Falls where you can try to catch a peek of the Brown Mountain Lights.

table, and the sites are located away from traffic. Along the park's nature trails you never know when you'll get a glimpse of a deer, flying squirrel, fox, or muskrat, and the lake offers great bass, crappie, and catfish fishing.

Where to Eat

Catawba Vale Cafe Restaurant. 130 N. Logan St; (828) 559-0661. Fresh salads and sandwiches are served along with Saturday afternoon jam sessions with local musicians. $

Countryside Bar-B-Que. 2070 Rutherford Rd.; (828) 652-4885. Countryside serves a variety of home-style dishes in addition to barbecue. $

Harvest Drive-In. 861 N. Main St.; (828) 652-4155. This is a really peachy 1950s drive-in. Enjoy childhood favorites like onion rings and a foot long hot dog—with a shake, of course. $

Where to Stay

Barn House Inn. 11611 Montford Cove Rd.; (866) 690-9182; www.barnhouseinn.com. This rustic blue barn-style inn is located on a piece of property that's just as quaint. Enjoy creek walking, swimming, hiking, and picnicking in

the gazebo. A fully equipped kitchen stocked with breakfast items, including homemade jellies and jams, local eggs, and honey, is waiting for you to check in. Families with children and pets are welcome. $$$–$$$$

Mountain Paradise Campground. 16823 US 221 North; (828) 756-4085; www.mountainparadisenc.com. If you are a kid, this is paradise. A rare waterslide at one of the pools, miniature golf, a playground, a fishing pond, and more are located on-site. $

Yogi Bear's Jellystone Park, Camp and Resort. 1210 Deacon Dr.; (828) 652-7208; www.jellystonemarion.com. Cabins and tent camping are both offered at this campground named for that funny bear that never seems to get enough to eat. $

For More Information

McDowell County Tourism Development Authority. (888) 233-6111; www.mcdowellnc.org.

Linville Falls

Located just off the Blue Ridge Parkway on US 221 is the town of Linville Falls and the **Linville Gorge Wilderness Area.** These 7,600 acres of land have been preserved as a natural area, but you can hike a number of trails for various views of the falls and the Linville River, which descends more than 2,000 feet in only 12 miles. The upper part of the falls rolls over 50 feet and disappears into the mountain, then the lower falls drops another 60 feet. If it's hot, hike down the rocks bordering the falls and wade in the cool waters, watching more adventurous hikers scale the vertical rocks. The gorge below the falls is part of Pisgah National Forest and is maintained for hunting and fishing. Two observation points, one on the east and one on the west side of the gorge, provide excellent panoramic views. You'll also come across plenty of picnic facilities around this area.

Jonas Ridge Snow Tubing (ages 5 and up)

Highway 181, Jonas Ridge; (828) 733-4155; www.jonasridgesnowtubing.com. $$$$.

Just about 10 minutes from Linville Falls in the Jonas Ridge community is a smaller snow-tubing park that includes 1 slope with 6 lanes. It's typically less crowed than the larger ski areas and tubing parks in the area.

Linville Caverns (ages 5 and up)

US 221 North, Marion; (800) 419-0540; www.linvillecaverns.com. Open daily 9 a.m. to 5 p.m. (until 6 p.m. in the summer, 4:30 p.m. Nov through Mar); weekends only Dec through Feb. $$; free for children under 5.

It's impossible to ignore the signs urging you to visit Linville Caverns, where the 52-degree year-round temperature is more than welcome during a humid North Carolina summer. The caverns, the only ones in the state that are open to the public, are located on US 221 near its intersection with the Blue Ridge Parkway. Get a lesson on stalagmites, stalactites, and other natural formations. In addition, you'll see unusual blind fish in the underground stream and experience total darkness. Guided tours on the marked trail are held about every half hour. One caution: The part of the tour that includes total darkness may frighten younger children (and some adults, too).

North Carolina **Skiing**

To the north of Linville is a skier's paradise. Between 5 and 8 feet of natural snow falls in this area each winter, depending on the elevation, but snowmaking machines provide good skiing conditions all winter long. You can call the **High Country Ski Report** at (800) 962-2322 or visit www.skinorthcarolina .com to get conditions at the area's ski resorts.

Where to Eat

Famous Louise's Rockhouse Restaurant. Highway 221 near Highway 183; (828) 765-2702. A favorite of the locals, Louise's has home-style cooking and killer pie. $

Spears Restaurant. Linville Falls Lodge, Highway 221 North near Highway 183; (800) 634-4421; www.linvillefallslodge.com. This restaurant serves what some call the best barbecue in the Carolinas, and the food has

stood the test of time, remaining open since 1979. $

Where to Stay

Linville Falls Lodge and Cottages. Highway 221 North near Highway 183; (800) 634-4421; www.linvillefallslodge.com. This is a small inn that also offers cottages. $$–$$$

Linville

Linville is located north of Linville Falls on US 221.

Grandfather Mountain (all ages)

Located on US 221, 1 mile from the Blue Ridge Parkway; (800) 468-7325; www.grandfather .com. Open daily 9 a.m. to 5 p.m. during winter; 9 a.m. to 6 p.m. in spring and fall; and 9 a.m. to 7 p.m. in summer. Closed Thanksgiving and Christmas. $$–$$$.

Don't let the similar names confuse you—Linville and Linville Falls are two different towns. Linville is known for one of the top scenic attractions in the North Carolina mountains—Grandfather Mountain. This is a great place to spend the day hiking and learning about nature. The 5,964-foot peak was named for its profile as it appears from about 7 miles north. As the name suggests, from this vantage point the mountain looks like a bearded grandfather. Grandfather Mountain has been recognized by the United Nations as an international reserve where people and nature live together in harmony. Enter the park off US 221 and you can drive through a lot of it, but you'll have to park at the visitor center and walk to get to the top. You'll also find picnic and limited camping facilities here. Food is available at **Mildred's Grill,** named for the famous bear that spent much of her life on Grandfather Mountain.

No matter what time of year you visit Grandfather Mountain, there is always plenty to do. As you drive into the park, the first attraction you come to is the nature museum, a small museum with a gift shop that kids will adore. At the shop they will find toys and all sorts of knickknacks related to animals, nature, and the Blue Ridge Parkway. The museum offers an unusual look at the area's natural past, with displays and films on nature and the mountains. You'll see gold nuggets, precious gemstones, a billion-year-old rock, and displays of rare plants and animals. The kids will surely want to have their picture taken with the big bear. They'll also love the

Celtic **Celebration**

A good time to visit Grandfather Mountain is the second weekend in July, when the **Highland Games** are held. While there are other Scottish celebrations in the state, this is one of the best. It includes traditional Scottish athletic competitions, spiced up with authentic Scottish music, dance, and other attractions from the Scottish tradition. For more information on the Highland Games, call (828) 733-1333 or log on to www.gmhg.org.

Daniel Boone exhibit. A variety of animals—including black bears and cubs, cougars, deer, and eagles—are on display in what resembles natural habitats. Many of these animals have been injured and will never be able to return to the wild.

The highlight of a visit to Grandfather Mountain is a stomach-rumbling walk across the **Mile-High Swinging Bridge.** It extends majestically over a natural gorge filled with hardwood trees and rhododendron. You'll find overlooks on both sides of the bridge if you can't make the walk across.

Seven Devils

Just north of Linville and off the beaten path on Highway 105 is Seven Devils.

Hawksnest (ages 5 and up)
2058 Skyland Dr.; (828) 963-6561; www.hawksnest-resort.com. $$$$.

Once a full-fledged wintertime resort, Hawksnest has downgraded its offerings but not its family fun. The park offers 4 slopes with multiple lanes for tubing only—no skiers allowed. In addition, a zip-line tour takes the more adventurous over valleys, forests, and creeks.

Banner Elk

From Seven Devils, take Highway 184 north to Banner Elk to find North Carolina's center for downhill fun.

Sugar Mountain Ski Resort (all ages)
1009 Sugar Mountain Dr.; (828) 898-4521; www.skisugar.com. $$–$$$$.

This ski resort is the area's largest, with 20 slopes and 8 lifts. A 1,200-foot drop provides plenty of thrills for the advanced skier, while lessons are offered for beginners. A ski school for kids ($$$$) offers lessons from 10 a.m. to 3 p.m. The resort also features tubing and ice skating. In warm months the slope offers scenic chairlift rides and biking trails.

For More Information

Avery/Banner Elk Chamber of Commerce. (800) 972-2183; www.averycounty.com.

Beech Mountain

Continue north from Sugar Mountain to find Beech Mountain, the highest incorporated town in the eastern US.

Genesis Wildlife Sanctuary (all ages)
206 Grassy Cap Creek Rd.; (828) 387-2979. Open daily 9 a.m. to 5 p.m. Free.

Sick, orphaned, and injured wildlife might find their way to this rehabilitation center and hospital in Beech Mountain. Some that are unable to be returned to the wild live in habitats located along a short trail. It's also home to Sir Walter Wally, the state groundhog. Visitors to the area are likely to meet one of the sanctuary's residents at many of the events and festivals held throughout the region.

Ski Beech (all ages)
1007 Beech Mountain Pkwy.; (800) 438-2093; www.skibeech.com. $$$–$$$$; children under 4 get a free lift ticket when accompanied by a ticketed adult.

Ski Beech, located on Highway 184 in Beech Mountain, north of Banner Elk, is at the highest elevation of the area's ski resorts and as a result offers the most natural snow. Its 15 slopes and 11 lifts tend to keep you on the slope more here. Skaters in the family will appreciate the ice-skating rink, and special programs are offered for children. A tube run provides additional adventure, and snowboarders will appreciate the freestyle terrain.

For More Information

Beech Mountain Chamber of Commerce. (800) 468-5506; www.beechmtn.com.

Parent's **Tip**

Kids under 12 can bring their plastic sleds to the hill at Beech Mountain Town Hall for sledding all winter long. It's free and parents can ride with children who can't ride alone.

Boone

From Beech Mountain head east on US 321. From Banner Elk take Highway 194 East. From Linville take the Blue Ridge Parkway to US 321.

Boone is a great central location for seeing this part of the Blue Ridge. Not only is there a lot to see and do in and around the city, but Boone also provides easy access to the Blue Ridge Parkway, the ski resorts, and other towns and attractions. The city is named for the famous frontiersman Daniel Boone, who had a cabin here from 1760 to 1769. Today there are thousands of lodging rooms, ranging from bed-and-breakfast inns to chain hotels.

Appalachian Ski Mountain (all ages)

940 Ski Mountain Rd.; (800) 322-2373; www.appskimtn.com. $$$$.

Just off the parkway near US 321 is another of North Carolina's ski resorts. Appalachian Ski Mountain has 9 slopes and 4 lifts. The resort is also home to the **French-Swiss Ski College.** The resort traditionally offers the best rates during its opening-anniversary period, when you ski for 1962 rates of $5 for an adult lift ticket, $2.50 for a junior lift ticket, and rentals for $6.50. Look for this special deal early in December.

Daniel Boone Native Gardens (ages 5 and up)

591 Horn in the West Dr.; (828) 264-6390; www.danielboonegardens.org. Open daily 10 a.m. to 6 p.m. $.

Head to the outdoor theater early to see the Daniel Boone Native Gardens, which features plantings unique to the area, native gardens, and unusual architecture. In addition to handsome hardscapes—a gatehouse, a complex of arbors and walks, and a reflecting pool—the garden features a bog garden, ferns, rhododendrons, and a whimsical meditation maze.

Hickory Ridge Homestead (all ages)

Located on the grounds at Horn in the West; (828) 264-2120. Hours vary according to showtimes.

Hickory Ridge is an 18th-century living-history museum highlighting the daily lives of mountain ancestors. Visitors get a glimpse into the past as interpreters in period clothing explain pioneer life and culture. Docents present regular demonstrations in hearthside cooking, weaving, and other crafts. Guests can explore the historic buildings on the grounds, such as the Tatum cabin, built in 1785, and learn how settlers survived brutal mountain winters.

Horn in the West (ages 5 and up)

591 Horn in the West Dr.; (828) 264-2120; www.horninthewest.com. Performances, which last about 2 hours, are held at 8 p.m. Tues through Sun from late June to mid-Aug. $$–$$$.

Daniel Boone's legacy and his contribution to the settlement of the area are portrayed in *Horn in the West,* a fabulous musical outdoor drama held at the Powderhorn Amphitheater just off US 421. The play, America's third-longest-running outdoor drama, running since 1952, is set during the time Boone lived here, when colonial unrest against British dominance was at its peak. The play reveals how Boone and his men struggled to settle this area and build the mountain culture that is still evident today. A favorite from the piece, for young and old alike, is a spectacular Cherokee Indian fire dance.

Wahoo's Adventures (ages 7 and up)

US 321; (800) 444-7238; www.wahoosadventures.com.

To schedule an active family adventure without doing all the planning yourself, call Wahoo's Adventures. No matter what kind of adventure you are looking for, Wahoo's can help you put it all together. Whitewater rafting trips are offered on 4 rivers in the area for different ages and skill levels. Full- and half-day trips are conducted, and picnics are prepared for you by the crew. If an overnight trip is more to your liking, that too can be arranged. The outfitter also plans four-wheel-drive trips, self-guided canoe trips, inner-tubing, and even cave exploration trips. Prices are as varied as the activities, so call ahead for information or to make reservations.

Where to Eat

Bandana's Bar B Que & Grill. 1475 Highway 105; (828) 265-2828; www.bandanas barbque.com. Bandana's features barbecue of all kinds—pork, chicken, turkey, and baby back and St. Louis ribs—in a relaxed family atmosphere. $$

Casa Rustica. 1348 Highway 105; (828) 262-5128; www.casarustica1981.com. This Italian restaurant has a neat casual atmosphere and good pizza. $

Dan'l Boone Inn. 130 Hardin St.; (828) 264-8657; www.danlbooneinn.com. If it's time for dinner, make sure you're hungry before you head to the Dan'l Boone Inn restaurant. One price gets you all you want to eat at this busy rustic inn. You won't have to worry about menus or deciding what you're going to eat because meals are served family-style, just like at Grandma's house. If they run out of mashed potatoes, don't worry—if you want seconds, you can have rice. There is plenty of variety on the dessert cart, too; save room if you can. $–$$$; children under 4 eat **free**

Mountain House Restaurant. 1601 Blowing Rock Rd.; (828) 264-4680; www.mountain houserestuarant.com. Get breakfast any time of day here. Steaks, seafood, salads, and sandwiches are also offered. $

Troy's 105. 1286 Highway 105; (828) 265-1344; www.troys105diner.com. This 1950s-style restaurant serves standard diner selections along with prime jukebox selections. $

Where to Stay

ADN Log Cabin Rentals. Blowing Rock, Boone, and Valle Crucis; (800) 237-7975. This agency describes their rentals as elegantly rustic cabins. Enjoy the hot tub on the porch or go inside and curl up on the elegant furnishings by the gas log fireplace. Video games, foosball, or other entertainment is available in each cabin. $$$$

Broyhill Inn & Conference Center. 775 Bodenheimer Dr.; (800) 951-6048; www.broy hillinn.com. First-class service and accommodations are trademarks here. Rooms and suites are offered, and the inn does as nice a job serving families as it does business clients. $$–$$$$

Hidden Valley Motel. 8725 Highway 105; (828) 963-4372; www.hiddenvalleymotel.com. Hidden Valley offers only 8 rooms nestled at the picturesque foot of a mountain. $

Highland Hills Motel and Cabins. 2748 Highway 105; (828) 264-2277; www.highland hillscabins.com. Rustic but beautiful and comfortable rooms are offered at Highland Hills.

Cabins overlook spectacular countryside and offer all the comforts of home. $–$$$

For More Information

Boone Convention and Visitor's Bureau. (800) 852-9506; www.visitboonenc .com.

Blowing Rock

Blowing Rock is south of Boone on US 321.

Blowing Rock is a small resort town whose population mushrooms from 1,800 in winter to more than 8,000 in the warm weather months, and you'll find plenty to do near here. Plan to spend several hours in the village shopping center downtown. There are a dozen antiques shops, a great sports novelty shop, and local craftspeople making candles, dulcimers, and other items.

Blowing Rock (all ages)

US 321 and Rock Road; (828) 295-7111; www.theblowingrock.com. Open 8:30 a.m. to 7 p.m. daily, Memorial Day weekend through Labor Day; 9 a.m. to 6 p.m. Sun through Thurs and 9 a.m. to 7 p.m. Fri and Sat, Sept and Oct; 9 a.m. to 5 p.m. daily, Nov and Dec; and 9 a.m. to 5 p.m. Sat and Sun, Jan through Mar. $–$$; free for children 3 and under.

Just south of the shopping district on US 321, learn how the town got its name at the Blowing Rock, where it snows upside down. The attraction is a large rock formation

The Legend of **the Blowing Rock**

The legend of the Blowing Rock seems to vary a little from one account to another. Here's a summary of one I found in *North Carolina Legends* by Richard Walser (North Carolina Division of Archives and History):

A maiden named Starlight, at the age of 16, convinced her father to allow courting by suitors on a particular day. Among the braves who came was Kwasind, who some said had deserted his wife in a far-off land. Believing this to be true, Starlight rejected the brave, who, in a profession of his love, threw himself off the peak now known as Blowing Rock. At that moment Starlight shrieked, "O strong West Wind, bring my lover back to me! O sweet South Wind, bear him up in your gentle arms." It worked, and the two were wed.

hanging over John's River Gorge. Plan to spend about an hour or so enjoying the views and walking the ridges and rock, as you discover the story of this mysterious formation. Legend says that a Cherokee brave who had thrown himself off the Blowing Rock was blown up out of the gorge to the Chickasaw maiden who had prayed for his return for three days. Today light objects thrown from the rock will be blown back up.

Mystery Hill (ages 5 and up)

129 Mystery Hill Ln., off US 321/221; (828) 263-0507; www.mysteryhill-nc.com. Open 9 a.m. to 8 p.m. daily, June through Aug; 9 a.m. to 5 p.m. daily the rest of the year. Closed Thanksgiving and Christmas. $$; free for children under 5.

If you spend any amount of time on US 321 in the Tweetsie area you probably noticed Mystery Hill, a hands-on science museum that lets visitors decide if these strange exhibits are natural phenomena or illusions. It doesn't appear there's much to the old wood-sided building, but it's worth stopping here to see rocks that glow in the dark and exhibits that defy gravity, such as a ball that rolls uphill, or leave your shadow on the wall. Even walking across the room in this mysterious house is a struggle. Also located on-site is a small American Heritage Museum and Indian artifact display.

Tweetsie Railroad (all ages)

300 Tweetsie Railroad Ln., off US 321; (800) 526-5740; www.tweetsie.com. Open 9 a.m. to 6 p.m. daily, generally mid-May through Aug, and weekends only in Sept and Oct. $$$$; free for children ages 2 and under.

You might think they need to beef up security when you take a ride on the Tweetsie Railroad, because it seems robberies occur on every single trip. Tweetsie, located just north of Blowing Rock, is a great park, especially for families with young children, where you take a trip back to the Old West. Enjoy dozens of great rides as you walk through the theme park, where you are more than likely to meet up with a gunslinger or a Native American chief. Visit a century-old general store and a blacksmith shop, and spend a little time in jail. Another option is the mining town, where the children can pan for gold or meet the animals in the petting zoo. But the biggest attraction here is old Number 12, a steam locomotive that takes you on a 3-mile journey around a mountain. You never know when robbers or Native Americans will hop on board, so stay alert. Plenty of traditional theme park rides provide hours of entertainment as well. In October enjoy a haunted house, visit a mad scientist's lab, and go trick-or-treating at the Tweetsie Railroad Halloween Festival, which features rides on the ghost train. While the escapades at Tweetsie might be amusing to adults and older children, they will seem very real to young children. Use your discretion when determining whether your children will enjoy a ride on the train.

Where to Eat

Bistro Roca. 143 Wonderland Trail; (828) 295-4008; www.bistroroca.com. Roca is classified as fine dining, but a wood-fired oven that produces gourmet pizzas makes it more than palatable for families. $

Blowing Rock Grille. 349 Sunset Dr.; (828) 295-9474; www.theblowingrockgrille.com. Looking for trout? Look here. The grill is a favorite hangout for locals. $

Canyons. 8960 Valley Blvd.; (828) 295-7661; www.canyonsbr.com. Asian, American, Mexican, and Southwestern dishes make for an interesting blend and a large selection on the menu. Sunday brunch features live jazz. $–$$

Knights on Main. 870 Main St.; (828) 295-3869; www.knightsonmainrestaurant.com. Knights serves breakfast, lunch, and dinner, offering great variety and a super-friendly atmosphere. $–$$$

Pssghetti's Italian Restaurant. 7179 Valley Blvd.; (828) 295-9855; www.pssghettis .com. Authentic Italian cuisine served in a restaurant with an inauthentic spelling. $$

Woodlands Barbecue and Pickin' Parlor. US 321 Bypass; (828) 295-3651; www .woodlandsbbq.com. We'll talk more about barbecue later, but you can get a pretty good plate here. $

Where to Stay

Because the ski slopes are located near here, there is no shortage of places to stay in Blowing Rock. Here's a short list of places you might look into first:

Alpen Acres Motel. 318 Old US 321; (828) 295-7981; www.alpenacres.com. This family-oriented motel with 19 rooms has a playground, and children stay **free.** $$–$$$

Alpine Village Inn. 297 Sunset Dr.; (828) 295-7206. Alpine is a very nicely decorated inn in a great location. While the inn caters to couples, it offers family rates and is more than suitable for children. $$

Blowing Rock Inn and Mountain Village. 788 N. Main St.; (828) 295-7921. Very cozy rooms are offered at this inn that also has several villas for rent. $$–$$$$

Blowing Rock Resort Rentals. 232 Ransom St.; (828) 295-9899. This company offers a wide variety of cottages, condos, and cabins throughout the area. $$–$$$$

Chetola Resort at Blowing Rock. N. Main St.; (800) 243-8652. With lodge rooms, condominiums, and a bed-and-breakfast, Chetola offers an indoor fitness center, massage therapy, kids' camp, and much more in some of the most luxurious accommodations in the Blue Ridge. $$$$

Hillwinds Inn. 315 Sunset Dr.; (828) 295-7660. Selections include standard rooms, suites, and cottages, some with fireplaces and full kitchens. Complimentary continental breakfast is offered, and pet-friendly rooms are available. $–$$$

The Village Inn. 7876 Valley Blvd.; (828) 295-3380. Beautifully landscaped, with a lake and the New River. Accommodations include guest rooms, suites, and cottages. Pet-friendly rooms are available. $$–$$$$

For More Information

Blowing Rock Chamber of Commerce. (800) 295-7851; www.blowingrock.com.

Back on the Parkway

The Blowing Rock area is one of the best places to explore the Blue Ridge Parkway. Nearby is a small lake where you can rent canoes and paddleboats, plus two great parks where you can have a picnic and let the kids run. **Moses Cone Memorial Park,** located at Milepost 297, has grills at the sites, stepping stones in the stream that runs through the park, and a big field that's great for tossing a football or baseball. **Julian Price Park,** also located at Milepost 297, features great hiking trails around the lake as well as boat rentals. Just south of the park is the **Linn Cove Viaduct,** the most complicated concrete bridge in the world. It took 15 million pounds of concrete and steel to wind the road around the cove without damaging the environment.

The Jeffersons

Heading north on the Blue Ridge Parkway, you escape a lot of the common tourist activity that you find in the larger towns. Two towns, Jefferson and West Jefferson, seem to blend into one.

Ashe County Cheese Factory (ages 3 and up)

106 E. Main St., West Jefferson; (336) 246-2501; www.ashecountycheese.com. The factory is open to the public 8:30 a.m. to 5 p.m. Mon through Sat, but you should get there by 2 p.m. to see cheese being made. Call ahead since they often stop production at least one day a week. Free.

Founded in 1930, this is North Carolina's only cheese factory. Forty-five-minute tours of the plant are conducted by the staff, who will show you how they make cheese. They demonstrate how they turn milk into cheddar, Colby, and several other types of cheese, totaling 50,000 pounds per week.

Amazing
North Carolina Facts

The New River, located in this area, is said to be the second-oldest river in the world. Along its banks you'll find park areas that offer fishing, picnicking, and primitive camping. Also, you can "canoe the New" by calling one of the area outfitters: **New River Outfitters,** (800) 982-9190; **Wahoo's Adventures** (see the Boone entry), (800) 444-7238; and **Zaloo's Canoes,** (800) 535-4027.

Ben Long **Frescoes**

The most popular area attraction is the collection of contemporary paintings by Ben Long at two local churches. The Blue Ridge Mountain Frescoes at **St. Mary's Episcopal Church,** 400 Beaver Creek School Rd., in West Jefferson (336-982-3076), and **Holy Trinity Episcopal Church,** 120 Glendale School Rd., in nearby Glendale Springs (336-982-3076), include *The Last Supper*, one of the largest frescoes in the country, and *Mary Great with Child*. Long, a Statesville native, has become known internationally, and his work is featured both in the US and in Italy. Admission is **free,** and the churches are open to the public during limited hours.

Mount Jefferson State Natural Area (all ages)

SR 1152, off Highway 163; (336) 246-9653; www.ncparks.gov. **Generally open during daylight hours. Free.**

The slopes and summit of this mountain area are home to an immensely diverse population of trees, shrubs, and wildflowers—a canopy of oak, shade rhododendron, mountain laurel, azaleas, and dogwoods. Wildflowers include trillium, pink lady slipper, and false lily of the valley. American chestnut trees were once abundant in the area, but the chestnut blight, introduced in the early 20th century, destroyed the species here and elsewhere. Rangers give occasional programs, and you can hike one of several trails. A picnic site with grills is available.

For More Information

Ashe County Visitors Center. (336) 246-9550; www.ashechamber.com.

Laurel Springs

Continue north on the Blue Ridge Parkway to Laurel Springs.

Doughton Park (all ages)

Blue Ridge Parkway at Milepost 241; (336) 372-4499. **Open May through Oct. Free.**

The largest recreation area on the parkway is Doughton Park. It includes all the standard park facilities, and you can also stay at **Bluffs Lodge** ($$$–$$$$), a rustic lodge that offers 24 rooms with scenic views of the mountains and surrounding meadows. A coffee shop

Agritourism

From Christmas trees to tomatoes, North Carolina is supporting a burgeoning business focused on buying fresh from the farm. Pick your own strawberries or hunt down your own pumpkin at one of North Carolina's farms and support that local economy. A comprehensive list of farms, roadside markets, and pick-your-own operations can be found at www.ncfarmfresh.com. Another site, www.naagr.gov, also includes listings for operations with barnyard animals, dairy products, hayrides, corn mazes, and more.

and crafts shop are located nearby. Here you can explore great scenic trails and several historic buildings. **Brinegar Cabin** and the **Caudill Family Homestead** give a glimpse of the secluded mountain life.

Wilkesboro

Worth a detour south off the Blue Ridge Parkway from Laurel Springs is the Wilkesboro area. Backtrack to Highway 18 and travel south.

Old Wilkes (all ages)

"Old Wilkes" is how local folk refer to their charming downtown area that is incredibly rich with history. Call (336) 667-3712 for more information. Tours are free; donations accepted.

Make an appointment or take a walking tour of Old Wilkes, which includes 13 buildings that are on the National Register of Historic Places. Some of the highlights of the tour are the Old Wilkes Jail, completed in 1860, which once held Tom Dooley, convicted of murdering his girlfriend and made famous in the ballad *Tom Dooley* by the Kingston Trio; the Wilkes County Courthouse, a 1902 Classical Revival building that is known for the Tory Oak on the front lawn from which British sympathizers were hanged; and the Robert Cleveland House, a log home built in the 1770s and moved behind the jail.

W. Kerr Scott Dam and Reservoir (all ages)

Highway 268, 499 Reservoir Rd.; (336) 921-3390; www.saw.usace.army.mil. Generally open during daylight hours. Free.

The reservoir, located on the Yadkin River and managed by the US Army Corps of Engineers, is accessible by taking Highway 18 through Wilkesboro to Highway 268 West. This 1,470-acre lake at the edge of the Blue Ridge Mountains offers a dozen sites for outdoor recreation. There are more than 55 miles of shoreline for everything from swimming to boating. Picnic facilities are located throughout the area, and you can also camp at Bandits Roost and Warrior Creek Park. **Berry Mountain Park,** located 5 miles west of Wilkesboro on Highway 268, is a good place to spend the day swimming and sunning on the beach. **Bloodcreek Overlook,** located about 2 more miles west, has a fishing pier as well as picnic facilities that include grills. A state fishing license is required to fish here.

Morganton

End your tour of western North Carolina by swinging back west and south from Wilkesboro along Highway 18 to the junction with I-40 at Morganton.

Other Things to See & Do
in the Blue Ridge Mountains

- **Backcountry Outdoors.** Brevard; (828) 884-4262; www.backcountryoutdoors.com

- **Brevard Music Center.** Brevard; (828) 884-2100; www.brevardmusic.org

- **Pisgah Forest Stables.** Brevard; (828) 883-8258; www.pisgahstables.com

- **Whitewater Equestrian Center.** Brevard; (828) 966-9646; www.funhorsebackriding.com

- **Jump Off Rock.** Hendersonville; (800) 828-4244

- **Western NC Air Museum.** Hendersonville; (828) 696-2482; www.wncairmuseum.com

- **Blowing Rock Stables.** Blowing Rock; (828) 295-7847

- **High Mountain Expeditions.** Blowing Rock; (800) 262-9036; www.highmountainexpeditions.com

- **Fun N Wheels.** Boone; (828) 262-3780

- **Magic Mountain Mini Golf and Arcade.** Boone; (828) 265-4653

- **Mast General Store.** Valle Crucis, (828) 963-6511; Boone, (828) 262-0000; Waynesville, (828) 452-2101; Hendersonville, (828) 696-1883; Asheville, (828) 232-1883; www.mastgeneralstore.com

- **Grassy Creek Speedway at Gem Mountain.** Spruce Pine; (828) 766-6007

- **Grandfather Trout Farm.** Banner Elk; (828) 963-5098

- **Judaculla Rock.** Cashiers; www.stayandplayinthesmokies.com

- **Redbone Willy.** Lawndale; (704) 538-3670; www.redbonewilly.com

- **From This Day Forward Outdoor Drama.** Valdese; (828) 874-0176

Morgantown is the home of the late US senator Sam Ervin Jr., who became famous for presiding over the Watergate hearings in the early 1970s. The area offers a number of opportunities for recreational outdoor activities.

The Beanstalk Journey (ages 4 and up)

220 Catawba Meadows Dr.; (828) 430-3440; www.thebeanstalkjourney.com. Open 11 a.m. to 5 p.m. Tues through Sun. $$$$.

This combination ropes course and zip-line takes participants through tree houses and over tree lines. It features a life-size Ewok Village, a rope spider web, and a 32-foot-tall beanstalk climbing tower.

South Mountains State Park (all ages)

Highway 18; (828) 433-4772; www.ncparks.gov. Generally open during daylight hours. **Free.**

South of Morganton off Highway 18 is South Mountains State Park, a great place for trout fishing, biking, or simply wading in the streams or stepping on stones. The 7,330 acres of this park are largely undeveloped, but a series of bridges and walkways along the trails make the park more accessible, especially for younger children. That's not to say there are no challenging trails here. Many of them are difficult, so check with the park office before heading out.

Tuttle Educational State Forest (all ages)

US 64; (828) 757-5608; www.ncesf.org. Generally open during daylight hours. **Free.**

Located north of Morganton off US 64 near Lenoir, the forest is a 170-acre park that offers a range of educational nature programs. In addition, there is a family campground as well as primitive campsites.

Where to Stay

Daniel Boone Campground. 7360 Highway 181 North; (828) 433-1200. Trailer and tent sites are here along with a nature trail, a playground, and a store so you can pick up any items you forgot. $

Rose Creek Campground. 3471 Rose Creek Rd.; (828) 438-4338. This will get the kids' vote. It has a waterslide, playground, and more. $

Steele Creek Park. 7081 Highway 181; (828) 433-5660; www.steelecreekpark.com.

Tent and RV sites are offered along the creek, where the kids can swim and play in tubes. The park also has a miniature golf course, swimming pool, and waterslide. $

For More Information

Burke County Travel and Tourism Commission. (828) 433-6793; www.discover burkecounty.com.

NC High Country Host. (800) 438-7500; www.highcountryhost.com.

The Northern Piedmont

Some of North Carolina's biggest metropolitan areas are located in the Northern Piedmont, and as a result there is no shortage of great things to see and do. Educational opportunities abound at the state capital and on the campuses of the state's leading universities. Here you'll also find one of the country's leading zoos, where you can come within an arm's length of a rare bird or any number of African and North American animals. In addition, some of the best parks are located here, as is a living-history 18th-century Moravian village.

Jim's
TopPicks in the Northern Piedmont

1. North Carolina Zoo, Asheboro

2. Chapel Hill

3. Old Salem

4. Wet 'n Wild Emerald Pointe, Greensboro

5. North Carolina Museum of Natural Sciences, Raleigh

6. SciWorks, Winston-Salem

7. Carolina BalloonFest

8. North Carolina Museum of History, Raleigh

9. Durham Bulls

10. North Carolina State Fair, Raleigh

THE NORTHERN PIEDMONT

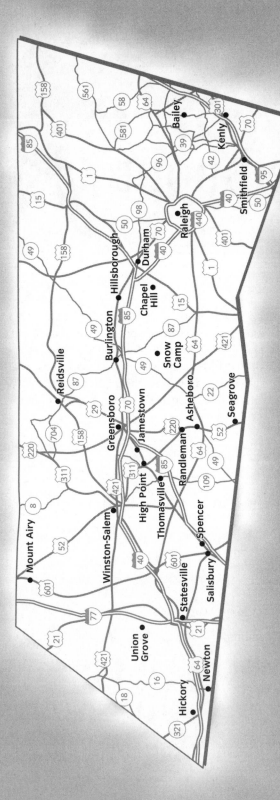

The highway system here is tops, which means you won't have much of a problem navigating this area. I-40 takes you here from the west and combines with I-85 at Greensboro. I-40 then runs south through Raleigh, and I-85 runs north into Virginia.

Hickory

Hickory is conveniently located on Highway 321 and I-40.

Leaving the Blue Ridge Mountains, you descend quickly into the Catawba River Valley, originally inhabited by the Catawba Indians, the "people of the river." The Hickory area, the westernmost point of the Northern Piedmont, is the first city you come to and has become known as a national furniture capital. So if you are looking for new or antique furniture, this is the place to come. While your chances of dragging the kids cheerfully into the **Hickory Furniture Mart** or other outlets are about as good as seeing a pig fly over US 321, they have that industry to thank for all the other funs things to see and do in this area.

Catawba Science Center (all ages)

243 3rd Ave. Northeast; (828) 322-8169; www.catawbascience.org. Open 10 a.m. to 5 p.m. Tues through Fri, 10 a.m. to 4 p.m. Sat and 1 to 4 p.m. Sun. $–$$; free for children under 3.

The Catawba Science Center will provide hours of entertainment and education with a wide variety of hands-on exhibits. Don't miss the exhibit on the life cycle of a live mountain stream or the displays on health and fitness. The Hall of Astronomy offers opportunities to learn about physics, light, and sound throughout the universe. Climb a mountain wall and check out the exhibits in the Science Courtyard. Kids can also take a walk down Energy Avenue, where they will create and launch rockets, give themselves a lift with a pulley system, and take a spin in Spin Circle.

Hickory Museum of Art (all ages)

243 3rd Ave. Northeast; (828) 327-8576; www.hickorymuseumofart.org. Open 10 a.m. to 4 p.m. Tues through Sat and 1 to 4 p.m. Sun. Free.

The city of Hickory has instituted a concerted effort over several decades to establish an art museum focused on American art to rival similar museums in bigger cities. And they have done just that. The museum contains a significant collection of contemporary folk art and classic American work from significant artists such as Romare Bearden and Herb Jackson. It also has an incredible collection of blown glass, including some amazing pieces by Dale Chihuly. Local clay works and pottery are also represented in the museum.

Where to Eat

Circus Hall of Cream. 2111 22nd St. Southwest; (828) 328-4214. This is a fun-themed ice-cream place. $

Four Peas in a Pod. 1640 10th Ave.; (828) 267-0202. Friendly service in a family atmosphere is a trademark of this restaurant. $

Hickory Smokehouse. 2450 N. Center St.; (828) 328-2300. Barbecue is the specialty here. $

J & S Cafeteria. 1949 13th Avenue Dr. Southeast; (828) 326-8983. This is a great place for families with a wide variety of tastes. $

Mama's Pizza and Pasta. 1322 Highway 70 Southeast; (828) 855-0550; www.mamaspizzanc.com. Two New York brothers (not their Mama) started this small restaurant with New York– and Chicago-style pizza. Get it by the slice or whole. $

Where to Stay

Park Inn Gateway Center Hotel. 909 Highway 70 Southwest; (800) 789-0686. You get a buffet breakfast in this very nice hotel. $$

Chain hotels here also include **Courtyard by Marriott, Comfort Suites, Hampton Inn, Holiday Inn Express,** and **Quality Inn and Suites.**

For More Information

Hickory Metro Convention & Visitors Bureau. (800) 849-5093; www.hickorymetro.com.

Newton

East and a bit south of Hickory is the town of Newton, the Catawba County seat, located off I-40.

Catawba County Museum of History (all ages)

30 N. College Ave.; (828) 465-0383; www.catawbahistory.org. Open 9 a.m. to 4 p.m. Wed through Sat and 1:30 to 4:30 p.m. Sun. Free.

The historical settler reenactments are a key program at this small history museum, located in the former Catawba County Courthouse in Newton's Downtown Square. The Catawba County Museum of History pays tribute to the brave settlers of the Catawba River Valley and their descendants who are responsible for establishing a world-renowned furniture industry. The significant collections include agricultural tools and implements forged from hand-dug iron ore, produced by the area's Scotch-Irish, German, and English settlers. Handcrafted household cupboards, wagon benches, and other furniture items are on display. You will also find military uniforms, including a British redcoat from the Revolutionary War era; Civil War weapons; and other objects. The museum has also re-created antebellum parlors and an early 20th-century medical office here. A gallery of looms, spinning wheels, and other items commemorates the area's textile heritage.

Historic Newton Tour (ages 5 and up)

Buildings on the tour are open 9 a.m. to 4 p.m. Tues through Fri, 10 a.m. to 4 p.m. Sat, and 2 to 5 p.m. Sun. Call (828) 465-0383 for more information. For a walking tour brochure, call (828) 465-7400. Free.

You'll find a number of historically significant sites on the Historic Newton Tour, which includes 105 buildings. Among the sites on the tour are Murray's Mill, a fully restored corn and gristmill; and St. Paul's Lutheran Church, a 2-story log, weather-boarded church that includes the balcony where slaves sat during services and a cemetery with tombstones in German dating back to 1771. Also on the tour is the Catawba County Museum of History.

Where to Eat

Geppetos of Newton. 114 N. College Ave.; (828) 464-7833. Pizza is the specialty of the house. $

Statesville

Continue east on I-40 or US 70 to where they intersect I-77, and you'll be in Statesville. US 64 and US 21 also converge here.

Carolina BalloonFest (all ages)

Statesville Regional Airport, I-40 West at exit 146 or exit 148. Call the Greater Statesville Chamber of Commerce at (704) 873-2892 or visit www.carolinaballoonfest.com for more information. $$.

Balloons fill the sky over Statesville each October as one of the oldest (second oldest in the country) and biggest balloon rallies on the East Coast gets under way. The Carolina BalloonFest, held in late October, is the city's best attraction. Thousands of spectators show up annually to watch the more than 50 beautiful, silent, colorful balloons ascend to the heavens. Standard festival amenities are also offered at the event, including a kids' fun zone, a trick-or-treat event, crafts, and even an adult feature—a wine festival. Balloon rides are also offered, of course.

Fort Dobbs (ages 5 and up)

438 Fort Dobbs Rd.; (704) 873-5866; www.fortdobbs.org. Open 9 a.m. to 5 p.m. Tues through Sat. Free.

Just north of Statesville on US 21 is Fort Dobbs, built in 1756 and named after Royal Colonial Governor Arthur Dobbs. The fort was constructed at a time when tension between the colonists and the British was rising and settlers came into increasing conflict with Native Americans. On many occasions colonists in the area, including Daniel Boone and his family, were forced out of their homes and sought refuge at the fort, which was attacked only once in more than 15 years. Today the fort, which includes little more than ruins and ground impressions, is the site of continual archaeological investigation. Archaeological finds and other artifacts are displayed along the trails and at the visitor center.

Kids @ Play (up to age 12)

1613 E. Broad St.; (704) 872-7508; www.iredellmuseums.org. Open Tues through Fri 11 a.m. to 4 p.m. and Sat 10 a.m. to 3 p.m. $; free for children under age 12.

Part of the Iredell Museums organization, this children's museum operates in Signal Hill Mall. Its art exhibit includes an abundance of art supplies to allow children to experiment with a variety of media. A music exhibit helps children explore instruments from around the world, including African drums, bells, xylophone, tambourine, and rain stick. A costume and puppet stage invites children into a "barn" equipped with a variety of diverse puppets to help children create their own puppet show. Nearby is a costume area and mirror where children dress up and put on their own performance. A child-size kitchen and cafe exhibit puts children to work setting a table, preparing and serving "meals" to friends and family, and cleaning up and vacuuming. A blocks exhibit exposes children to architecture, and the nature exhibit includes live fish, snakes, and painted turtles.

Love Valley Arena (all ages)

Highway 115, north of I-40; (704) 592-2299; www.lovevalley.com. Prices vary by activity.

During the summer months Statesville's Love Valley Arena features old-fashioned rodeos and other events. Love Valley is known throughout the state as a cowboy's paradise, complete with a saloon, hitching posts, and a general store, and it attracts horse enthusiasts year-round. During the **Tar Heel Classic Horse Show,** held in May, you can get a look at Tennessee Walkers, Arabians, and quarter horses as they go through various events and judging. Among the fun-filled rodeo events are junior competitions and events with a frontier theme.

Museum of Arts and Heritage (all ages)

134 Court St.; (704) 873-4734; www.iredellmuseums.org. Open 10 a.m. to 5 p.m. Mon through Fri. Free.

The Museum of Arts and Heritage is located in the former 1920s courthouse in downtown Statesville. It exhibits the work of local and regional artists and displays a permanent collection of art and historical items, including paintings, drawings, Audubon prints, sculptures, pottery, and even an Egyptian mummy. This, along with the courthouse architecture, really makes it worth the stop.

Union Grove

Usually Union Grove isn't much more than a place to stop for a quick bite and a tank of gas while traveling along I-77. However, in May that all changes. That's when the small, unassuming town comes alive and plays host to the biggest bluegrass festival in the state.

Old Time Fiddler's and Bluegrass Convention (all ages)

Fiddler's Grove Campground, Highway 901 west of I-77; (828) 478-3735; www.fiddlersgrove .com. Held each May; check website for dates. $$$$.

One of the state's more unusual annual events is the Old Time Fiddler's and Bluegrass Convention, held each May near the town of Union Grove, located north of Statesville. It is the oldest event of its kind in the nation, running since 1924, and attracts musicians from around the country. The weekend-long event features continuous performances and competitions in all areas of bluegrass music, from clogging to fiddling. There are more than 50 bands that compete for various titles, including the coveted Fiddler of the Festival award. Whether you're an experienced fiddler wishing to sharpen your skills or a beginner who has never held a fiddle before, the convention has a class—and often an instrument— available for you. Booths are situated throughout the campground, offering a variety of musical and craft items for sale.

For More Information

Statesville Convention and Visitors Bureau. (704) 878-3480; www.visitstatesville .org.

Salisbury

Salisbury is located southeast of Statesville at the junction of US 70 and I-85.

Salisbury, the largest city in western North Carolina until the early 1900s, was once a center for trade and politics. Today the city celebrates its rich heritage with eight separate historic districts where you can take a walk back in time.

Dan Nicholas Park & Campground (all ages)

6800 Bringle Ferry Rd.; (704) 216-7803; www.dannicholas.net. Open generally during daylight hours. Free; fee for some activities.

This 400-acre park just southeast of Salisbury offers a big lake for paddleboating and fishing. Live animals in a petting barn and nature center are eager to greet the kids. The park also offers miniature golf, a carousel, gem mining, and a miniature train ride. You'll also find standard park amenities such as tennis courts, picnic shelters, a playground, volleyball, horseshoes, and ball fields. There are also 80 sites for tents and campers.

Lazy 5 Ranch (all ages)

Located on Highway 150 west of Salisbury; (704) 663-5100; www.lazyfiveranch.com. Open 9 a.m. to one hour before sunset. Mon through Sat and 1 p.m. to one hour before sunset Sun. $$. Reservations for wagon rides ($$) are recommended. Lazy 5 does not accept credit or debit cards.

Drive through this exotic zoo in your car or a horse-drawn wagon, but expect to see more than horses and cows. A road winds around 185 acres that include hundreds of exotic animals in somewhat natural habitats. There's also a petting zoo and a playground.

Salisbury Heritage Tour (all ages)

When you get to Salisbury, head to the Visitors Information Center, located in the Gateway Building, 204 E. Innes St. (800-332-2343; www.salisburync.gov).

Here you can pick up a **free** brochure or audiotapes (or download the tour in an MP3 file from the website) for the Salisbury Heritage Tour and the Salisbury National Cemetery Tour. The sites that you won't want to miss are Josephus Hall House and the 1820 federal-style home of the chief surgeon of the Salisbury Confederate Prison. A Civil War cannon rests on the lawn in front of the home, which has been renovated with Greek and Victorian touches. **Free** tours by costumed guides are given on weekends. Another interesting home is the **Old Stone House,** an impressive two-story stone structure built in 1766. On the second story you'll find two openings believed to be gunports used to fight off hostile Native Americans. In all there are 142 points of interest on the tour, which can be taken by trolley on Saturday April through October.

Waterworks Visual Arts Center   (all ages)

123 E. Liberty St.; (704) 638-1882; www.waterworks.org. Open 10 a.m. to 5 p.m. Mon through Fri (until 7 p.m. on Tues and Thurs) and 11 a.m. to 3 p.m. Sat. Free.

Originally located in the city's first waterworks building, the center is now across the street from the police station in another refurbished building. The center offers regional and national gallery exhibitions, studio classes, workshops, and lectures. The sculpture gallery invites visitors to participate in the art experience through touch, sound, fragrance, and sight.

Barbecue **Battle**

Since we're coming up on the halfway point in the book, we'll pause for a moment and mention **Lexington,** which has gained considerable notoriety for its barbecue. The town, located on US 64, holds an annual barbecue festival in October, and restaurant guides proclaim Lexington to be the "Barbecue Capital of the World," listing 15 barbecue restaurants. The reason I put this in the middle of this guide is that there is some debate in the state over what is and is not "barbecue." In Lexington, you see, they serve western North Carolina barbecue, made of pork shoulder, cooked *sloooowly* over hickory coals, and topped with a tomato-based sauce without mayonnaise. In the east the whole pig is used and topped with a vinegar-based sauce. For more information about Lexington's festival, call (336) 236-4218.

Great Train **Day Trip**

Amtrak operates two Piedmont train routes from Charlotte to Raleigh with seven stops in between. So if you find yourself in any one of these cities, you can combine a train trip with an attraction you want to see in one of the other cities. Rates range from $8 to $32 per person, and each summer a promotion has permitted children to ride free. Call (800) 878-7245 for details or visit www.amtrak.com.

Where to Eat

Christo's Family Restaurant. 431 Innes St.; (704) 637-9050. Christo's offers subs, salads, pasta, and pizza. $

D.J.'s. 1502 W. Innes St.; (704) 638-9647; www.djsrestaurant.com. A local favorite, D.J.'s serves an eclectic blend of Italian, Greek, and American, including steak and seafood. $$$

Sweet Meadow Cafe. 118 W. Innes St.; (704) 637-8715. This quaint cafe serves contemporary cuisine with a twist. An eclectic menu includes crab cakes and red beans and rice. Fresh breads are made daily, and works by local artists are on display. $–$$

Where to Stay

You'll probably want to stick with the larger chain hotels if your trip calls for a stay in the Salisbury area. You'll find all of them there. Several B&Bs in the area do not allow children under the age of 12.

For More Information

Rowan County Convention and Visitors Bureau. (800) 332-2343; www.visitsalisbury nc.com.

Spencer

Just north of Salisbury on US 70 is the town of Spencer, named for a railroad executive.

Historic Spencer Shops (all ages)

Located on S. Salisbury Avenue; (704) 636-2889; www.nctrans.org. Open 9 a.m. to 5 p.m. Mon through Sat and 1 to 5 p.m. Sun, Apr through Oct; 10 a.m. to 4 p.m. Tues through Sat and 1 to 4 p.m. Sun, Nov through Mar. $$; train rides additional.

Everything you want to know about transportation you can learn at the **North Carolina Transportation Museum** at Historic Spencer Shops, a sprawling and fun family attraction. The Spencer Shops was once the largest steam locomotive servicing station operated by the Southern Railway. Built in 1896 and now a State Historic Site, it features exhibits on the development of vehicles, from the dugout canoe to the airplane. You can also see vintage automobiles and take a train ride through the 57-acre facility that includes 13 buildings.

Thomasville

Thomasville is northeast of Spencer, just off I-85.

You might not plan an entire vacation around the town of Thomasville, but it is a beautiful, charming town to pass through. Thomasville's symbol is the World's Largest Duncan Phyfe Chair. You will know you are in furniture country when you stop at the town square to see the faux wood-framed chair that rests majestically on a granite pedestal for a total height of 30 feet with a seat 10½ feet wide.

In addition, the town is home of the oldest remaining railroad depot in the state, also located in the town square. Next, head north on I-85 to find a rest stop that makes a great place for a picnic and a chance to see the **North Carolina Vietnam Veterans Memorial.** Located down a short trail, the memorial features crepe myrtles and brick walls in honor of the 216,000 North Carolinians who served in Vietnam and the 1,600 who died or are missing.

For More Information

Thomasville Convention and Visitors Bureau. (800) 611-9907; www.thomasville tourism.com.

High Point

High Point, north of Thomasville off I-85 or US 70, is North Carolina's main furniture-manufacturing center, with 125 furniture plants.

All-a-Flutter Butterfly Farm (all ages)
7850 Clinard Farms Rd.; (336) 989-4507; www.all-a-flutter.com. Family days are Sat at 10 a.m. and Wed at 3 p.m., late Apr to late Sept. $.

Fine **Furniture**

Thomasville and High Point are famous for fine—and huge—furniture. The 18-foot chair in Thomasville was once promoted as the World's Largest Chair. But officials discovered it was technically the World's Tallest Duncan Phyfe Chair—apparently another chair had it beat. The World's Largest Chest of Drawers is located in High Point. It's the 4-story home of the High Point Jaycees, but once served as the chamber office and was known as the bureau of information.

If you've ever been to a wedding during which the couple releases butterflies, they may have gotten them here. But the operators have developed a significant and fun educational program in conjunction with the wedding business. They present demonstrations of all stages of butterfly development from caterpillar to chrysalis to emergence of an adult butterfly. Plus you get a chance to hand-feed the colorful creatures. The program, which covers the monarch, its lifecycle, and the nectar plants on which it feeds, is presented in a small flight house. Laughter also emerges as audience members dress up as part of the show. Tip: Wear bright clothes, especially warm colors, and you just might make a new friend.

Carolina Dynamo (all ages)

McPherson Stadium, 6105 Townsend Rd.; (336) 316-1266. $–$$; free for children under 2.

One of the bright spots on the family fun scene in High Point is the Carolina Dynamo, a soccer team that springs into action each April. Each home game brings an array of promotional events, including a fans' kick for $15,000 toward the purchase of a new car and a kids' competition for soccer gear. D. D., the 8-foot soccer dog, comes out of his house in the 10,000-seat stadium to give away premium items.

Doll and Miniature Museum of High Point (all ages)

101 W. Green Dr.; (336) 885-3655. Open 10 a.m. to 4 p.m. Tues through Sat and 1 to 4 p.m. Sun. $.

Anyone who has ever played with dolls will love the Doll and Miniature Museum, adjacent to the furniture center. Here you will find one of the greatest collections of dolls anywhere. It features more than 2,500 dolls, miniatures, and artifacts from around the world. This exquisite collection took Angela Peterson more than 50 years of travel to put together, and it includes many costumes, shadow boxes, and dollhouses she made herself. As you enter the main gallery, you'll see dozens of glass cases filled with china dolls, along with dolls made of papier-mâché, wax, and tin, some dating back to the 1800s. A 3-foot-high Shirley Temple doll may prompt some stories from Grandma. Among the most interesting in the collection are an unusual doll made of seaweed and the dressed fleas you have to look at under a magnifier. And don't forget the more modern collection of Barbie dolls and the Pillsbury Doughboy.

High Point City Lake Park (all ages)

602 W. Main St., Jamestown; (336) 883-3498; www.highpointnc.gov. Open generally during daylight hours; activities vary by season. Free; fee for some activities.

Access to High Point's (and one of the state's) best parks is located in nearby Jamestown. The 340-acre lake is open for boating, fishing, and other fun. You can rent a fishing boat, a paddleboat, or a canoe or take a tour on the 30-passenger excursion boat. For the younger set, there are amusement rides, including a carousel and train. A waterslide and the largest outdoor swimming pool in the state create more water fun, and you'll want to make time for miniature golf and the playgrounds.

High Point Museum and Historical Park (ages 5 and up)

1859 Lexington Ave.; (336) 885-1859; www.highpointmuseum.org. The museum, house, and grounds are open 10 a.m. to 4:30 p.m. Thurs through Sat and 1 to 4 p.m. Sun. Free.

The High Point Museum and Historical Park is the epicenter of cultural life in High Point. It manages the museum and other historical points of interest in the area. At the museum examine woodworking tools dating back to the 19th century as well as local artifacts and Civil War items. Also on the grounds is the John Haley House, an early brick Quaker house and the oldest structure still standing in Guilford County. Built in 1786, the house has been fully restored. The grounds also include a weaving house, the Hoggett House built in 1801, and a blacksmith shop.

Piedmont Environmental Center (all ages)

1220 Penny Rd.; (336) 883-8531; www.piedmontenvironmental.com. Trails and outdoor exhibits are typically open during daylight hours. Free.

Located at High Point City Lake, this nature preserve, with a staff of naturalists, includes a nature store and a center with small animal exhibits. There is also access to the Greenway Trail, an 8-mile walk. In addition, the center conducts hands-on family workshops on topics such as stargazing, birding, cultivating wildflowers, and mushrooms.

Where to Eat

Carolina Diner. 201 Eastchester Dr.; (336) 869-0660. This is a good family-style diner for breakfast, lunch, or dinner. $

The Dog House. 662 N. Main St.; (336) 886-4953. Belly on up to the counter for a dog with great chili. This local favorite since 1950 is open only for lunch. $

Kepley's Barbecue. 1304 S. Main St.; (336) 884-1021. Some say Kepley's is in the running for the best barbecue in the state. $

Plaza Cafe. 336 S. Main St.; (336) 886-5271. Get an omelet for breakfast or lunch at this popular spot. Salads and sandwiches are also on the menu. $$

Where to Stay

Atrium Inn. 425 S. Main St.; (888) 928-7486. Children under 18 stay free in this smaller standard hotel that was renovated in 2006. $$$–$$$$

Biltmore Suites Hotel. 4400 Regency Dr.; (888) 412-8188. This is an upscale facility that caters largely to business travelers. Suites are available. $$$$

For More Information

High Point Convention and Visitors Bureau. (336) 884-5255; www.highpoint.org.

Winston-Salem

Northwest of High Point, via Highway 109 near I-40, is Winston-Salem, a city of arts and site of one of the most impressive restorations of early American life.

Children's Museum of Winston-Salem (ages 8 and under)

390 S. Liberty St.; (336) 723-9111; www.childensmuseumofws.org. Open 10 a.m. to 4 p.m. Tues through Sat and 1 to 5 p.m. Sun, Memorial Day through Labor Day and on school holidays. $.

This children's museum focuses on literature and the arts. Regularly scheduled story times become interactive experiences through a host of exhibits, props, and displays that teach youngsters about science, nature, history, and more. An arts and crafts room also helps stimulate their creativity.

Historic Bethabara Park (all ages)

2147 Bethabara Rd.; (336) 924-8191; www.bethabarapark.org. Building tours ($) are 10:30 a.m. to 4:30 p.m. Tues through Fri and 1:30 to 4:30 p.m. Sat and Sun, Apr through mid-Dec. Admission to the grounds is **free.**

Historic Bethabara Park, located north of town off University Parkway, was a Moravian settlement that actually preceded the establishment of Salem. It's a great place for outdoor activities, to have a picnic, or to stroll along the walking trails, but history is alive here. Its 175 acres are a wildlife preserve, but the park is also part museum, telling the story of a group of Moravians who bravely settled the village beginning in 1753. Visit Palisade Fort, originally built in 1756 during the French and Indian War and reconstructed on its original site. You'll also find the 1788 Gemeinhaus, a church; a 1782 Potter's House; and an 1803 Brewer's House.

Museum of Anthropology (ages 5 and up)

Located behind Kentner Stadium off University Parkway, Wake Forest University; (336) 758-5282. Open 10 a.m. to 4:30 p.m. Tues through Sat. **Free.**

Get to know people from around the world at the Museum of Anthropology, located on the campus of Wake Forest University. This is the only museum of its kind in the Southeast. The museum is dedicated to the study of world cultures and includes exhibits related to these studies. Featured are costumes, clothing, tools, and more, all depicting human development around the world. The museum also relates some of the greater achievements of the people from the Americas, Africa, Asia, and the Pacific. Even young kids will love the Discovery Room, which helps them explore anthropology through hands-on activities.

Old Salem (ages 5 and up)

527 S. Main St.; (888) 348-5420; www.oldsalem.org. Open 9:30 a.m. to 4:30 p.m. Tues through Sat and 1 to 4:30 p.m. Sun. Hours of some facilities and exhibits may vary. $$–$$$$.

Winston-Salem's most popular attraction is Old Salem, a living-history 18th-century Moravian village from which the modern city emerged. You'll want to spend most of the day here as costumed guides take you through the community from which the city evolved. More than 80 structures, dating back to 1766, have been fully and meticulously restored. The most popular among kids is **Winkler Bakery,** where fresh sugar cakes, gingerbread cookies, and other tasty goodies are made using early methods and recipes. You can also see the Boys School; the John Vogler House, which includes a collection of 19th-century toys; a structure that served as a meat market and firehouse; Shultz shop, the shoemaker's shop; and more. A film on Moravian life is presented in a theater inside Vierling Barn. In addition, you can take a half-hour carriage ride ($$$) on the cobblestone streets of the district.

You can also see the nation's largest collection of furniture and decorative arts of the South here at the **Museum of Early Southern Decorative Arts.**

Reynolda House Museum of American Art (ages 5 and up)
2250 Reynolda Rd.; (336) 758-5150; www.reynoldahouse.org. Open 9:30 a.m. to 4:30 p.m. Tues through Sat and 1:30 to 4:30 p.m. Sun. Closed Thanksgiving, Christmas, and New Year's Day. $$; admission to the gardens is free.

Three centuries of American art are on display at Reynolda House Museum of American Art, located off Reynolda Road near Wake Forest University. The museum is located on the country estate and model farm built by tobacco magnate R. J. Reynolds and his wife, Katherine Smith Reynolds. The house, built in 1917, is filled with beautiful paintings, prints, sculptures, and furnishings, some of which date back to the 17th century. Also included is a ladies' costume collection that dates back to nearly 1900. Japanese cherry trees on the grounds bloom with magnificent color in late March, but a visit to the garden and greenhouses is fun anytime. Family-oriented workshops are held the first Sunday of each month.

SciWorks (all ages)
400 W. Hanes Mill Rd.; (336) 767-6730; www.sciworks.org. Open 10 a.m. to 4 p.m. Mon through Fri and 11 a.m. to 5 p.m. Sat. $$; free for children under 2.

Science lovers will get their fill in Winston-Salem at SciWorks, a 45,000-square-foot science center and environmental park that lets kids and adults discover how everything from the human body to a computer works. Here guests conduct experiments themselves, while staff members put on displays designed to astonish. Learn about the sea at the aquariums, at the touch tank, and through CD-ROM computer programs of undersea adventure. The center also includes a 120-seat planetarium that presents various shows year-round. Take a walk or have a picnic in the 34-acre park. Here you're likely to come face-to-face with a deer or river otter, and the kids get a chance to meet farmyard animals.

Southeastern Center for Contemporary Arts (ages 10 and up)
750 Marguerite Dr.; (336) 725-1904; www.secca.org. Open 10 a.m. to 5 p.m. Tues through Sat and 1 to 5 p.m. Sun. Free.

More low-key adventure awaits you at the Southeastern Center for Contemporary Arts, located in the English-style manor house of the late industrialist James G. Hanes. The kids are likely to be more drawn to this center than other art museums because of its more relaxed and engaging approach and innovative programming. Although this is a center for Southeast arts, you can enjoy fascinating works from around the world in changing exhibits from well-known artists. In addition, the museum presents occasional interpretive programs on exhibits as well as performing arts programs. A wide array of contemporary crafts are also on display and for sale at the Centershop.

Tanglewood Park (all ages)

4061 Clemmons Rd.; (336) 778-6300; www.tanglewoodpark.org. Open daily 7 a.m. to dusk. $–$$$.

While there are a number of hotels and other accommodations in the area, the most popular place to stay is Tanglewood Park, a great outdoor recreational facility operated by Forsythe County, about 10 minutes from downtown Winston-Salem. It offers a bed-and-breakfast inn in an old manor house as well as cottages and a neat campground. Both welcome children. The park has 1,100 acres for golf, tennis, swimming, horseback riding, hiking, studying nature, and fishing. Included are 2 top-rate golf courses and a par-3 course for families who just want to get out on the course for a couple hours. You'll also find miniature golf and horse stables.

Where to Eat

Mary's, Of Course!. 723 Trade St. Northwest.; (336) 725-5764. Funky and fun! Sunday brunch is the time to go to Mary's, Of Course! Located in an artsy space in the Old Salem area. $

Old Fourth Street Filling Station. 871 W. 4th St.; (336) 724-7600; www.theoldfourth streetfillingstation.com. Originally a gas station, this restaurant offers some of the best food and atmosphere in town. Choices range from salads to filet mignon. $$$

Old Salem Tavern Dining Room. 736 S. Main St. in Old Salem; (336) 748-8585; www .oldsalemtavern.com. Servers wear Moravian costumes and serve traditional Moravian dishes along with more typical fare. You'll want to make reservations for dinner here. $$

Village Tavern. 2000 Griffith Rd., (336) 760-8686; 221 Reynolda Village Rd., (336) 748-0221; www.villagetavern.com. Pasta, fish, and chicken are the mainstays of the menu here. The menu also includes grown-up healthy options for kids. $–$$

The Vineyards Restaurant. 120 Reynolda Village; (336) 748-0269. This restaurant fits in very well with its location at Reynolda Village. $$

West End Cafe. 926 W. 4th St.; (336) 723-4774; www.westendcafe.com. This is very casual, but it still offers great atmosphere near Old Salem. $$

Where to Stay

Brookstown Inn. 200 Brookstown Ave.; (336) 725-1120; www.brookstowninn.com. Fresh-baked cookies every night. Wow! And children under 12 stay **free.** This historic inn is located in a restored factory and is very nice, with exposed brick and beams on high ceilings. $$$$

The Hawthorne Inn and Conference Center. 420 High St.; (800) 972-3774. While

Amazing
North Carolina Facts

The eastern gray squirrel was selected as the state mammal in 1969. You'll find them everywhere from hardwood forests to backyards throughout the state.

this hotel caters largely to business travelers, it's a great place for the family. Suites and efficiencies are available. $$$$

For More Information

Winston-Salem Convention and Visitors Bureau. (800) 331-7018; www.visitwinston salem.com.

Mount Airy

If you're staying in the triad area—Winston-Salem, High Point, or Greensboro—a great day trip is less than an hour northwest on US 52, where you'll find Mount Airy.

The town was made famous as the model for Mayberry in the popular television series *The Andy Griffith Show.* Griffith, the show's star (who later became the title character in television's *Matlock*), was born and raised here until he left to attend college in Chapel Hill. His house, at 711 E. Haymore St., and the **Andy Griffith Playhouse,** at 218 Rockford St., have been preserved as landmarks and are on the town's tour of historical places. Memorabilia from the show and Griffith's career can be found throughout the town, but his house is now a rental property. In addition, the playhouse is the venue for productions throughout the year. At the **Andy Griffith Museum** adjacent to the theater you'll find a variety of memorabilia from his career. Unless the kids have seen Andy in reruns, they aren't likely to know who he is, but if a tour of "Mayberry" is something Dad just has to do, take a squad car tour. For $35 a car load, tourists can go to all the sites in a car just like Andy and Barney rode in. Call (336) 789-6743 for more information.

Hanging Rock and Pilot Mountain State Parks (all ages) 🏕️ 🏕️ 👫 🏊

Hanging Rock is on Hanging Rock Road, and Pilot Mountain is at 1792 Pilot Knob Park Rd. Both parks are open sunrise to sunset daily, year-round. **Free.**

To the south and west of Mount Airy you will find two state parks that are great for hiking, picnicking, and other recreational activities. **Hanging Rock State Park** (336-593-8480), located off Highway 89, provides a great opportunity for picnicking, hiking, camping, and swimming. Six rustic cabins are available for rent in advance.

An interesting granite formation pokes 1,400 feet out of the earth at **Pilot Mountain State Park** (336-325-2355), located off Highway 52. Here a number of recreational activities are available in addition to a family campground ($), which operates on a first-come, first-served basis.

Where to Eat

Snappy Lunch. 125 N. Main St.; (336) 786-4931. The Snappy Lunch was mentioned on *The Andy Griffith Show*, and Andy ate there as a young boy growing up in Mount Airy. It's famous for its pork chop sandwich. $

Where to Stay

The Mayberry Motor Inn. US 52 Bypass North; (336) 786-4109. This hotel takes advantage of "Mayberry's" fame with a themed property that includes a 1960s squad car in the parking lot. $$

For More Information

Call the town visitor center at (800) 576-0231 for more information about Mount Airy, or visit www.visitmayberry.com.

Greensboro

North Carolina's third-largest city, with a population of 200,000, is easily accessible from I-85 and I-40.

Greensboro regularly rates as one of the most desirable places in the country to live in national surveys. The Piedmont Triad International Airport has made it one of the Southeast's more economically successful business centers, with businesses ranging from textiles to tobacco to service-related industries such as insurance. For the visitor it hosts a wide variety of activities that include outdoor sports, among them golf and tennis, as well as spectator sports that include Atlantic Coast Conference basketball action, Class A baseball, and arena football. Greensboro is a center for arts, history, and culture as well.

ArtQuest (all ages)

200 N. Davie St.; (336) 333-2610; www.greenhillcenter.org. Public hours are 12:30 to 7 p.m. Tues through Sat. $.

ArtQuest, located in Green Hill Center, is a spectacular hands-on children's gallery that offers creative learning and fun with interactive exhibits. Morning hours are often reserved for group tours, but it's open to the public the rest of the time. Families have the opportunity to discover the excitement of making art together through activities like building a castle or working on the loom. Wednesday from 5 to 7 p.m. is **free** family night.

Blandwood Mansion and Carriage House (ages 5 and up)

447 W. Washington St.; (336) 272-5003; www.blandwood.org. Open 11 a.m. to 4 p.m. Tues through Sat and 2 to 5 p.m. Sun. $–$$.

Historical elegance is only a short drive away at Blandwood Mansion and Carriage House, a 19th-century Italian villa. The house, originally built as a farmhouse in the late 18th century, was redesigned and totally renovated in 1844. Blandwood served as home for former North Carolina governor and Whig party politician John Motley Morehead and today still contains many of its original furnishings. Docents lead tours through the grounds and gardens. The adjacent carriage house serves as the site for many formal receptions and meetings.

Bur-Mil Park (all ages)
5834 Bur-Mil Club Rd.; (336) 373-3800. Generally open during daylight hours. Free.

This city/county park includes standard park facilities but also features a significant wildlife education facility and program. Visitors can take lessons on everything from fly fishing to landscape design. At the center of the park, in a renovated barn, is the Frank Sharpe Jr. Wildlife Education Center. Borrow a fishing rod here or browse through the permanent and rotating exhibits on local wildlife and the environment.

Carolina Theatre (all ages)
310 S. Greene St.; (336) 333-2605; www.carolinatheatre.com.

This historic landmark puts an old twist on a popular pastime. Built in 1927, the historic Carolina Theatre once hosted some of the era's most famous vaudeville performers, as well as being a first-run movie house for silent films. Despite the decline of vaudeville, the dwindling of downtown's popularity, and even a fire, the theater has returned to its old glory and continues to welcome audiences in a rich atmosphere of days gone by. It now hosts film and live presentations.

Celebration Station (all ages)
Just off I-40 at 4315 Big Tree Way; (910) 316-0606; www.celebrationstation.com. Open 11 a.m. to 11 p.m. Mon through Thurs and 11 a.m. to midnight Fri and Sat. Fees vary by activity.

Find more than water fun at Celebration Station, a great family entertainment center with locations in a handful of cities around the country. The park includes miniature golf, bumper boats, go-karts, batting cages, arcade games, a pizza restaurant, and a snack bar where you can grab a foot-long hot dog or a salad. The center is set up so each age group has its own area, making the activities safe for young children as well as their older siblings. It's also a lot of fun, especially if you have toddlers, to order a pizza and listen to the entertainment from the Dixie Diggers, an animated musical band of animals.

Charlotte Hawkins Brown State Historic Site (ages 5 and up)
Located off I-85, northeast of Greensboro, at 6136 Burlington Rd., Sedalia; (336) 449-4846; www.nchistoricsites.org/chb. Open 9 a.m. to 5 p.m. Mon through Sat. Free.

Your journey through historical Greensboro continues into the 21st century at the Charlotte Hawkins Brown State Historic Site. North Carolina's first official site to honor an

African American and a woman, it is the former location of the Palmer Institute, a prep school that Brown founded in 1902 when she was only 19 years old. Eventually the school grew to 350 acres, included a farm, and received full accreditation by the Southern Association of Colleges and Secondary Schools. Today you can see displays about the school, Brown's life, and the civil rights movement. Also included are her home and grave site.

Garden Variety (all ages)

(336) 373-2199; www.greensborobeautiful.org. Open 8 a.m. to sunset daily. Free.

Three of the state's most beautiful and intriguing botanical gardens are located in Greensboro. The **Bog Garden,** located at the corner of Hobbs and Starmount Farms Roads, provides an interesting twist to this swampy land. The marsh has been transformed into a beautiful area that includes more than 8,000 trees, shrubs, ferns, bamboo, and wildflowers. A wooden walkway leads through the bog, where plants are labeled for visitors' education. **Bicentennial Gardens,** completed in 1976 to commemorate the nation's bicentennial and located at 1105 Hobbs Rd. off Highway 29 North, features spectacular rose gardens as well as a fragrance and herb garden. It's hard to find a time of year when this garden isn't bursting with color. A favorite among kids is the **Greensboro Arboretum,** located on Wendover Avenue, which features 17 acres of gardens, including a butterfly garden and 11 other labeled plant collections.

Greensboro Children's Museum (ages 1 to 10)

220 N. Church St.; (336) 574-2898; www.gcmuseum.com. Open 9 a.m. to 5 p.m. Tues through Sat, 9 a.m. to 8 p.m. Fri, and 1 to 5 p.m. Sun. $$.

This bright, colorful museum is a great place for families to spend hours. It is a wonderland of exciting exhibits that are the perfect size for kids and their imaginations. It includes themed learning stations for children ages 1 to 10. Visitors can swing by the kid-size ATM at the bank, drive a fire truck, sound the siren on a police car, and bring a DC-9 jet in for a landing. Kids can help with a house under construction or deliver the mail in a US postal jeep. Whatever's in your town is likely to be in theirs. The Tot Spot offers activities to stimulate even the youngest children. The museum's newest attraction is an outdoor edible schoolyard.

Greensboro Cultural Center at Festival Park (ages 5 and up)

200 N. Davie St. Admission to all the museums and galleries is free, but hours vary. Call each facility for hours of operation or other details.

Greensboro's downtown arts district is centered around the Greensboro Cultural Center that features 5 galleries offering a variety of visual art experiences. The **African American Atelier** (336-333-6885) exhibits original artwork by local African-American artists and provides educational programs to the community's youths. The **Green Hill Center for North Carolina Art** (336-333-7460) features changing exhibits and programs that include works in glass, ceramics, jewelry, and painting. The **Greensboro Artists' League Gallery and Gift Shop** (336-333-7485) includes a sales gallery as well as changing exhibits of the works of artists in the triad area. The **Guilford Native American Art Gallery** (336-273-6605) has contemporary Native American arts and crafts on display and for sale. The **Mattye Reed African American Heritage Center** (336-334-7108) is a satellite center located on the campus of North Carolina A&T State University. This museum has a seemingly unending collection of cultural exhibits from more than 30 African nations, New Guinea, and Haiti. Also at Festival Park is space for concerts, plays, and other celebrations and events.

Greensboro Historical Museum (ages 5 and up)

130 Summit Ave.; (336) 373-2043; www.greensborohistory.org. Open 10 a.m. to 5 p.m. Tues through Sat and 2 to 5 p.m. Sun. Free.

Get a glimpse into the lives of some of the area's more prominent residents at the Greensboro Historical Museum. Among those residents is Greensboro native William Sydney Porter, who gave his account of the city's occupation by Union troops in the stories he wrote under the name O. Henry. Other displays highlight the lives of First Lady Dolly Madison and famed television journalist Edward R. Murrow. The museum, housed in a Romanesque church built in 1892, also features changing exhibits and displays on early transportation, military history, and Native American settlements. Learn about the famous sit-in at the Woolworth lunch counter in 1960 that helped launch the national civil rights movement and other significant contributions the city made in race relations. Confederate artwork, weapons, clothing, photos, and other documents offer a timeline for the city.

Guilford County Courthouse National Military Park (all ages)

2332 New Garden Rd.; (336) 288-1776; www.nps.gov/guco. The park is open 8:30 a.m. to 5 p.m. daily. Free.

Much of Greensboro's roots are tied to the city's most popular historical attraction, the Guilford County Courthouse National Military Park. It is the country's first Revolutionary War park and features more than 200 acres of wooded trails, monuments, and memorials. It memorializes a bloody battle at Guilford Courthouse, then the county seat, that occurred in March 1781. In that battle American major general Nathaniel Greene, for whom the city is named, lost control of the area to the British—but in the process took out more than a quarter of their troops. The British soon lost North Carolina as a result. The entire battle is re-created at the visitor center through an audiovisual display and exhibits of period artifacts. A film, exhibits, and audio tour will take you through it all.

The International Civil Rights Center & Museum (ages 6 and up)

134 S. Elm St.; (336) 274-9199; www.sitinmovement.org. Open Tues through Sat 10 a.m. to 6 p.m. and Sun 1 to 5 p.m. $–$$.

One of the most poignant stories in the struggle for civil rights is told at this unique museum. The story begins with four black students from North Carolina A&T State University who walked into the Greensboro Woolworth on a February day in 1960 and ordered lunch. That action started a national sit-in movement that literally changed the country. Today that store has been converted into a center and museum dedicated to telling the story of the civil rights movement. Three levels of exhibits document the efforts of those students and others who contributed to change a society. Through one-hour guided tours, visitors begin to understand the history and the effects of segregation from 18th- and 19th-century slavery to the Jim Crow South.

Natural Science Center (all ages)

4301 Lawndale Dr.; (336) 288-3769; www.natsci.org. Open 10 a.m. to 4 p.m. Mon through Sun. $$.

Make a day out of a visit to the Natural Science Center of Greensboro. It's a real treat to visit this hands-on museum, zoo, and digital theater. At HealthQuest learn about all the fascinating and sometimes freaky things our bodies do and why. If your kids like dinosaurs, and they probably do, they'll love visiting the fine dinosaur gallery as much as they'll like the snakes and amphibians at the herpetarium and the crabs and sea urchins in the touch tank. Here and at the touch labs they'll learn a lot about minerals and gems. The kids can meet animals up close at the petting zoo, where they will find donkeys, rabbits, goats, and more. They can also see a black bear and a jaguar at the zoo. The Omnisphere digital theater presents a variety of natural science shows on what was once a planetarium dome.

Afterward you can spend the afternoon at **Country Park** (336-545-5343) adjacent to the science center. The park offers fishing at 2 stocked lakes, paddleboats, playgrounds, fields for running and playing, and trails for hiking and jogging. It's also a great place for a picnic. Admission to the park is **free,** and it is open 8 a.m. to sunset daily.

Tannenbaum Park (all ages)

2200 New Garden Rd.; (336) 545-5315; www.guilfordbattlegroundcompany.org. The heritage center is open 9 a.m. to 5 p.m. Tues through Sat. The park closes at 4:30 p.m. in winter. Call for information on the center or a schedule of living-history events at Hoskins House. Free.

Learn more about the state's history from the Revolutionary War period to the early 1800s at Tannenbaum Park, near the National Military Park. At the heart of the park is **Hoskins House** (circa 1778). It is nearly 45 percent original but has been restored to what historians believe to be its original condition. Occasional living-history programs bring the house—including the kitchen, barn, and blacksmith shop—alive with demonstrations from interpreters. The **Colonial Backcountry Farm** is host to field crop and gardening exhibits and presentations. The **North Carolina Colonial Heritage Center** at the park provides an opportunity for hands-on participation in learning about backcountry life. Here visitors can try on colonial clothes, feel the weight of a real musket, and see up close how colonial people made their clothes and furnishings.

Wet 'n Wild Emerald Pointe (all ages)

Off I-85 at 3910 S. Holden Rd.; (800) 555-5900; www.emeraldpointe.com. Hours vary according to season and weather. $$$–$$$$.

Those who want to get in on some action themselves and cool off during the warm summer months can head to Wet 'n Wild Emerald Pointe. Splash and play here at the Carolinas' largest water park, which offers 22 waterslides, rides, and attractions, including an

Spectator Sports

Greensboro has much to offer sports lovers. **Forest Oaks Country Club** (800-999-5446), located at 4600 Forest Oaks Dr., is the site of the **Wyndham Championship,** one of the richest and most prestigious golf tournaments on the PGA tour. Well-known golf stars come out for this event each October to compete for the purse.

In addition to pro golf, the **Greensboro Coliseum Complex** (336-373-7474), located at 1921 W. Lee St., is the site of a number of college events as well as the frequent host to the Atlantic Coast Conference basketball tournament. The **ACC Hall of Champions,** adjacent to the coliseum, features audiovisual and interactive displays on all the ACC teams. The coliseum additionally hosts such non-sporting events as the Ringling Bros. and Barnum & Bailey Circus, trade shows, flea markets, and more.

NewBridge Bank Park at 408 Bellemeade St. (336-268-2255) is the home of the Greensboro Grasshoppers, a Class A affiliate of the Florida Marlins. This state-of-the-art facility features a huge, open-air concourse that includes a kids' play park. The Grasshoppers have special promotions practically every game night. These include giving away hats, pennants, and other novelties. They also have special picnic packages that combine your dinner with a seat at the game. Check the local media for the dates of special dollar nights to attend a game in the 7,500-seat stadium at a bargain price.

exciting Sky Coaster ride that lets you fly suspended under a giant arch. (The Sky Coaster requires an additional charge.) With ominous names like Dragon's Den and Dr. Von Dark's Tunnel of Terror, realize older children will be as happy to head here as the young ones, who will love Happy Harbor and Splash Island.

Where to Eat

Anton's Restaurant. 1628 Battleground Ave.; (336) 273-1386; www.cellarantons.com. This Italian restaurant is popular among local folk. You'll find a good variety of American dishes—steak, seafood, and chicken—in addition to the classic Italian food. $$

Arigato. 1200 S. Holden Rd.; (336) 299-1003; www.arigatos.net. Japanese food prepared at your table—who could ask for more? You'll also find a sushi bar, of course. $$

Darryl's Wood Fired Grill. 3300 High Point Rd.; (336) 294-1781; www

.darrylswoodfiredgrill.com. After a big plate of ribs, the kids can get their mug shot taken inside the jail or dress up like a firefighter. $$$

Fincastles. 215 S. Elm St.; (336) 272-8968; www.fincastles.com. Get a big juicy burger where owner J. Bird is rumored to break out in song right at your table. $

Gate City Chop House. 106 S. Holden Rd.; (336) 294-9977; www.chophouseofnc.com. While this is fairly upscale and a little on the pricey side, it does have a children's menu. $$$

Lucky 32. 1421 Westover Ter.; (336) 370-0707; www.lucky32.com. Lucky 32, near UNC Greensboro, serves Southern cuisine with flair. $$

Yum Yum Better Ice Cream Co. 1219 Spring Garden St.; (336) 272-8284. This 100-year-old Greensboro institution located near the UNC campus serves ice cream and hot dogs served with chili, slaw, and onions if you like. $

Where to Stay

Battleground Inn. 1517 Westover Ter.; (800) 932-4737; www.battlegroundinnnc .com. This is a good, affordable place to stay that's centrally located. Some of the inn's 48 rooms feature whirlpool tubs. It's a lauded as a great choice for business travelers, but it has all the conveniences that will appeal to families, as well. Other **free** amenities are

high-speed Internet access, complimentary continental breakfast, and use of the fitness facility. $$

O. Henry Hotel. 624 Green Valley Rd.; (336) 854-2000; www.ohenryhotel.com. This more upscale hotel is conveniently located and has a pool, business center, game room, exercise facilitiy, and suites. There is a **free** shuttle to and from the airport that will also take you to the hotel's sister restaurants up until 11 p.m. each day. The hotel offers transportation of up to 11 people at a time to area attractions for a fee. $$$

Park Lane Hotel at Four Seasons. 3005 High Point Rd.; (800) 942-6556. This is one of the nicer hotels in Greensboro. Look for a little pampering here. $$$$

The Proximity Hotel. 704 Green Valley Rd.; (336) 379-8200, (800) 379-8200; www .proximityhotel.com. The Proximity was the country's first LEED Platinum hotel—the US Green Building Council's highest recognition in the Leadership in Energy and Environmental Design (LEED) rating system, the nationally accepted benchmark for the design, construction, and operation of high-performance green buildings. $$$$

For More Information

Greensboro Area Convention and Visitors Bureau. (800) 344-2282; www.greens boronc.org.

Reidsville

Head north from Greensboro on US 29, and you'll find the town of Reidsville, home of one of the prettiest plantations in the state.

Chinqua-Penn Plantation (ages 5 and up)

2138 Wentworth St.; (336) 349-4576; www.chinquapenn.com. Open 10 a.m. to 5 p.m. Wed through Sat and 1 to 5 p.m. Sun. $$$; **free** for children under 6.

This is the beautifully preserved home of businessman and farmer Thomas Jefferson Penn. The 27-room mansion, built in 1925, is filled with an extensive collection of artwork and furnishings from Russia, Egypt, China, and France. Some pieces date as far back as 1100 BC. Outside, the gardens reflect the same eclectic taste, from the fountains to the pagoda gardens.

Jamestown

Jamestown is just south of Greensboro on US 29.

Mendenhall Plantation (ages 5 and up)

603 W. Main St.; (336) 454-3819; www.mendenhallplantation.org. Open for tours 11 a.m. to 3 p.m. Tues through Fri., 1 to 4 p.m. Sat, and 2 to 4 p.m. Sun. $.

Mendenhall is the early 19th-century Quaker plantation of Richard Mendenhall. It consists of a number of interesting structures, a museum, and one of only two false-bottom wagons still in existence. The wagon was used to transport escaped slaves during the operation of the Underground Railroad.

Randleman

From Jamestown, jump on I-85 to I-73/US 220 to get to Randleman.

Richard Petty Museum (ages 5 and up)

142 Academy St.; (336) 495-1143; www.pettyracing.com. Open 9 a.m. to 5 p.m. Mon through Sat. $; free for children age 6 and younger.

This museum is a tribute to the king of NASCAR. Petty won 7 Winston Cup Championships during his career, and today the museum, located in his hometown, houses a fine collection of memorabilia commemorating his career. Included are a number of cars he raced, his trophies, and tons of other awards and recognitions he received. You can also see on video some of the most exciting moments of his career, in addition to photos that include his crash at Daytona Speedway.

Amazing North Carolina Facts

Richard Petty won his first stock car race in 1960 at the age of 22 on a half-mile dirt track at the **Mecklenburg County Fairgrounds.**

Asheboro

Continue south on US 220 to reach Asheboro.

North Carolina Zoo (all ages)

4401 Zoo Pkwy.; (800) 488-0444; www.nczoo.org. Signs lead you right to the zoo from US 220 or 64, or Highway 49. Open daily 9 a.m. to 5 p.m. Apr through Oct, and 9 a.m. to 4 p.m. the rest of the year, except Christmas. $$–$$$, free parking.

One of the best family attractions in the state is the North Carolina Zoo, one of the largest walk-through zoos in the world. Great care has been taken to create this natural-habitat zoo to present the best possible views of the animals on display in what could be their natural habitats. While you can walk through the zoo, a tram allows you to go back and see your favorite parts over and over. The North American Region, with more than 200 acres, features 10 different exhibits that cover everything from deserts to swamps to prairies. In this region you'll see bison in an 11-acre exhibit, roadrunners, rattlesnakes, and polar bears diving into a huge tank of water, as well as puffins, sea lions, and more at play. Also part of the North American Region is the Red Wolf Species Survival Plan, one element of the zoo's commitment to save the endangered animal and reintroduce it into the wild.

Next journey to Africa at the zoo's 500-acre region that includes 9 exhibits. Among those is a 37-acre African Plains exhibit that includes some of the largest animals that naturally roam the plains of the African continent. Here antelope graze an open plain, giraffes tower at treetop level, and elephants get up close and personal. In this region you also get a chance to look massive gorillas in the eye and muse at the antics of monkeys and baboons. One of the best parts of the African exhibit is the R. J. Reynolds Forest Aviary, including more than 1,700 tropical plants and 100 birds. A carousel and 4-D adventure ride round out this great experience. There is a picnic area located at the main entrance, and snack bars and refreshment stands are scattered throughout the park. Lockers are also provided.

Where to Eat

America's Roadhouse. 818 E. Dixie Dr.; (336) 633-1234; www.americasroadhouse .com. This restaurant offers a wide selection from seafood to ribs. $–$$

Taste of Asia. 127 E. Taft Ave.; (336) 626-7578; www.tasteofasia.biz. You can get great Thai food here in a friendly, unassuming atmosphere. $–$$

Where to Stay

Zooland Family Campground. 3671 Pisgah Covered Bridge Rd.; (336) 381-3422. This campground offers 200 sites, 2 pools, miniature golf, a game room, playgrounds, and modern bathhouses. $

Chains located here include **Best Western, Comfort Inn, Fairfield Inn and Suites, Hampton Inn,** and **Holiday Inn.**

For More Information

Randolph County Tourism Development Authority. (800) 626-2672; www.visit randolph.org.

Seagrove

Seagrove, south of Asheboro on US 220, and the surrounding area could well be the pottery capital of the world.

Seagrove Area Potteries (ages 5 and up)

For more information call the Pottery Museum at (336) 626-0364 or visit www.seagrove potterymuseum.org.

The Seagrove Area Potteries bring to life a tradition that has been passed down through the ages. In this area, you'll find something in the neighborhood of 100 potteries where potters work and put their wares on sale. Pottery was first made here by Native Americans in the 1500s. Today's works have been refined, thanks to modern technology, but some of the potters here now come from families that have practiced the craft since the late 18th century. Here you can purchase a whole set of dishes, a pottery bird feeder, or a museum-quality piece. The annual **Pottery Festival,** sponsored by the Friends of the Pottery Museum, is held in Seagrove each November on the Sunday before Thanksgiving. In addition to pottery, the crafts of doll making, candle making, wood carving, and more are demonstrated.

Burlington

If you choose to head east instead of south from Greensboro, I-40 or US 70 will take you to Burlington.

The city of Burlington has grown to become a shopping mecca for North Carolina residents, but it offers plenty of history and other attractions for your family to enjoy.

Alamance Battleground State Historic Site (ages 5 and up)

Located on Highway 62 South off I-85/40 on Alamance Battleground Road; (336) 227-4785; www.nchistoricsites.org. Open 9 a.m. to 5 p.m. Mon through Sat. Free.

Start a historical tour of the Burlington area at the Alamance Battleground State Historic Site. This is the site where Royal Governor William Tryon in 1771 led the North Carolina Militia into a battle against 2,000 Regulators, an army of colonial reformers who protested taxes, corrupt officials, and the lack of representation. Learn more about the battle and the Regulator movement at the site. The visitor center presents an audiovisual display as well as other historical information. In addition, the **John Allen House,** a log home typical of this area in the late 1700s, has been restored and contains its original furnishings.

Cedarock Historical Farm (all ages)

Highway 49 South, 4252 Cedarock Park Rd.; (336) 570-6759. Typically open during daylight hours. Free.

A great way to spend part of an afternoon is at Cedarock Historical Farm. This is a unique 414-acre park that features a rolling terrain full of cedar trees and rock outcroppings, hence its name. Now restored to its original condition, the farm and its buildings were originally constructed in 1830 by John and Polly Garrett. Today a variety of livestock is kept on the farm, including goats, sheep, and cattle. A museum includes antique farm equipment and demonstrations of long-lost farming techniques.

City Park (all ages)

Located at S. Church Street and Overbrook Road; (336) 222-5030. The park generally is open during daylight hours. Free.

When you are in Burlington, make sure you visit City Park, especially if you have young children. This 76-acre park offers miniature golf and amusement rides ($) in addition to traditional park facilities such as picnic tables and a pool. But the centerpiece of the park is a **Dentzel Menagerie Carousel** made in 1910. This is a beautiful piece of work. The carousel has 46 hand-carved animals, no two alike. Included are 26 horses with real horse-hair tails and a variety of other bright animals ranging from pigs to reindeer. Other rides, including a train and boats, are smaller and great for younger children and even toddlers.

Where to Eat

The Cutting Board. 2619 Alamance Rd.; (336) 226-0291; www.cuttingboard.com. Standard American dishes, especially steak, are offered in a sea-themed setting. $

Where to Stay

You'll find a number of large chain accommodations near I-40 and I-85.

For More Information

Burlington Convention and Visitors Bureau. (800) 637-3804; www.ci.burlington.nc.us.

Snow Camp

From Burlington take Highway 87 South to Snow Camp.

Snow Camp Amphitheatre (all ages)

Located on SR 1005 south of Burlington; (800) 726-5115; www.snowcampdrama.com. Evening shows are presented at 8:30 p.m. from mid-June through late Aug. Write to PO Box 535, Snow Camp, NC 27349 for tickets. $–$$$.

Although Snow Camp is a small town, it boasts one of the best drama societies in the state. The most popular annual production is *Sword of Peace,* which is presented alternately with *Pathway to Freedom*. Much of Alamance County's history is presented in William Hardy's *Sword of Peace,* a tribute to the Quakers and their role in the American Revolution. In this action-packed production, Simon Miller, a Quaker miller, must decide whether his faith allows him to take part in the Revolution. In *Pathway to Freedom,* playwright Mark R. Sumner tells the fictional story of the son of a slave-owning family and how he became involved with the Underground Railroad. In addition to these wonderful annual productions, Snow Camp also presents other plays that are especially appropriate for children. In the past such greats as *The Sound of Music* have been presented, and Saturday mornings are reserved for young children with productions such as *Cinderella*.

Where to Eat

Ye Old Country Kitchen. Located on Drama Road at the amphitheater; (336) 376-6991. You can eat at the buffet here before going to the play. $

Ye Old Ice Cream Shop. On Drama Road at the amphitheater; (919) 376-6948. Not only will you find ice cream here, but also roasted peanuts and other confections. Outside, crafts and other displays are set up during performances. $

Chapel Hill

Three cities to the east of Burlington—Raleigh, Durham, and Chapel Hill—lie in a geometric shape known as the Triangle. If you visit this area in the winter months, you should be aware that you are in college basketball country. The state's three main universities are located in the Triangle area, making for a long-standing rivalry among the teams vying for the Atlantic Coast Conference basketball championship. For years it has been one of the favorite athletic competitions for North Carolina residents.

Ackland Art Museum (ages 5 and up)

101 S. Columbia St. near Franklin Street; (919) 966-5736; www.ackland.org. Open 10 a.m. to 5 p.m. Wed, Fri, and Sat; 10 a.m. to 8 p.m. Thurs; and 1 to 5 p.m. Sun. Free.

Take a stroll through the oak trees that line the brick walks of the UNC campus to the Ackland Art Museum. Here you'll find a wide range of art—paintings, sculptures, drawings, photographs, and furnishings. Works in the museum's permanent collections come from Europe and Asia as well as the US. Art from the Renaissance to the present is represented in addition to North Carolina pottery and folk art. Regular programs for children are also scheduled.

Carolina Basketball Museum (all ages)

450 Skipper Bowles Dr.; (919) 843-9921; www.tarheelblue.com. Open 10 a.m. to 4 p.m. Tues through Fri and 9 a.m. to 1 p.m. Sat. Free.

Located in the Koury Natatorium adjacent to the Smith Center, the Carolina Basketball Museum tells the story of one of the most legendary college basketball programs in the nation. Artifacts, jerseys, balls, trophies, videos, photos, and more capture the college days of the likes of Michael Jordan, Phil Ford, James Worthy, and others whose names still figure prominently in the world of basketball.

Kidzu Children's Museum (ages 1 to 8)

123 W. Franklin St.; (919) 933-1455; www.kidzuchildrensmuseum.org. Open 10 a.m. to 5 p.m. Tues through Sat and 1 to 5 p.m. Sun. $; free for children under age 2.

Kidzu offers an interactive, fun learning environment for children up to age 8 through storytelling, art, crafts, music, and permanent and traveling exhibits, such as Mister Roger's Neighborhood. First opened on Franklin Street in 2006, it relocated to a temporary home in University Square on W. Franklin Street in the summer of 2011. The museum hopes to open its permanent location at Wallace Plaza by 2014.

Morehead Planetarium and Science Center (all ages)

250 E. Franklin St.; (919) 962-1236; www.moreheadplanetarium.org. Open 10 a.m. to 3:30 p.m. Tues through Sat and 1 to 4:30 p.m. Sun. $$.

The most easily accessible attraction is Morehead Planetarium, once used by NASA as a training center for astronauts and now one of the largest planetariums in the country. Part of the university, the planetarium houses a rare projector that casts nearly 9,000 stars onto the inside of the planetarium's 68-foot dome. In addition to the 350-seat theater, there are a host of related exhibits, art galleries, a digital theater, observatory, a science shop, rose gardens, and a huge sundial. Special programs for children are held most weekends. Call for a schedule of shows.

North Carolina Botanical Garden (all ages)

Old Mason Farm Road; (919) 962-0522; www.ncbg.unc.edu. Open 8 a.m. to 5 p.m. Mon through Fri, 9 a.m. to 6 p.m. Sat, and 1 to 6 p.m. Sun. Free.

This is the largest natural botanical garden in the Southeast and consists of 600 acres of naturally preserved land. There are miles of walking trails and collections of North Carolina and southeastern plants arranged in habitats in natural settings. Here you will also see carnivorous plants, aquatic plants, herb gardens, and more in 10 acres of display gardens. Gigantic chess pieces as tall as your children are just an example of the creative sculptures at this great garden. A LEEDS-certified education center built largely from materials on the property provides space for exhibits and programs.

University of North Carolina

Chapel Hill is home of the University of North Carolina, the nation's first state-supported university, chartered in 1789. This great town is, for all intents and purposes, the university—the city's population of 40,000 includes a largely diverse collection of 24,000 students and professors from across the country, making Chapel Hill a uniquely cosmopolitan town. Franklin Street, which forms the northern edge of the university campus, is full of opportunities for a wide variety of shopping and dining, while the campus provides a multitude of cultural and popular attractions. Limited parking is available on campus, but you can use one of the municipal lots on Rosemary or Franklin Street.

There are a few formal exhibits on the 700-acre campus, and the campus itself is well manicured with big oaks, gardens, courtyards, centuries-old buildings, and, of course, the quad. Sights include the **Morehead Patterson Bell Tower** on South Road, south of the art museum, and the **Dean E. Smith Center,** located on Skipper Bowles Drive on the southern part of campus, the home of the Tar Heels and named for the longtime men's basketball coach. Other famous locations include **Old Well,** where a sip of water is expected to bring good luck, and performance places **Memorial Hall** and the **Paul Green Theater.** Plan ahead, use connections, or count on luck at the door to get tickets to a game on campus, but the Dean E. Smith Center is host to other special events and concerts. Football tickets are easier to come by if you get them as soon as the schedule is finalized in early summer.

Where to Eat

Breadmen's. 324 W. Rosemary St.; (919) 967-7110; www.breadmens.com. Breadmen's serves great burgers and such, as well as breakfast all the time. $

Crooks Corner. 610 W. Franklin St.; (919) 929-7643; www.crookscorner.com. Crooks Corner for years has enjoyed a reputation for providing the best Southern cuisine in the state. $$$

Mama Dip's Traditional Country. 405 W. Rosemary St.; (919) 942-5837; www.mama dips.com. Get your fried chicken here. Try the ribs or even the chitterlings. $

Il Palio Ristorante. 1505 E. Franklin St.; (919) 929-4000; www.sienahotel.com. This is probably the best Italian restaurant in the town and the state. It can be great for a romantic dinner, but it also has a children's menu. Make reservations. $$$

Spanky's Restaurant & Bar. 101 E. Franklin St.; (919) 929-5098; www.spankysrestau rant.com. A tradition at Chapel Hill, the menu at Spanky's features burgers and its famed brown-sugar baby back ribs, and it has a kids' menu. $$

Top of the Hill Restaurant. 100 E. Franklin St.; (919) 929-8676; www.topofthehillrestau rant.com. Overlooking Franklin Street from the third-floor patio, this microbrewery offers casual, upscale dining. $$

Where to Stay

Chapel Hill offers a selection of upscale hotels, all with a taste of the town. For more moderately priced accommodations, you'll have to look for hotel chains.

Carolina Inn. 211 Pittsboro St.; (800) 962-8519; www.carolinainn.com. This is a classic historic hotel located on the campus and is *the* place to stay. Make sure you eat at Carolina Crossroads, the restaurant in the hotel. $$$$

The Siena Hotel. 1505 E. Franklin St.; (919) 929-4000; www.sienahotel.com. This is another of Chapel Hill's AAA four-diamond hotels. Expect great service and accommodations here. $$$$

For More Information

Chapel Hill/Orange County Visitors Bureau. (888) 968-2060; www.chocvb.org.

Hillsborough

North of Chapel Hill on Highway 86 is the historic town of Hillsborough.

Hillsborough is listed on the National Register of Historic Places and has more than 100 structures from the late 18th and 19th centuries, some of which provided a backdrop for a number of events during the Revolutionary War. Most notable is the site of the Constitutional Convention of 1788, where delegates demanded a Bill of Rights before they would ratify the Constitution. In addition, the town was significant in the Civil War and served as headquarters for Confederate general Joseph E. Johnston, who later negotiated terms of the South's surrender with Union general William T. Sherman.

Occaneechi Village Restoration (ages 5 and up)
Cameron Street on the Eno River; (919) 304-3723; www.occaneechi-saponi.org. Free.

This project of the Occaneechi Band of the Saponi Nation is still in development, but you can visit now. Its village was reconstructed with a palisade (stockade fence), huts, a cooking site, and a sweat lodge, just as it was in this general area during the late 17th century. During that period tribes in south-central Virginia and western North Carolina used it along their trading path. Future years will bring more attractions to the site.

Orange County Historical Museum (ages 5 and up)
201 N. Churton St.; (919) 732-2201; www.orangehistory.org. Open 11 a.m. to 4 p.m. Tues through Sat and 1 to 4 p.m. Sun. Free.

The museum illustrates much of Hillsborough's past, depicting history and lifestyles from the time Native Americans inhabited the Eno River area through the Civil War. It was the site of the 1788 North Carolina Constitutional Convention. A gallery features works by a different artist every month.

Where to Eat

Andy's Burgers and Fries. 601 Hampton Pointe Blvd.; (919) 732-3734; www.andys burgers.net. This fun 1950s-style diner serves burgers, shakes, onion rings, and other similar fare. $

Kelsey's Cafe. 126 W. King St.; (919) 732-1155. Simple dishes come from this downtown diner that's a popular breakfast destination. $$

Where to Stay

Southern Country Inn. 122 Daniel Boone St.; (919) 732-8101. You'll find great hospitality at this hotel that also has a campground out back. $–$$

For More Information

Alliance for Historic Hillsborough. (919) 732-7741; www.historichillsborough.org.

Durham

Although Durham is noted for its athletic heritage at Duke University and tobacco-industry history, it is just as notable as a "city of medicine." The university opened its medical school in 1930, there are five major hospitals and a number of pharmaceutical research companies located here, and the city is largely connected to Research Triangle Park, said to be the world's largest university-related research park. To reach Durham from Hillsborough, take I-85 South.

Bennett Place State Historic Site (ages 5 and up)

4409 Bennett Memorial Rd.; (919) 383-4345; www.nchistoricsites.com. Open 9 a.m. to 5 p.m. Tues through Sat. Free.

Like most major cities in the state, Durham has a rich history. It was at Bennett Place State Historic Site that the Civil War effectively ended. Union general William T. Sherman and Confederate general Joseph E. Johnston met at this farmstead in 1865, 17 days after Confederate general Robert E. Lee surrendered at Appomattox. Following meetings in Hillsborough, the Durham meeting set up the largest surrender of the war. Although fighting continued in the west, this was the conclusion to the bloody War Between the States. Today the farmhouse and outbuildings have been restored, and the grounds also include a museum and interpretive center. Exhibits concentrate on North Carolina's role in the war, and uniforms, flags, and weapons are on display. A surrender reenactment is presented each April.

Duke Homestead State Historic Site (ages 5 and up)

2828 Duke Homestead Rd.; (919) 477-5498; www.nchistoricsites.com. Open 9 a.m. to 5 p.m. Tues through Sat and 1 to 5 p.m. Sun. Free.

Long before Durham was a medical center, its roots were deeply embedded in the tobacco industry. Much of this history is available for viewing at the Duke Homestead State Historic Site and Tobacco Museum. The site includes the Duke home, constructed in 1852, plus tobacco barns and 2 early tobacco factories. The museum chronicles the history of the tobacco industry and production, and cigarette manufacturing. A moving mannequin plants tobacco and helps bring the industry into perspective, as does a film about the Duke family and their tobacco empire.

Duke Lemur Center (all ages)

3705 Erwin Rd.; (919) 489-3364; www.lemur.duke.edu. Reservations required. $$–$$$$.

This is the world's largest sanctuary for rare and endangered prosimian primates. It was established in 1966 on 85 acres in Duke Forest (about 10 minutes from the Duke University campus) to study and help preserve these adorable animals that live naturally on the island of Madagascar. Family-oriented tours take visitors through the facilities to learn about these fascinating animals. A separate tour, costing $95 per person, takes participants ages 10 and over behind the barriers to get up close and personal with lemurs.

Duke University

Duke University is located on another beautiful campus. Its stately architecture indicates its rich history and legacy as one of the leading private universities in the country. For more information, visit the university website at www.duke.edu.

Duke University Chapel   (all ages)

Located on Chapel Drive; (919) 681-1704; www.chapel.duke.edu. Tour the church 8 a.m. to 10 p.m. daily, 8 a.m. to 8 p.m. in summer, or attend a nondenominational worship service at 11 a.m. Sun. Free. (Of course, donations are accepted.)

At Duke University you'll find a number of interesting attractions, most notable of which is Duke University Chapel in the west campus. This 1,800-seat chapel, constructed in the 1930s, was the last of the great collegiate Gothic projects. It features a 5,033-pipe organ with 5 keyboards and a 50-bell carillon. Its 77 intricate stained-glass windows depicting stories from the Bible are also noteworthy.

Nasher Museum of Art at Duke University   (ages 5 and up)

Located on Campus Drive in the East Campus; (919) 684-5135; www.nasher.duke.edu. Open 10 a.m. to 5 p.m. Tues, Wed, Fri, and Sat; 10 a.m. to 9 p.m. Thurs; and noon to 5 p.m. Sun. $.

Nasher Museum of Art at Duke University is most notable for its fine collection of medieval sculpture, but it is also host to a lovely collection of stained glass and an extensive collection of pre-Columbian exhibits and classical objects. The museum's Chinese jade is quite unusual. American and European paintings, prints, and drawings round out the trip to the museum.

Sarah P. Duke Gardens   (all ages)

Anderson St.; (919) 684-3698; www.hr.duke.edu/dukegardens. Open 8 a.m. to dusk daily. Free.

Here you find 55 acres of beautifully kept gardens, both natural and landscaped. There are more than 1,500 kinds of plants along the paths. The walks feature pathways with bridges, grottoes, court lawns, waterfalls, and pavilions. Such a wide variety of plants exists here that you'll find color in bloom practically all year long. In addition, there is an Asiatic Arboretum.

Durham Bulls   (all ages)

Durham Bulls Athletic Park, Blackwell Street; (919) 768-6000; www.durhambulls.com. $–$$.

One of the most popular attractions for Durham residents are these legendary boys of summer who turn out at the Durham Bulls Athletic Park, the home of the Durham Bulls, a Class AAA baseball affiliate of the Tampa Bay Devil Rays. The Bulls received national attention in 1987 with the release of the movie *Bull Durham,* starring Susan Sarandon, Kevin Costner, and Tim Robbins. Even before the release of the film, area residents helped set attendance records at what is North Carolina's most famous baseball team's stadium.

North Carolina Museum of Life and Science (all ages)

433 Murray Ave.; (919) 220-5429; www.ncmls.org. Open 10 a.m. to 5 p.m. Tues through Sat and noon to 5 p.m. Sun, Memorial Day through Labor Day. $$–$$$.

This is a great interactive museum that features a range of exhibits from railroads to aerospace. Included is a display of *Apollo 15* and *Enos,* the first US spacecraft to orbit Earth. The museum's nature center is the best part of the museum. Indoor and outdoor exhibits allow visitors to see a variety of wildlife and learn more about it through hands-on activities. The kids can hold a box turtle or hear a rabbit's snappy heartbeat. They won't, however, want to hold the black bears, red wolves, and other large animals on display in attractive, well-maintained displays. There is also a farmyard where kids can pet the animals, a great tropical butterfly house, and a half-mile-long dinosaur trail of life-size replicas.

Wheels Family Fun Park (all ages)

715 Hoover Rd.; (919) 598-1944. Hours vary according to season. Fees vary by attraction.

Wheels Family Fun Park is the largest of Durham's several small amusement parks, with more than 8 acres of fun and adventure. The park features the basic amusement park facilities, such as bumper cars, go-karts, and video games, but it also has a skating rink and a miniature golf course.

Where to Eat

Bombay Grille. 2223 E. Highway 54; (919) 544-6967; www.bombaygrille.com. Don't be afraid to try new things; at least that's what I tell my kids. You may have to ask for mild dishes at this Indian restaurant that is expanding to other locations in North Carolina. $$

Bullock's Bar-B-Que. 3330 Quebec Dr.; (919) 383-6202; www.bullocksbbq.com. You can check out the pictures of the famous folk who have dined here on what is in the running for the best eastern barbecue in the state. $

Elmo's Diner. 776 9th St.; (919) 416-3823; www.elmosdiner.com. You'll find an Elmo's in Chapel Hill, too, and they pay special attention to kids. You'll find everything from breakfast to burgers, shakes, and malts. $–$$

Foster's Market. 2694 Durham–Chapel Hill Blvd.; (919) 489-3944; www.fostersmarket

.com. Sara Foster opened this as a specialty and take-out food store, but you can also grab a bite on the porch. $

Nikos Taverna. 905 W. Main St.; (919) 682-0043; www.nikostaverna.com. Greek food is served in a historic warehouse in Brightleaf Square. $$

Where to Stay

Brookwood Inn & Suites at Duke University. 2306 Elba St.; (919) 286-3111. This is a very contemporary hotel. Children stay **free.** $$–$$$

Carolina Duke Motor Inn. 2517 Guess Rd.; (800) 438-1158. Even if you're a little more budget conscious, you'll still find good service and clean rooms here. $

Millennium Hotel. 2800 Campus Walk Ave.; (919) 383-8575. You could walk to the university from this hotel, but it would be a long one. Still, it's one of the nicer hotels in Durham, with some efficiencies. $$$

Washington Duke Inn and Golf Club. 3001 Cameron Blvd.; (919) 490-0999. This is a four-star hotel with impeccable service and first-class amenities. Expect to pay for it. $$$$

For More Information

Durham Convention and Visitors Bureau. (800) 446-8604; www.durham-nc .com.

Raleigh

I-40 draws drivers from east and west, merging into the sometimes confusing loop, I-440, that encircles this capital city.

Raleigh, with a population of more than 300,000, has been voted the best place in America to live by both *Fortune* and *Money* magazines. It's just as good a place to visit. Raleigh offers all the expected amenities of a big city—the arts, the culture, and the entertainment—and great museums and other educational opportunities at the state's largest university and at the government complex abound. What's more, it has plenty of good old-fashioned Southern hospitality. The city was founded in 1792 and named for Sir Walter Raleigh, who is credited with founding the first English colonies in the Carolinas. While there are big buildings and lots of traffic, one of the first things you'll notice is the abundance of oak trees that add to the city's charm.

Carolina Hurricanes (all ages)

RBC Center, 1400 Edwards Mill Rd.; (919) 861-2323; www.carolinahurricanes.com. $$$–$$$$.

Hockey fever overtook the city of Raleigh in 2002 as the Carolina Hurricanes slapped their way into the Stanley Cup Finals and then grabbed the Stanley Cup in 2006. The RBC Center has been the home of the 'Canes since October 1999, and it also is home court for North Carolina State's basketball team.

Executive Mansion (ages 5 and up)

200 N. Blount St.; (919) 807-7950. Free.

An impressive mansion built in the Victorian style of architecture, the Executive Mansion was constructed largely of handmade bricks and has housed 26 families since its completion in 1891. Self-guided tours of the home are permitted on an irregular basis. The Capital Area Visitors Center, located in the North Carolina Museum of History, also conducts guided tours with advance notice. Call for hours or other information.

Frankie's Fun Park (all ages)

11190 Family Fun Park Dr.; (919) 433-7888; www.frankiesfunpark.com. Open 10 a.m. to 10 p.m. Mon through Thurs, 10 a.m. to midnight Fri and Sat, and 11 a.m. to 10 p.m. Sun. Fees charged for various attractions.

Frankie offers go-karts for several ages and skill levels, bumper boats, miniature golf, laser tag, a batting cage, a fun house, and an arcade.

Historic Homes (ages 5 and up)

Maps of Raleigh's historic sites are available at the visitor center (919-834-0887) located at 500 Fayetteville St. or download them from the website at www.visitraleigh.com.

The **Historic Oakwood** neighborhood (919-807-7950) is a 20-block area of Victorian homes built in the late 1800s, bordered by Delson, Edenton, Boundary, and Watauga Streets. Just west of downtown on Hargett Street is the **Joel Lane House** (919-833-3431), which was built in the 1760s and is Raleigh's oldest dwelling. In 1782 representatives of the newly formed legislature selected this site as the capital and purchased 1,000 acres of the Lane plantation to create the city of Raleigh. The furnishings in the home are authentic to the period. Just north of downtown at 1 Mimosa St. you will find **Mordecai Historic Park** (919-857-4364), a former antebellum plantation. Here you can get a glimpse of 19th-century life and see the cabin where Andrew Johnson, the nation's 17th president, was born. Modest fees are charged for some tours and activities. The Oakwood neighborhood can be toured at any time. The Lane House is open on an irregular basis, and Mordecai Park is open 10 a.m. to 4 p.m. Mon through Sat and 1 to 4 p.m. Sun. Trolley tours ($–$$, **free** for children age 6 and under) originate from Mordecai Park on Sat from Mar through Dec from 11 a.m. to 2 p.m.

Kazoom Children's Theater (ages 2 to 7)

431 Peace St.; (919) 829-0822; www.carolinapuppets.com. Showtimes vary. $.

Children are engaged at this innovative puppet and storytelling theater. Children from the audience participate in the production songs and dances in each of the themed shows.

Marbles Kids Museum (all ages)

201 E. Hargett St.; (919) 834-4040; www.marbleskidsmuseum.org. Open 9 a.m. to 5 p.m. Tues through Sat and noon to 5 p.m. Sun. $$–$$$.

Marbles is a children's museum that focus on child development through communication, creativity, and play. Interactive experiences include Castaway Cove, Around Town, the high finance of Moneypalooza, and Storybook Forest. While most of the exhibits focus on children under the age of 10, it also has an IMAX theater which will please kids of all ages.

North Carolina Museum of Art (ages 5 and up)

2110 Blue Ridge Rd.; (919) 839-6262. Open 10 a.m. to 5 p.m. Tues, Wed, Thurs, Sat, and Sun and 10 a.m. to 9 p.m. Fri. Guided tours are conducted at 1:30 p.m. daily. Free, with a charge for special exhibitions.

Several miles north of the university is the North Carolina Museum of Art, housing the permanent art collection of the state as well as changing exhibits. The museum contains paintings and sculptures dating back 5,000 years that come from as far away as Egypt. Included are works by Raphael, Monet, Botticelli, and others. The newest part of the museum includes a stunning contemporary building constructed with techniques that utilize natural light to enhance exhibits and conserve energy. Along with it opened Museum Park, which includes sustainable landscaping that is intertwined with newly acquired outdoor sculptures.

North Carolina Museum of History (all ages)

5 E. Edenton St.; (919) 807-7900; www.ncmuseumofhistory.org. Open 9 a.m. to 5 p.m. Tues through Sat and noon to 5 p.m. Sun. Free.

The North Carolina Museum of History, which is surprisingly unstuffy and fun for a history museum, is divided into four sections, each depicting a part of North Carolina's history. Included are displays that present a chronological history, the role of women in the state's history, and folklife. Artifacts tell North Carolina's story from the earliest settlements on Roanoke Island, as well as the state's role in the Revolutionary and Civil Wars. A replica of a drugstore gives insight to early 20th-century Carolina life, while the North Carolina Sports Hall of Fame delivers artifacts and audiovisual displays about North Carolina's sports greats. You'll also find the Capital Area Visitors Center here.

North Carolina Museum of Natural Sciences (all ages)

11 W. Jones St.; (919) 733-7450; www.naturalsciences.org. Open 9 a.m. to 5 p.m. Mon through Sat and noon to 5 p.m. Sun. Free, with a charge for some special exhibitions.

Located in the capitol complex, this massive collection of exhibition spaces is devoted to the study of natural history. Visitors here get an opportunity to explore the natural world by looking at things that are uniquely North Carolina. Among the most amazing exhibits is *Prehistoric North Carolina,* which includes Willo, a 66-million-year-old dinosaur with a fossilized heart and the only acrocanthosaurus on display in the world. (You can teach the kids to say akro-cantho-saurus on the way.) Live animals are part of the *Mountains to the Sea* exhibit that presents North Carolina's five distinct habitats. Many of the collections from the old museum once located on Edenton Street are also part of the new facility that spans a city block stacked into 5 stories. Begin your visit by methodically visiting each of the 4 stories that are connected by escalators. Reach the top to explore the arthropod zoo and a butterfly house.

North Carolina State Fairgrounds (all ages)

1025 Blue Ridge Rd.; (919) 821-7400. $–$$.

The best time to visit Raleigh is in the fall, when the North Carolina State Fairgrounds, near the university, come alive with the excitement of the annual state fair. The fair is a traditional festival featuring rides, games, and farm-related events and exhibitions. It is usually held for 10 days in the middle of October. When the fair isn't in town, the grounds are host to a flea market on the weekends and a variety of other shows, including livestock and pet shows. Rodeos are also periodically held here, and the fairgrounds are the Raleigh venue for the Ringling Bros. and Barnum & Bailey Circus.

North Carolina State University

Leaving downtown, take Hillsborough Street to North Carolina State University; (914) 515-2011; www.ncsu.edu.

With 30,000 students, this is the state's largest institution of higher learning. The university is almost a completely separate town. The campus, noted for its redbrick walkways and buildings, is host to Wolfpack basketball, football, and other sports. In addition, it provides venues for concerts, theater, and the arts. Also worth a visit is the **NCSU J. C. Raulston Arboretum** (919-515-3132), which features 6,000 different kinds of plants from 55 countries. Located off Old Hillsborough Street at 4301 Beryl Rd., the arboretum also includes a Victorian gazebo and a Japanese garden, with guided tours at 2 p.m. Sun from mid-Apr to mid-Oct. Admission is **free.**

Pullen Park   (all ages)

520 Ashe Ave.; (919) 831-6468. Generally open during daylight hours. Free, with fees for some attractions.

Part of Raleigh's Parks and Recreation Department, Pullen Park offers a train ride through the amusement park, a kiddie boat ride, pedal boats, and a 1912 Dentzel Menagerie Carousel. Of course, you'll also find standard park attractions such as tennis courts, softball fields, a swimming pool, and picnic and playground areas. Pullen Park is also home of TV Land's tribute statue of Andy and Opie Taylor honoring *The Andy Griffith Show*.

State Government Complex   (all ages)

Open 8 a.m. to 5 p.m. Mon through Fri, 9 a.m. to 5 p.m. Sat, and 1 to 5 p.m. Sun. Free.

A good place to start a visit to Raleigh is downtown. In addition to the state government complex, you'll find museums, restaurants, shopping, street vendors, and more. The **State Capitol** (919-733-4994) is located in the geographic center of downtown. Built in the late 1830s in the Greek Revival style, it houses the governor's office, cabinet offices, historic

Keep Your Feet **Off the Carpet!**

No one walks on the bold red carpet centered on the impressive marble staircase that leads to offices, exhibits, and viewing galleries in the North Carolina Legislative Building. Instead, the staircase is roped off with stanchions at the top and bottom while pedestrian access is provided by two steep, narrow staircases that lead up three stories. A docent said not even the governor is allowed on the carpet. In fact, she said, when presidents have visited the Legislative Building they, too, were directed around the carpeted stairs. The building was designed in 1960 by the famous architect Edward Durell Stone, who also designed New York's Radio City Music Hall, Museum of Modern Art, and Kennedy Center.

Area **Parks**

If you're looking for an opportunity for outdoor recreation, two lakes are within easy driving distance from Raleigh, as are a handful of city and county parks. In Wake Forest find **Falls Lake State Recreation Area,** located on Creedmoor Road. It is one of the largest recreation facilities in the state and offers camping, hiking, fishing, swimming, a picnic area, playgrounds, boat rentals, and interpretive nature programs. Hours vary according to season. Call (919) 676-1027 for more information.

Southwest of Raleigh is **Jordan Lake Recreation Area,** located on State Park Road. Just take US 64 west out of Raleigh. One of the largest summertime homes of the bald eagle in the eastern US, Jordan Lake is a great place to study nature. The 15,000-acre recreation area offers a full-service marina as well as opportunities for camping, fishing, and swimming. Hours vary according to season. Call (919) 362-0586 for more information.

legislative chambers, and the state library. The state **Legislative Building** (919-733-7928) is located across Bicentennial Plaza and is home to the North Carolina General Assembly. Devoted solely to the legislative branch, the General Assembly gives visitors an opportunity to view the legislative process with viewing galleries that overlook both chambers of the legislature.

Where to Eat

Andy's Pizza. 1302 E. Milbrook Rd., (919) 872-6797; 4217 Six Forks Rd., (919) 781-9043. The staff makes pizza night even more fun than it already is. $

Angus Barn. 9401 Glenwood Ave.; (919) 787-3535; www.angusbarn.com. The Angus Barn is known far and wide for its quality steaks. $$–$$$

Kanki. 4325 Glenwood Ave., (919) 782-9708; 4500 Old Wake Forest Rd., (919) 876-4157; www.kanki.com. Food is prepared at your table at this Japanese restaurant. $$$

The Pit. 328 W. Davie St.; (919) 890-4500. Whole hog barbecue comes out of the smokers here. $

Poole's Diner. 426 S. McDowell St.; (919) 832-4477; www.poolesdowntowndiner.com. Poole's started as a pie shop in the 1940s. Now it's one of the city's most popular downtown dining locations. $$

Where to Stay

Milner Inn. 1817 Capital Blvd.; (888) 331-5500. This is a small inn for the budget-minded. $$

The Plantation Inn Resort. 6401 Capital Blvd.; (919) 876-1411. Located near Research Triangle Park, this resort offers top-quality amenities, including 2 restaurants. $$$$

Velvet Cloak Inn. 1505 Hillsborough St.; (919) 828-0333; www.thevelvetcloak.com.

Located between the university and downtown, the Velvet Cloak provides elegance and convenience plus an indoor pool. $$$

For More Information

Greater Raleigh Convention and Visitors Bureau. (800) 849-8499; www.visitraleigh.com.

Smithfield

Travel southeast from Raleigh to I-95 and US 70 to find Smithfield.

Ava Gardner Museum (ages 3 and up)

325 E. Market St.; (919) 934-5830; www.avagardner.org. Open 9 a.m. to 5 p.m. Mon through Sat and 2 to 5 p.m. Sun. $$.

Your kids might not know exactly who Ava Gardner was (she may be before your time, too, for that matter, but your parents will know), yet they'll probably get a kick out of a visit to the Ava Gardner Museum, located in her hometown of Smithfield. The museum was opened in 1991, a year after the actress died, as a tribute to her. Exhibits include the posters from her 57 films as well as photographs that show her as a child through her years as a seductive leading lady of the 1940s and '50s. You will find other memorabilia from her life at this unique museum, too.

Bentonville Battleground (ages 5 and up)

South of Smithfield on US 701; (919) 594-0789; www.nchistoricsites.org. Open 9 a.m. to 5 p.m. Mon through Sat, Apr through Oct; 9 a.m. to 5 p.m. Tues through Sat, Nov through Mar. Free.

This is the site of the largest battle ever fought in the state. The fierce Civil War battle raged for three days, but Union troops eventually beat down Confederate forces, and a month later the war ended in the Carolinas. More than 4,000 men were killed, wounded, or went missing in the battle. Many of them were taken to the farm home of John and Amy Harper, which was turned into a field hospital. The house still stands and is furnished as a field hospital. A section of Union trenches and a cemetery remain as stark reminders of the battle. Other exhibits on display at the site's visitor center include a fiber-optic map and artifacts from the battle.

Where to Eat

Becky's Log Cabin Restaurant. 2491 US 70 East; (919) 934-1534; www.beckyslogcabin.com. This is a good steak house with a neat, rustic atmosphere among a big selection of chain restaurants. $$

Where to Stay

Log Cabin Motel. 2491 US 70 East; (919) 934-1534. This is the home of Becky's Log Cabin Restaurant. Pets are welcome in the 61 rooms here. $$

Village Motor Lodge and Restaurant. 198 Mallard Rd.; (800) 531-0063. A swimming pool, playground, and restaurant make this a great accommodations option. $$

For More Information

Johnston County Visitors Bureau. (800) 441-7829; www.johnstoncountync.org.

Other Things to See & Do
in the Northern Piedmont

- **Hickory Dickory Dock.** Hickory; (828) 322-3625; www.hickorydickorydock .net

- **Fun Station.** Statesville; (704) 838-0440; www.funstation2000.com

- **Mayberry Shazzam Family Entertainment Center.** Pilot Mountain; (336) 368-9900; www.mayberyshazzam.com

- **The Barn Dance.** Greensboro; (336) 685-9200; www.thebarndance.com

- **Grand Prix.** Greensboro; (336) 664-6222

- **Ice House.** Greensboro; (336) 852-1515; www.greensboroice.com

- **American Classic Motorcycle Museum.** Asheboro; (336) 629-9564

- **I-85 Golf and Baseball.** Burlington; (336) 578-2391

- **University Lake.** Chapel Hill; (919) 942-8007

- **Triangle SportsPlex.** Hillsborough; (919) 644-0339; www.trianglesportsplex .com

- **Adventure Landing.** Raleigh; (919) 872-1688; www.adventurelanding.com

- **Battlezone Laser Adventure.** Raleigh; (919) 847-4263

- **Clemmons Educational State Forest.** Clayton; (919) 553-5651; www.dfr .state.nc.us

- **Tag Ur It.** Smithfield; (919) 209-0851; www.bbamusements.com

Kenly

Kenly is located in Johnston County just off I-95, 15 minutes north of Smithfield.

Tobacco Farm Life Museum (ages 5 and up)

709 Church St., 1.5 miles east of Kenly; (919) 284-3431; www.tobaccofarmlifemuseum.org. Open 9:30 a.m. to 5 p.m. Tues through Sat. $$; children age 4 or younger get in free.

Life on the tobacco farm is the subject on display at the bright Tobacco Farm Life Museum. The exhibits at the museum illustrate how tobacco farming improved the life of the farm families who did it. Visit the Depression era of the 1930s and examine artifacts that relate to the farmers' struggles. On display are schoolbooks, medical equipment, and household goods as well as tobacco farming equipment and outbuildings.

Bailey

North of Kenly and east of Raleigh you'll find Bailey.

Country Doctor Museum (all ages)

6642 Peele Rd.; (919) 235-4165; www.countrydoctormuseum.org. Open 10 a.m. to 3 p.m. Tues through Sat. $.

More everyday life from the late 19th century is waiting at the Country Doctor Museum, chartered in 1967 in honor of the tradition of the family doctor. It consists of 2 restored offices of country doctors. It's easy to appreciate how the medical field has progressed when you see the artifacts here. On display are apothecary jars, old stethoscopes, and saws and knives used at battlefield hospitals. Docents lead tours of the 3 buildings that make up the museum.

The Southern Piedmont

I n North Carolina's Southern Piedmont your family will be treated to some of the biggest, best, brightest, tallest, and loudest experiences the state has to offer. At the heart of the region is the state's biggest city, which features major-league sports, the state's largest amusement park, and what is one of the world's best science centers. Not far away enjoy down-home fun at the state's largest county fair or visit a small textile community that is set to brighten your Christmas season. The region extends east into the Carolina heartland, where you'll find some of the country's premier golf courses and discover the unusual art of hollerin'.

Jim's
TopPicks in the Southern Piedmont

1. Carowinds, Charlotte

2. Children's Theater of Charlotte

3. Charlotte sports

4. Discovery Place, Charlotte

5. Reed Gold Mine, Stanfield

6. Crowders Mountain State Park, Gastonia

7. Christmastown USA, McAdenville

8. Daniel Stowe Botanical Garden, Belmont

9. Morrow Mountain State Park, Albemarle

10. Lowe's Motor Speedway, Harrisburg

THE SOUTHERN PIEDMONT

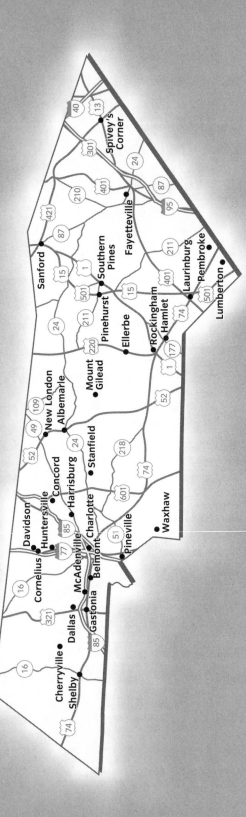

Growth has made travel within some cities difficult, but getting around in this region isn't totally unpleasant. From the north, I-77 bisects Charlotte and intersects with I-85, which runs northeast to Greensboro and southwest into South Carolina. To get to the eastern part of the region from Greensboro, take US 220. From the Triangle area take US 15/501. US 74 runs along the southern part of the region, and I-95 is a good route to use when traveling the eastern part.

Shelby

Shelby is located along US 74 at the western end of the Southern Piedmont.

Cleveland County Fair (all ages)

1751 E. Marion St. (US 74 Business); (704) 487-0651; www.ccfair.net. The fair traditionally runs for 10 days from late Sept through early Oct. $–$$; an additional fee is charged for many of the attractions, but you can buy combo passes ($$–$$$).

Thousands of people roll into Shelby in the fall for the state's largest county fair, which has run continually since 1954. The Cleveland County Fair is state's biggest and best traditional agricultural event, featuring carnival rides, games, exhibitions, livestock shows, and contests. Plenty of homegrown food and country crafts will also be on hand for you to buy. During the rest of the year, the fairgrounds host a number of festivals and horse shows.

Where to Eat

Alston Bridges Barbecue. 620 E. Grover St.; (704) 482-1998. This is one of two Bridges barbecue restaurants in Shelby, and the debate over which is best is a constant. $

Red Bridges Barbecue Lodge. 2000 E. Dixon Blvd.; (704) 482-8567; www.bridgesbbq .com. You'll pass this on the main strip in Shelby, so even if you're not hungry when you pass by, stop and take some home for later. $

Satterfields. 4702 E. Dixon Blvd.; (704) 734-0400. People come from miles around to eat at this restaurant, which features a variety of selections from pasta to blackened dishes. $$

For More Information

Cleveland County Department of Tourism. (704) 484-8521; www.clevelandcounty .com.

Cherryville

The small town of Cherryville is about a 20-minute drive through the country northeast of Shelby on Highway 150.

C. Grier Beam Truck Museum (ages 3 and up)
111 N. Mountain St.; (704) 435-3072; www.beamtruckmuseum.com. Open 10 a.m. to 3 p.m. Thurs and Sat, and 10 a.m. to 5 p.m. Fri. **Free.**

There is a small but unique museum in Cherryville. Check out the old big rigs at the C. Grier Beam Truck Museum, opened in 1982 in a former gas station that once served as the headquarters for Carolina Freight Carriers Corporation. The museum commemorates the history of trucking, and you will see trucks dating back to 1929 and displays that look back at the origins of trucking.

Dallas

Dallas is southeast of Cherryville on Highway 279, just east of US 321.

Gaston County Museum of Art and History (ages 5 and up)
131 W. Main St.; (704) 922-7681; www.gastoncountymuseum.org. Open 10 a.m. to 5 p.m. Tues through Fri and 10 a.m. to 3 p.m. Sat. **Free.**

Step back into the 1800s at one of the four-star hotels of the time at the Gaston County Museum of Art and History. Housed in the former Hoffman Hotel, built in 1852, the museum is at the center of the historic district in the former county seat. Since 1984 the museum has been working to renovate the hotel to show how it evolved through several periods. It is now occupied by displays emphasizing the county's textile heritage as well as the largest collection of horse-drawn carriages in North Carolina. You are also likely to see one of many changing art exhibits here or to want to play in the hands-on parlor. In addition, you can get a brochure with information on buildings included in the district's walking tour.

Gastonia

Gastonia is just south of Dallas on US 321.

Crowders Mountain State Park (ages 5 and up)
Find this park by following the signs from US 74; (704) 853-5375. The park is generally open during daylight hours, year-round. **Free.**

A good place to spend a quiet afternoon hiking or canoeing is at Crowders Mountain State Park. The mountain's stone face, jutting 800 feet above the surrounding area, is an attraction for adventurous mountain climbers. You might even see experienced rappellers taking on the mountain's challenging terrain. Several trails that are easier to navigate await families, and you can fish in the lake or rent a canoe. The park office periodically offers interpretive nature presentations and has a small but engaging nature exhibit hall.

Schiele Museum of Natural History and Planetarium
(ages 3 and up)

1500 E. Garrison Blvd.; (704) 866-6900; www.schielemuseum.org. Open 9 a.m. to 5 p.m. Mon through Sat and 1 to 5 p.m. Sun. $; free for children under 4. Admission fee also charged for programs, special exhibits, and planetarium shows.

Head east on US 74 and right on Garrison Boulevard to the Schiele Museum of Natural History and Planetarium. The museum is continuing its mission of educating Gaston County students, and it has grown to become a staple for the community. Within the museum's walls is North Carolina Hall, showing the six regions of North Carolina during various seasons. On top of the cave in one three-dimensional diorama, a bobcat wags its tail every few minutes. Look carefully in the cave to discover bats on the ceiling. The Hall of Earth and Man presents life as it developed over the last 500 million years. It's almost as if the saber-toothed tiger in one exhibit is alive. The museum's space theater presents shows on the arts, history, travel, and ecology, along with more conventional planetarium shows. Outside the museum discover more on the Trail for All Seasons, the Eighteenth-Century Backcountry Farm, and the Catawba Indian Village. Interpretive and living-history programs are scheduled at the Schiele Museum throughout the year.

Where to Eat

RODI. 245 W. Garrison Blvd.; (704) 864-7634; www.rodiworld.com. Authentic Mediterranean cuisine is served, and live music is scheduled periodically. $$

Gaston County has become more or less famous for its restaurants known as **fish camps.** They serve, almost exclusively, deep-fried fish along with hush puppies and slaw.

Several are located on and near S. New Hope Road. Check out one of the following:

Captain's Cap. 3140 Linwood Rd., (704) 865-7433; 670 Park St., Belmont, (704) 825-4103; www.thecaptainscap.com. With 2 locations in the area, Captain's Cap also serves calabash-style seafood. $$

Christmastown **USA**

Located between I-85 and US 74 is the town of **McAdenville,** better known as Christmastown USA. Each December this small textile community turns on more than 350,000 green, red, and white lights on homes, in trees, and around the small lake in the center of town. Speakers play carols, and churches present Nativity scenes in one of the state's (and perhaps the nation's) most spectacular Christmas displays. The lights come on in early December and stay on until late in the month from 5 to 9:30 p.m. Monday through Friday and 5 to 11 p.m. Saturday and Sunday. Because the exact dates vary from year to year, call (704) 824-3190.

Catfish Cove. 1401 Upper Armstrong-Ford Rd.; (704) 825-3332. $–$$

Graham's Fish Fry. 4539 S. New Hope Rd.; (704) 825-8391. $–$$

Twin Topps. 4547 S. New Hope Rd.; (704) 825-2490. $–$$

Where to Stay

Most of the large chains are represented just off I-85 in Gastonia, making for easy access to the towns located near here, as well as Charlotte.

For More Information

Gaston County Department of Tourism. (800) 849-9994; www.gastontourism.com.

Belmont

Heading east on US 74 from Gastonia will take you to Belmont, but S. New Hope Road is a quicker route to our next stop.

Daniel Stowe Botanical Garden (ages 3 and up)

6500 S. New Hope Rd.; (704) 825-4490; www.dsbg.org. Open 9 a.m. to 5 p.m. daily. $$.

About 110 of the 400 acres of beautiful rolling meadows and woodlands donated to be developed as a garden are now open at this facility, which is quickly developing a reputation as one of the finest gardens in the Southeast. Themed gardens include walks, fountains, and plaques describing the flora and fauna. Kids shouldn't miss the tunnel fountain, but they better move through it quickly or face getting wet! The 1-mile Meadowood Walk allows for exploration of butterflies and other native animals and plants. A stained-glass dome tops off the visitor center, which houses a great gift shop for kids and adults and serves as a base for hands-on workshops and other events. An orchid conservatory displays a dazzling collection of orchids and other tropical plants.

For More Information

Gaston County Travel and Tourism. (800) 849-9994; www.gastontourism.org.

Charlotte

The "Queen City" is North Carolina's largest city and it's the epicenter for arts, culture, and big-league sports. With a population of more than a half million, Charlotte became a national financial leader in the late 1980s and early 1990s. This growth only strengthened the financial stability created through Charlotte/Douglas International Airport, which opened the city to the world and made it a transportation hub for the Southeast. But this growth has meant more than additions to the uptown (not downtown) skyline. The city has seen a proverbial boom in the creation of more fun things to see and do.

Bechtler Museum of Modern Art (ages 5 and up)

420 S. Tryon St.; (704) 353-9200; www.bechtler.org. Open 10 a.m. to 5 p.m. Mon and Wed through Sat and noon to 5 p.m. Sun. $$.

Among the newest facilities on the art scene is this modern art museum located on the new campus known as the Levine Center for the Arts. The works were donated by artist Andreas Bechtler and include his work as well as an extensive collection that he inherited from his parents and accumulated himself. Works include those of Niki de Saint Phalle, Andy Warhol, and other mid- and late-20th-century artists.

Billy Graham Library (ages 3 and up)

4330 Westmont Dr.; (704) 401-3200; www.billygrahamlibrary.org. Open 9:30 a.m. to 5 p.m. Mon through Sat. Free.

This impressive display, reflective of a presidential library experience, was established to tell the story of one of America's best-known religious leaders. Billy Graham, who grew up on a farm near the library, became so prominent that he would preach to stadiums full of people and would counsel US presidents and foreign kings, queens, and other heads of state. The library includes a moving journey through audiovisual exhibits that tell his life story and the impact it has had on a wide variety of people. The site also includes his restored home place and prayer garden.

Carowinds (all ages)

Located off I-77 South on the state line, 14523 Carowinds Blvd.; (800) 588-2600. Open 10 a.m. to 8 p.m. daily June through late Aug, Sat and Sun only mid-Mar through May and Sept through mid-Oct. $$$$.

This is the state's largest theme park, packed with a day full of fun and adventure for everyone in the family. As you walk through the main gate, you may be greeted by your favorite characters from television and film, past and present, including Peanuts characters. A county fair section has games and rides for all ages, including bumper cars, a carousel, and more.

Some of the rides and attractions for younger guests include the Carolina Goldrusher, a wooden mine train rollercoaster; Woodstock Express; Carolina Skytower, an air-conditioned cabin that travels up a 320-foot tower; Ricochet, which takes riders through continuous twists and turns and other traditional rises like a carousel; and Rip Roarin' Rapids, a soggy whitewater rafting expedition. Boo Blasters on Boo Hill will be fun for the older set, too. The truly adventurous will want to experience Vortex, a stand-up roller coaster; Nighthawk; Drop Zone, which drops visitors 174 feet at more than 50 mph; or even the Intimidator, the tallest, fastest coaster in the Southeast. Cool off at Boomerang Bay, which includes several great waterslides and more. For a break in the action, you'll want to catch some of the shows at the park, including popular and Christian music concerts in the palladium. **Free** kennels are provided if your pet is with you, and picnic facilities are available if you aren't lured into one of the park's dozens of food stands and restaurants.

Charlotte Museum of History/Hezekiah Alexander Homesite
(ages 5 and up)

3500 Shamrock Dr.; (704) 568-1774; www.charlottemuseum.org. Open 10 a.m. to 5 p.m. Tues through Sat (and Mon in summer) and 1 to 5 p.m. Sun. $–$$; free for children ages 5 and under.

Like most towns in the Old North State, Charlotte has a rich historical heritage. To get a glimpse of this history, start at the Charlotte Museum of History and Hezekiah Alexander Homesite. Built in 1774, the home is the oldest dwelling in Mecklenburg County. The 5,000-square-foot stone house includes a museum with exhibits that concentrate on the history of the city. In the 2-story springhouse you'll see a hand-hewn log kitchen with a working stone fireplace. Tours are offered daily at 1:15 and 3:15 p.m. Docents dressed in 18th-century costumes lead visitors through the buildings and grounds, discussing artifacts and furnishings found in the buildings and illustrating the everyday lives of the Alexanders.

A 36,000-square-foot museum building includes an extensive exhibits program that tells the story of Charlotte-Mecklenburg from the 18th to the 20th century. A changing exhibit space is located on the second floor. The American Freedom Bell, a 7-ton ground-level bell guests can ring themselves in honor of those who fight for the freedom of America, is also on display. It acts as a permanent reminder that Charlotte was the location of the first official declaration of freedom from British rule.

Charlotte Nature Museum (best for younger children)

1658 Sterling Rd.; (800) 935-0553. Open 10 a.m. to 5 p.m. Tues through Sat, 10 a.m. to 5 p.m. and noon to 5 p.m. Sun; closed Thanksgiving and Christmas. $$.

This museum has a number of hands-on exhibits, such as games and push-button displays, to help explain natural history and also features a puppet theater; a butterfly pavilion; an exhibit called *Insect Alley*; a live animal room that includes owls, snakes, and other nocturnal creatures; and a nature trail. You'll also want to see the talking Grandpa Tree, a mechanical replica of a tree that helps explain some of nature's wonders during special programs that are held nearly every weekend.

Children's Theater of Charlotte (ages 4 and up)
300 E. 7th St.; (704) 973-2828; www.ctcharlotte.org. Prices vary by production.

A really first-class place to take the kids for exposure to the performing arts is the Children's Theater of Charlotte. The theater is largely dedicated to the arts in education and is heavily involved with the Mecklenburg County school system. Many of the plays are performed by local children; however, the playbill includes several professionally produced productions annually. In the past the theater has presented such gems as *Winnie the Pooh, Treasure Island,* and *Charlotte's Web,* in addition to creative holiday and seasonal productions. It's located in ImaginOn.

Discovery Place (all ages)
301 N. Tryon St.; (800) 935-0553; www.discoveryplace.org. Open 9 a.m. to 5 p.m. Mon through Fri, 10 a.m. to 6 p.m. Sat, and noon to 5 p.m. Sun. IMAX shows are held during operating hours and during evening hours on weekends. Discovery Place is closed Thanksgiving, Christmas, and Easter. $$–$$$.

Whatever has drawn you to Charlotte, you won't want to miss a chance to see Discovery Place, a national-award-winning, hands-on science and technology center. The complex also includes the Charlotte Observer IMAX Dome Theatre. Though the center has been in Charlotte for more than 20 years, recent renovations have brought a range of new exhibits. Younger children can tinker and play in KidScience, while everyone in the family can conduct experiments in the Life Lab or dive into the aquariums at World Alive. Lie on a bed of nails, and push, pull, and lift all in an exploration of scientific phenomena. The IMAX, considered to be the best motion-picture system in the world, is composed of the largest screen in history and a 6-track sound system. Presentations at the IMAX are scheduled throughout the year at this domed version of the technology. A variety of traveling exhibits that explore everything from mummies to space are also scheduled throughout the year.

Freedom Park (all ages)
1900 East Blvd.; (704) 336-2663. Generally open during daylight hours. **Free.**

Before or after you visit the Charlotte Nature Museum, you can get away from the hustle and bustle of city traffic at adjacent Freedom Park, one of Charlotte's oldest parks and a longtime favorite for school field trips. Take along a picnic lunch. The kids will be thrilled

Amazing
North Carolina Facts

Charlotte is known as the City of Trees, and one tree you'll see a lot of in this area is the dogwood. The dogwood blossom was chosen as the state flower in 1941.

with a walk around the lake, skating on one of the park's trails, or playing on the park's playground. The park is the site of **Festival in the Park,** another of Charlotte's big annual celebrations. The festival, held in late September, is a huge arts, crafts, and entertainment event.

Harvey B. Gantt Center for African American Arts and Culture (ages 5 and up)

551 S. Tryon St.; (704) 547-3700; www.ganttcenter.org. Open 10 a.m. to 5 p.m. Tues through Sat and 1 to 5 p.m. Sun. $$.

Exhibition and performance spaces make up this center named for Charlotte's first African-American mayor. It hosts various traveling exhibitions that honor African-American art. Its most significant permanent collection came from a retired librarian and freelance writer who held works by Romare Bearden, Henry Ossawa Tanner, and Jacob Lawrence. The John and Vivian Hewitt Collection was purchased by Bank of America and toured the country before coming back to Charlotte, where it is housed permanently.

ImaginOn: The Joe and Joan Martin Center (all ages)

300 E. 7th St.; (704) 973-2780; www.imaginon.org. Open 10 a.m. to 7 p.m. Tues through Thurs and 10 a.m. to 5 p.m. Fri and Sat. Free, with fees charged for activities and presentations.

Sprawling across a city block, ImaginOn is part library, part theater space—a partnership between the national-award-winning Charlotte-Mecklenburg Public Library system and the Children's Theater of Charlotte. It's fun just to visit this innovative colorful building. But upon exploring you find a cozy section for toddlers and preschool-age children that includes more than 12,000 books and a range of audiovisual materials, computers, games, and activities. The Listening Post enables children to listen to stories and music. An indoor "garden" with cozy seating and flooring gives babies and toddlers a chance to explore. A separate space for children ages 5 through 12 includes over 30,000 books, computers with assistance software and skill-building games and activities, and an audiovisual alcove with over 3,500 videos, music, and books on CDs.

Levine Museum of the New South (ages 5 and up)

200 E. 7th St.; (704) 333-1887; www.museumofthenewsouth.org. Open 10 a.m. to 5 p.m. Mon through Sat and noon to 5 p.m. Sun. $$; free for children ages 5 and under.

Focused on history after the Civil War, the Levine's centerpiece exhibit is From Cotton Fields to Skyscrapers, which illustrates the area's history and how it grew from a primarily farming area to a banking center. Visitors get this story from audio, video, and artifacts from people who actually lived the history from 1865.

Mint Museum at Levine Center for the Arts (ages 5 and up)

500 S. Tryon St.; (704) 337-2000; www.mintmuseum.org. Open 10 a.m. to 9 p.m. Tues, 10 a.m. to 6 p.m. Wed through Sat, and 1 to 5 p.m. Sun. $$; free Tues 5 to 9 p.m.

Big-League **Sports**

Charlotte began to develop a significant sports entourage in 1993, when it was awarded an NFL expansion team, the **Carolina Panthers.** Almost immediately the city began construction of the 72,000-seat Bank of America Stadium. A policy of selling privilege seat licenses has made it difficult to get tickets, but the organization has committed to keeping a certain number of single-game seats available for every game. Tickets for single games, on sale in spring when the NFL season schedule is completed, go quickly through Ticketmaster outlets. Call (704) 358-1644 for more information.

In 2004 Bob Johnson, founder of the Black Entertainment Network, bought an NBA franchise for the city to replace the Charlotte Hornets team, which made its way to New Orleans. For a year the **Charlotte Bobcats** played at the city's old coliseum, while the team, in partnership with the city, built a new state-of-the-art arena in the city's center. Built with the region's rich basketball history and cultural heritage in mind, there are fun things to do at **Time Warner Arena** regardless of the event. Exhibits and displays, as well as a kids' interactive center, welcome all. In more recent history, Johnson sold the team to basketball legend and North Carolina native Michael Jordan. Individual tickets for Bobcats games can be purchased online at www.charlotte bobcatsarena.com, by phone at (800) 495-2295, or at the arena's on-site box office.

Time Warner Arena is also home to the **Charlotte Checkers,** a professional hockey affiliate of Raleigh's Carolina Hurricanes and a member of the American Hockey League. Despite hockey's rough-and-tumble reputation, the organization makes games a great family-oriented event complimented by the state-of-the-art arena. For more information on tickets, contact the Checkers at (704) 342-4423 or visit www.go checkers.com.

The AAA affiliate of the Chicago White Sox, the **Charlotte Knights,** is Charlotte's, even though its home field is in nearby Fort Mill, South Carolina. The stadium is located off I-77 South just across the state line. You can get general admission seats inexpensively here ($$). The park also has a playground and even a miniature golf course. Lots of family fun is offered in the form of postgame fireworks, concerts, and more.

This Mint Museum is the uptown sister facility of the original Mint Museum located on Randolph Road. It was established here in 2010, moving into a new, much-heralded cultural campus. At the uptown facility is the Museum of Craft and Design that includes works by Chihuly and other renowned artists who work in glass, clay, fiber metal, and other media. A variety of American, European, and contemporary art is also on display.

Mint Museum of Art   (ages 5 and up)

2730 Randolph Rd.; (704) 337-2000; www.mintmuseum.org. Open 10 a.m. to 9 p.m. Tues, 10 a.m. to 6 p.m. Wed through Sat, and 1 to 5 p.m. Sun. $$; **free** Tues 5 to 9 p.m.

Built in 1836 as the first branch of the US Mint, the building in which the museum is housed later served as a Confederate headquarters, a hospital, and an assay office. In 1933 it was moved from its original location uptown and opened as North Carolina's first museum of art 3 years later. You'll see a complete set of gold coins minted there, American and European paintings, pre-Columbian art, historic costumes, and ancient Chinese ceramics. It holds more than 27,000 items in its collection. You'll also see life-size paintings of King George III and his queen, Charlotte, for whom the city was named. Seeing the queen's carriage will round out your trip to the museum.

NASCAR Hall of Fame   (all ages)

400 E. Martin Luther King Blvd.; (704) 654-4400; www.nacarhall.com. Open 10 a.m. to 6 p.m. daily. $$$.

The Hall of Fame opened in Charlotte in 2010, beating out several other competing racing cities for the honor. The dazzling hall is more than a stuffy museum of trophies and typical audiovisual displays. It includes simulators, interactive touch-screen displays, and dramatic video productions in addition to the hall of honor and archives associated with the sport's rich history. Kids and adults alike can repair simulated engines, take the pit crew challenge, and experience the thrill of driving in a stock car. NASCAR fans can trace the sport's history from Junior Johnson's days of running moonshine to the life and tragic death of the hall's first inductee, Dale Earnhardt.

Ray's Splash Planet   (all ages)

215 N. Sycamore St.; (704) 432-4729; www.rayssplashplanet.com. Open 10 a.m. to 7:30 p.m. Mon, noon to 7:30 p.m. Tues through Fri, 9 a.m. to 6:30 p.m. Sat, and 1 to 6:30 p.m. Sun. $$.

Ray's is a one-of-a-kind indoor water park and fitness center. The water park contains 117,000 gallons of water and a host of adventure. A 3-story slide, in the form of a double figure 8, is encircled by The Orbiter, which takes guests on a leisurely ride around the park. Saturation Station features 4 slides, interactive water play, and a tumble bucket. Moon Beach is a state-of-the-art gradual beach-like entry pool, and there are 2 lanes for lap swimming. The fitness center includes an aerobics and dance room, cardiovascular theater, free weights, and resistance equipment.

Worth **More Time**

While you're in the Charlotte area, plan to spend some time exploring the towns along I-77, north of the city, as well as Lake Norman, the largest artificial lake in North Carolina. Built by Duke Power Company to accommodate its hydroelectric and nuclear power plants, **Lake Norman** is a big draw for boating and fishing enthusiasts from across the state. Ten public access areas around the 32,500-acre lake are perfect for camping, swimming, and fishing. Duke Power has also established a 1,400-acre public park north of Huntersville. **Lake Norman State Park** is located in the town of Troutman (704-528-6350). You'll find a variety of large hotels in the Lake Norman area, and **Lake Norman Rentals** in Mooresville (800-408-5997) can help you find larger places for a vacation stay. For more information contact the **Lake Norman Convention and Visitors Bureau** at (704) 987-3300 or visit www.lakenormancvb.org.

Uptown Charlotte

If you visit Charlotte, make sure to save a couple hours to explore what the marketing pundits like to call uptown, which has become a burgeoning arts center. Frescoes by Ben Long can be found at Bank of America Corporate Center and at TransAmerica Square, both on Tryon Street. Make sure to visit **The Green,** which runs between Tryon and College Streets near the Wachovia Atrium and the Charlotte Convention Center. It's a unique park themed on literature. Bronze works depicting characters from literature, poems on bronze placards written by local schoolchildren, fountains, and hidden speakers that spill out whimsical sounds adorn the park. Bricks also contain fun word puzzles. Trendy restaurants and upscale shops also fill the uptown area. Architectural high points include **Founders Hall,** with a 10,000-square-foot glass atrium accessible from College Street or through Bank of America Corporate Center on Tryon Street, as well as Wachovia Atrium and Hearst Tower. The **Blumenthal Performing Arts Center** is adjacent to Bank of America Corporate Center and includes 2 theaters for the Charlotte Symphony, Broadway Lights Series plays, and other presentations. The art deco **Hearst Tower** is really cool because the top is actually bigger than the bottom. **Spirit Square,** 345 N. College Street, includes performance and exhibition space that includes **The Light Factory** (704-333-9755; www.thelightfactory.org), a dynamic museum of film and photography. The **Levine Center for the Arts** is a spectacular campus of museums and presentation spaces, including the **Knight Theater.** The open, contemporary design, including a cantilevered fourth story, makes this worth the stop on its own.

US National Whitewater Center (all ages, with restrictions)

820 Hawfield Rd.; (704) 391-3900, www.usnwc.org. **Generally open during daylight hours. $$–$$$$.**

On our route to Charlotte, we cross the Catawba River. Since it cuts through the low-lying Piedmont, it was never meant for whitewater rafting, at least until 2006. That's when the US National Whitewater Center opened a sprawling, man-made rafting facility just off I-85 in Charlotte. Integrated with miles of biking and hiking trails, the US Olympic Committee has designated the center an official training site, but there's plenty there for the average family.

The center includes the world's largest man-made recirculating river, which forms a 2-hour Class III/IV rafting adventure for ages 12 and above. For the younger set, there's whitewater kayaking for ages 8 and above and flat-water kayaking for all ages. Additionally, there's a climbing center for everyone over age 4. And finally, a restaurant provides a panoramic view of the facility in addition to selections that range from soup to salmon to steak. Keep in mind when planning that World Cup, Olympic Trials, and other competitions are held here and may limit availability to the public.

Where to Eat

All of Charlotte's top hotels have top restaurants, plus there are top chains such as **The Cheesecake Factory, Ruth's Chris,** and **Carrabba's**, and you won't have any trouble finding something to satisfy everyone in the family. Here are some of our favorites:

Baoding. 4722 Sharon Rd.; (704) 552-8899; wwwbaodingsouthpark.com. Baoding is not only a great Chinese restaurant, it's also the name of the city in China that is Charlotte's sister city. $$

Fuel Pizza Cafe. Multiple locations; www.fuelpizza.com. After running around Charlotte all day, you can gas up at this filling station–themed pizza chain. $

Lupie's Cafe. 2718 Monroe Rd.; (704) 374-1232. It doesn't look like it, but Lupie's has great burgers and home-style meals. You won't regret stopping here. $

Mert's Heart & Soul. 214 N. College St.; (704) 342-4222; www.mertsuptown.com. Comfort food is served here in an atmosphere of Southern blues. $$

The Open Kitchen. 1318 W. Morehead St.; (704) 375-7449. This is a classic Italian place where you'll feel right at home. $–$$

Pike's Soda Shop. 1930 Camden Rd.; (704) 372-0092; www.pikessodashop.com. Old-fashioned soda shop fare is served at Pike's. $$

Price's Chicken Coop. 1614 Camden Rd.; (704) 333-9866; www.priceschickencoop .com. The Chicken Coop is carry-out only but don't miss this treat. $

Rock Bottom Restaurant & Brewery. 401 N. Tryon St.; (704) 334-2739; www.rock bottom.com. Rock Bottom turns into a young-adult hangout at night, but by day and early evening it serves a great selection of burgers, sandwiches, and full entrees. $$

Where to Stay

While you can find economical accommodations in the Charlotte area along the interstates leading into the city, expect to pay top dollar for accommodations in the city, especially uptown. Here are some of the city's top places to stay:

Amazing North Carolina Fact or Fiction

More than 70 people on Lake Norman have reported seeing the Carolina version of Scotland's Loch Ness Monster, "Normie," since 2000. Sightings have reported the creature at as large as 30 feet long with a snakelike body and short legs.

Ballantyne Resort. 10000 Ballantyne Commons Pkwy.; (704) 248-4000. Ballantyne Resort is a luxury resort located in South Charlotte. $$$$

The Dunhill Hotel. 237 N. Tryon St.; (704) 332-4141. Listed on the National Register of Historic Places, this uptown hotel offers first-class treatment. $$$$

Morehead Inn. 1122 E. Morehead; (704) 376-3357. This is a historic bed-and-breakfast that will accommodate children. $$$$

OMNI Charlotte Hotel. 132 E. Trade St.; (800) 843-6664. If you want to splurge uptown, this AAA four-diamond hotel will do nicely. $$$$

The Park Hotel. 2200 Rexford Rd.; (704) 364-8220. If the Westin isn't the city's best hotel, the Park is. Even though it is quite large, it's still very comfortable. $$$$

Plaza Hotel on Carowinds. 225 Carowinds Blvd., Fort Mill, South Carolina; (803) 548-2400. If you are planning a Carowinds trip, you can find several chains on the North Carolina side. On the South Carolina side, you will find the Plaza Hotel. $$$$

The Westin Hotel. 601 S. College St.; (704) 375-2600. This is one of Charlotte's largest, and possibly best, hotels. You should expect top-notch service from the staff here, as you would at any Westin. $$$$

For More Information

Charlotte Convention and Visitors Bureau. (800) 722-1994; www.visitcharlotte .com.

Huntersville

Just minutes north of Charlotte (as long as it's not rush hour) on I-77 is the town of Huntersville, a burgeoning bedroom community whose population has grown by leaps and bounds in recent years.

Carolina Raptor Center (all ages)

600 Sample Rd.; (704) 875-6521; www.carolinaraptorcenter.org. Open 10 a.m. to 5 p.m. Tues through Sat and noon to 5 p.m. Sun. $$; children under 5 free.

Located in the Latta Park Nature Preserve, the center opened in 1980 as a haven for injured eagles, hawks, and other birds of prey. Today it is a sprawling center that combines fun and education. After the birds have been rehabilitated, some are released into the wild, while others are put on display in a natural wooded area and used for educational demonstrations. A 25,000-foot outdoor eagle aviary gives visitors an opportunity to see these remarkable birds of prey up close—closer than ever possible in the wild.

Carolina Renaissance Festival (ages 5 and up)

16445 Poplar Tent Rd.; (704) 896-5544; www.royalfaires.com. Open weekends 10 a.m. to 5:30 p.m. late Sept through early Nov. \$\$–\$\$\$; children under 5 free.

The Carolina Renaissance Festival is quickly becoming one of the area's biggest attractions. Sixteenth-century Europe is re-created during weekends in the fall. Don't be surprised to find yourself at the edge of a jousting contest or in the middle of a sword fight. You can enjoy the antics of the court jester and see knights dressed in full armor. Finding a feast fit for a king, complete with big turkey legs, won't be any problem, either. And when you finish eating, you can browse through acres of shops and galleries.

Discovery Place Kids (ages 1 to 7)

105 Gilead Rd.; (704) 372-6261; www.discoveryplacekids.org. Open 9 a.m. to 5 p.m. Tues through Sat and noon to 5 p.m. Sun. \$\$.

This bright satellite location of Charlotte's science center focuses on exhibits for younger children. All based on the theme "I Can," exhibits focus on developing cognitive and motor skills. These include experiences in building, gardening, and working in a variety of environments. Kids can climb into the clubhouse, check out a puppet show, and play with water.

Duke Energy's Energy Explorium (ages 5 and up)

1339 Hagers Ferry Rd.; (704) 875-5600; www.dukeenergy.com. Open 9 a.m. to 5 p.m. Mon through Fri and noon to 5 p.m. Sat. Free.

Located at McGuire Nuclear Plant, the Explorium presents hands-on exhibits where you can throw the switches on model nuclear and coal-fired plants. Power a television by converting your body's energy on a treadmill, play computer games, and figure out how much energy you get for a dollar. You can also burn off some energy on a mile-long nature trail.

Latta Plantation Nature Center (ages 5 and up)

5225 Sample Rd.; (704) 875-1391; www.lattaplantation.org. The park is open during daylight hours and facilities are free. The Latta House (704-875-2312) is open 10 a.m. to 5 p.m. Tues through Sat and noon to 5 p.m. Sun, Apr through Sept. \$; free for children ages 5 and under.

Huntersville's sprawling Latta Plantation is a 19th-century cotton plantation located in the Latta Park Nature Preserve. The 1,090-acre park borders Mountain Island Lake and includes an interpretive center, equestrian center, and hiking and horse trails. In addition, the park presents living-history tours of the James Latta house on the first and third Thursday of each month. The 2-story Federal-style house, built in 1800, is elaborately decorated to match the intricate detail of the architecture.

Scottish Heritage Center at Rural Hill Plantation (all ages)

4431 Neck Rd.; (704) 875-3113; www.ruralhillplantation.org. Open 9 a.m. to 5 p.m. Mon through Sat. $; special events have special times and prices.

Rural Hill Plantation is home away from home for area Scots. It's the historic homestead of Major John and Violet (Wilson) Davidson, who saw Rural Hill grow to become one of the most prosperous plantations in the Carolina piedmont. They raised 10 children who continued their legacy. The original home has not survived, but a reproduction stands instead. Original remnants include a smokehouse, ash house, well house, barn, chicken shed, and granary. Two of the last remaining one-room schoolhouses in Mecklenburg County—one for white and one for African-American children—are also located on the Rural Hill property.

The plantation hosts several fun events throughout the year, such as the Sheep Dog Trials in November, the Amazing Maize Maze, a 1760 Carolina Thanksgiving, and the Loch Norman Games each April. World-class athletes compete in various competitions, including the caber toss, and there are contests in bagpipe, fiddle, harp, and Scottish dance. More than 90 Scottish and Scots-Irish clans and organizations bring their banners to demonstrate their support and share family genealogy and heritage exhibits with visitors.

Where to Eat

Acropolis Cafe & Grille. 20659 Catawba Ave., Cornelius; (704) 894-0191; www.acropoliscg.com. Sandwiches, salads, and Greek specialties are offered here. $

Big Al's Pub and Grubberia. 8301 Magnolia Estates Dr.; (704) 987-6582; www.bigalspubandgrubberia.com. Big Al can whip up everything from burgers and sandwiches to Italian dishes in a very casual atmosphere. $–$$

Buzzy & Bear's Grill. 9709-B Sam Furr Rd.; (704) 895-2692; www.buzzyandbearsgrill.com. If you can't tell by the name, this is a fun place to get brats or a hot dog. Buzzy and Bear, the owners, might even show up. $

Fuddruckers. 16625 Statesville Rd.; (704) 896-8390; www.fuddruckers.com. This chain serves huge burgers and the like. Fix them up anyway you like at the dressing bar. $

Where to Stay

Davidson Village Inn. 117 Depot St., Davidson; (704) 892-8044. Kids stay **free** at this inn, near the very picturesque Davidson College. $$$$

Pineville

Pineville is southeast of Charlotte off Highway 16.

James K. Polk Memorial (ages 5 and up)

308 S. Polk St.; (704) 889-7145; www.nchistoricsites.org. Open 9 a.m. to 5 p.m. Tues through Sat and 1 to 5 p.m. Sun. **Free.**

The birthplace and childhood home of the 11th president of the US, the James K. Polk Memorial features exhibits on his life and times. You can see an audiovisual display here as well as take a guided tour of the home. The reconstructed house is typical of those during Polk's childhood. The kitchen and house are authentically furnished with period pieces from the early 1800s. The Mecklenburg Chapter of the Daughters of the American Revolution erected a stone monument for our 11th president at the site in 1904. Picnic facilities are available.

Zuma Fun Center (all ages)

10400 Cadillac St.; (704) 552-7888; http://zumafuncenters.com. Open noon to 9 p.m. Mon through Thurs, noon to midnight Fri, 10 a.m. to midnight Sat, and noon to 9 p.m. Sun. You can choose to pay per activity ($), or if you'll be there all day consider purchasing an unlimited-access wristband ($$$ per person).

To give the kids a treat for lunch or dinner, Zuma Fun Center is always a big hit. The amusement center/restaurant offers delicious pizza and a chance to let the kids run off some steam. Everyone in the family might want to ride go-karts or bumper boats or even play a round of miniature golf. Younger children can play in Harry's Clubhouse, a play park with rides designed especially for them, and older kids can brush up on their batting at the cages.

Waxhaw

Take Highway 16 south from Pineville to reach Waxhaw.

Cane Creek Park (all ages)

5213 Harkey Rd.; (704) 843-3919; www.co.umon.nc.us. Generally open during daylight hours, daily during summer and weekends only the rest of the year. $; other fees vary by activity.

Amazing
North Carolina Facts

A historical marker on Highway 75 says that Andrew Jackson was born in Union County in North Carolina, but most encyclopedias and historical accounts say he was born in Waxhaw, South Carolina. The place of Jackson's birth has been debated since 1815, with a total of four states, and Ireland, claiming his birth.

To enjoy outdoor recreation for a day, or even a weekend, try Cane Creek Park. The park offers an opportunity to wet a line at the trophy bass lake, rent a paddleboat, take a swim in cool, clear water, or even play a round of miniature golf. Cane Creek also offers 3 campgrounds to accommodate tents or recreational vehicles, with prices ranging from $15 to $30 per night. You can also enjoy miles of scenic hiking trails or splashing around in a canoe or rowboat. The park also offers sports equipment rental.

Museum of the Alphabet (ages 5 and up)
6409 Davis Rd.; (704) 843-6000. Open 9 a.m. to noon and 1 to 3:30 p.m. Mon through Sat. Admission is free, but donations are accepted.

Where in the world did words come from? That question is answered at the Museum of the Alphabet, an unusual but enticing collection of exhibits that trace the early origins of written communication from ancient times through the development of the Roman alphabet to our English alphabet today. You can also see a working model of the first printing press, displays on alphabets of foreign languages, and descriptions of the systems of alphabets created for the hearing- and sight-impaired.

Harrisburg

You can get to Harrisburg via I-85 from Charlotte, or you can also reach it from the Lake Norman area.

Backing Up Classics (ages 5 and up)
4545 Highway 29, Concord; (704) 788-9500; www.backingupclassics.com. Usually open 7 days a week, 8 a.m. to 6 p.m. Mon through Fri, 8 a.m. to 1 p.m. Sat, and 10 a.m. to 5 p.m. Sun, but hours may vary according to activity at the speedway. $$–$$$.

Next to Lowe's Motor Speedway near the border of Harrisburg and the city of Concord, you can visit Backing Up Classics. Step back into the 1950s at this unique museum that presents classic cars and dragsters from years gone by. You will also see memorabilia and cars from the sport of racing. The gift shop features a huge selection of unique 1950s and race-related souvenirs and gifts.

Lowe's Motor Speedway (ages 7 and up)
555 Concord Pkwy. South; (704) 455-3200 for ticket information or (704) 455-3204 for more information on tours; www.lowesmotorspeedway.com. Tours ($, children ages 2 and under free) are held 9 a.m. to 5 p.m. Mon through Sat and noon to 5 p.m. Sun, except when racing events are scheduled.

Thousands of NASCAR fans from across the country flock here each May and October to watch their favorite drivers negotiate speeds up to 200 mph at one of the country's premier racing facilities. The Coca-Cola 600, held each Memorial Day weekend, draws a huge crowd—second only in size to the Indianapolis 500, which is held the same day. As crowds roll in by recreational vehicle, truck, and car, the entire area lights up with races and activities all month long. A family-oriented event in downtown Charlotte called **Speed Street** takes place three days before the race and includes NASCAR simulators, music, food, and other activities. Racing excitement also picks up in October, culminating in the running of the Bank of America 500. If you plan on getting a ticket to one of the major races, be aware that these cars are very loud. Even the adults will need earplugs, and the noise is likely to bother children who are sensitive to it.

In addition to these major sporting events, Lowe's Motor Speedway hosts the **Legends Car Summer Shootout** ($–$$$) each Tuesday during the summer. Legends cars are small replicas of 1937 and 1940 Fords and Chevrolets. Games, other spectator events, activities, and entertainment from the world's fastest mascot, Lug Nut, are part of the show.

Other events held at the speedway include a regular schedule of events at a straight, four-wide hot rod track, events at the short dirt track, auto shows, motorcycle racing, go-kart racing, and tours of this spectacular facility. On these tours, you visit the garages, pits, and winner's circle. When the track is not in use, you can take a trip around the track through driving schools sponsored by various race teams. Finally, pick out a gift at the gift shop for the Nextel Cup fan in your life.

Concord

Concord is just a hop, skip, and jump from Harrisburg on either US 49 or Highway 29.

Concord Mills (all ages)

8111 Concord Mills Blvd.; (704) 979-5000; www.concordmills.com. Open 10 a.m. to 9 p.m. Mon through Sat and noon to 7 p.m. Sun.

This sprawling center offers more than just shopping. In addition to 200 stores, it includes a NASCAR simulator, a huge game room, an indoor amusement park for younger children, a Build-a-Bear Workshop, and restaurants. It has a 24-screen movie theater and a Bass Outdoor Pro Shop that features an outdoor RV center. There is also a NASCAR Speedpark featuring an array of rides, go-karts, bumper boats, minigolf, and more. Of course, you'll find standard mall fare including a food court, outlet stores, and specialty shops all laid out like what else but a race track.

Frank Liske Park & Soccer Complex (all ages)

4001 Stough Rd.; (704) 920-2700. Open generally during daylight hours. Free; fees charged for some activities.

Located near the center of the county, this park has just about everything one would hope to find at a park. Fishing is allowed in the 10-acre lake, and paddleboats are available for rent. Guests can play a round of miniature golf, and there are plenty of playgrounds, picnic shelters, and walking and fitness trails.

Great Wolf Lodge (all ages)

10175 Weddington Rd.; (704) 549-8206; www.greatwolf.com. $$$$.

Two giant stone wolves stand sentinel over this massive resort located just off I-85. In addition to fun accommodations that may include the children's separate "log cabin," there is literally enough to do for days. It all starts at the indoor/outdoor water park with giant slides, a wave pool, a splash park, a pool with water basketball, and other sports in a balmy 84 degrees indoors year-round. Guests gather around the big stone fireplace of the Great Northwoods–themed hotel lobby on a nightly basis for a story time by animatronic characters. The lodge is the home of the only Magiquest center in the area, in which children can use special wands to trip surprises, like a song from a raccoon in a tree, throughout the resort. Purchase of Magiquest wands also permits admission into a complete Magiquest live-action adventure game. You might think miniature golf, an arcade, and a game room especially for teens might round out the experience, but there's more—3 restaurants, shopping, crafts, and even a kid-size spa, called Scoops, on the property bring nonstop fun.

Where to Eat

Troutmans' Bar-B-Q. With 5 locations, has established quite a reputation in the area. The locations and their respective phones numbers are 362 Church St. North (704-786-5213); 1875 Highway 601 (704-786-9714); 1096 Highway 29 North (704-786-6317); 8335 W. Franklin St., Mount Pleasant (704-436-9806); and 530 S. Cannon Blvd., Kannapolis (704-938-6001). $

Where to Stay

Mayfair Motel. 1516 Highway 29 North; (704) 786-1175. This affordable motel has a playground in addition to a pool and refrigerators in some rooms. $$

Stanfield

Stanfield is east of Charlotte on Highway 24/27.

Reed Gold Mine (ages 3 and up)

9621 Reed Mine Rd.; (704) 721-4653; www.nchistoricsites.org. Open 9 a.m. to 5 p.m. Tues through Sat, Apr through Oct; 10 a.m. to 4 p.m. Tues through Sat and 1 to 4 p.m. Sun, Nov through Mar. The museum is free, and the panning area is open on a seasonal basis for a nominal fee.

Some say there could still be gold in Stanfield. You can try to find some of it as you pan for gold at Reed Gold Mine, off Highway 200. The brown highway signs may confuse you, so from Concord, take US 601, then turn south onto Highway 200. Here you will experience

Amazing
North Carolina Facts

At the age of 12, Conrad Reed discovered a 17-pound gold nugget in Little Meadow Creek, and it was, in fact, used as a doorstop for three years. When it was identified as gold, Conrad's father, John, opened the mine for business.

the country's first gold rush, which started with the discovery of a nugget (big enough to be used as a doorstop) near here in 1799. North Carolina remained the leader in gold production until the California gold rush in 1848. Today visitors at the site can see a film on more of this history, exhibits on the mining process, and the tools the miners used, as well as the underground tunnels of the nation's first gold mine.

For More Information

Cabarrus County Convention and Visitors Bureau. (800) 848-3740; www.cabarrus cvb.com.

Albemarle

From the Reed Gold Mine, Highway 24/27 will take you to the historic town of Albemarle, near the border of the Uwharrie National Forest.

While this isn't a famous tourist area, Albemarle offers a handful of attractions, mainly ample opportunity to enjoy the outdoors. But first take a trip to the historic downtown area, which served as a cultural and commercial haven for the rural area in the late 1800s and early 1900s. The Stanly County Chamber of Commerce (704-982-8116) can provide you with a walking map of the downtown area, where you'll see many charms from the late 19th and early 20th centuries. You can get a glimpse of the art deco style of architecture of the 1920s at the **Albemarle Opera House** or at the **Alameda Theater,** where silent films once played. Both are located near E. Main Street.

Morrow Mountain State Park (all ages)

SR 1719; (704) 982-4402; www.ncparks.gov. The park opens at 8 a.m. and generally closes at dusk. Admission to the park is free, but there are fees for some activities.

North of downtown find Morrow Mountain State Park, which offers the beautiful crystal-clear waters of the adjacent Lake Tillery. The landscape of this area, located in the heart of the foothills, is interesting. Because they were formed by volcanic eruptions thousands of years ago, the hills have resisted erosion and maintained a rugged appearance against a beautiful backdrop of green in the spring and summer. You'll find a number of trails in the park, ranging in length from a half mile to 6 miles. A small natural-history museum, located at the center of the park, explains the development of the region and includes exhibits on the wildlife and the vegetation that occupy the area. A family camping area can accommodate tents and recreational vehicles year-round, but there are no facility hookups. Water, showers, and toilets are available nearby. If you want to stay for a week, you can rent one of 6 cabins in the park, from April through October. In addition to the natural bounty, the park also has a swimming pool and boat and canoe rentals.

For More Information

Stanly County Convention and Visitors Bureau. (800) 650-1476; www.stanlycvb .com.

New London

Take US 52 north to New London from Albemarle.

Cotton Patch Gold Mine (all ages)

41697 Gurley Rd.; (704) 463-5797; www.cottonpatchgoldmine.com. Open 9 a.m. to 5 p.m. Fri and Sat, and 1 to 5 p.m. Sun. $–$$.

More camping facilities and a shot at striking it rich are available north of Albemarle at the Cotton Patch Gold Mine, located just off US 52 at Highway 740. The campground accommodates tent camping as well as full hookups for recreational vehicles, in addition to providing restrooms and showers. You can pan for gold and other minerals here with buckets of dirt that are provided.

Mount Gilead

Head southeast from Albemarle on Highway 73 to Mount Gilead.

Town Creek Indian Mound (ages 5 and up)

509 Town Creek Mound Rd., off Highway 73; (910) 439-6802; www.nchistoricsites.org. Open 9 a.m. to 5 p.m. Tues through Sat and 1 to 5 p.m. Sun. Free.

Town Creek Indian Mound was a ceremonial center for the Creek Indian Nation that occupied the area as early as 1450. The site, which served as a meeting place for religious ceremonies and even for executions of enemies 300 years ago, has been rebuilt nearly to completion over the past 50 years. The earthen mound—a sort of stage—is encircled by a wall constructed of logs, bound together by cane, and several other structures made of dirt, sticks, and thatch. Presentations are held to explain the structure, the history of the Native Americans, and the research that has been done in the area.

Where to Stay

Cardinal Pines Plantation Inn. 1570 Lilly's Bridge Rd.; (800) 711-1134. This is a very small, historic bed-and-breakfast that would be suitable only for quieter children. $$

Ellerbe

From Mount Gilead, head southeast onto Highway 73 and turn south on US 220.

Runners from all over the Southeast come to the small town of Ellerbe each April for one of the state's most demanding marathons. The 26-mile course, which is extremely hilly, has enjoyed increasing success over the past several years.

Rankin Museum of American Heritage and Natural History
(ages 5 and up)
131 E. Church St.; (910) 652-6378; www.rankinmuseum.com. Open 10 a.m. to 4 p.m. Tues through Fri and 2 to 5 p.m. Sat and Sun. $.

The Rankin Museum is a heralded collection that offers you an opportunity to travel back in time all over the world. This diverse collection of exhibits and artifacts is used to explain the heritage of North America, South America, Central America, and Africa. Here you'll see displays such as a fierce polar bear, a Central American jaguar, and a host of moose, elk, and caribou. In addition, the museum features displays on Native American life and a fine mineral collection.

Rockingham

US 220 south from Ellerbe is the route to Rockingham.

Rockingham Dragway (ages 3 and up)
2152 Highway 1; (910) 582-3400; www.rockinghamdragway.com. Prices vary by event.

Although it lost status as a hub for NASCAR racing in 2004, high-speed action is still here in Rockingham. The Rockingham Dragway is host to IHRA drag racing action. In addition, the racetrack holds sports car, motorcycle, and go-kart races as well as auto shows and other events throughout the year.

Hamlet

US 74 will take you southeast out of Rockingham to Hamlet.

National Railroad Museum (ages 5 and up)

120 Spring St.; (910) 582-2383; www.nationalrrmuseum.tripod.com. Open 11 a.m. to 4 p.m. Sat and 1 to 5 p.m. Sun. **Free.**

This museum relocated from the old Seaboard Air Line Railway depot, built in 1900. It is now in a larger space that displays an extravagant model train layout that features the Orange Blossom Special and the Silver Meteor on a layout that represents the town. The exhibit is designed as the system appeared in the early 20th century. The museum also includes artifacts, photographs, and maps preserving the railway's heritage, which was once crucial to the area, along with the Railroad Hall of Fame.

Southern Pines

To get from Hamlet to Southern Pines, take US 1 North.

Weymouth Woods Nature Preserve (ages 3 and up)

1024 N. Fort Bragg Rd.; (910) 692-2167. The park is typically open during daylight hours. The museum is open 8 a.m. to 5 p.m. daily. **Free.**

The Weymouth Woods Nature Preserve, south of Southern Pines, offers an introspective look at the natural features of the area. Here you will find 900 acres of wildflowers, wildlife, and peaceful rolling streams. The preserve includes more than 4 miles of hiking trails, a beaver pond, and a nature museum. At the museum you can see how the area evolved and listen to a night-sounds display that highlights the nocturnal wildlife of the Sandhills region. Each Sunday in the spring and summer a nature study program is presented by a naturalist.

Golf Capital **of the World**

Known as the Golf Capital of the World, Pinehurst/Southern Pines and the surrounding area offer the best amenities for those who play golf, and much more. In addition to world-class golf competition, the area also supports tennis competitions and equestrian events throughout the year. International cycling teams have also begun training here. You'll find more than 40 championship golf courses in the area, not to mention dozens of plush resorts. Pinehurst Number Two was the site of the 1999 and 2005 US Open Championship.

Where to Eat

Ice Cream Parlor. 176 NW Broad St.; (910) 692-7273. In addition to ice cream, this shop specializes in old-fashioned hand-pattied burgers served Southern-style with mustard, chili, slaw, and onions. $.

Sweet Basil. 134 NW Broad St.; (910) 693-1487. Sweet Basil is popular for its soups, salads, and sandwiches. $$

Where to Stay

Pinehurst Resort. 80 Carolina Vista Dr., Pinehurst; (910) 235-8507; www.pinehurst .com. Most Southern Pines accommodations are more suitable for couples, but a short drive away is one of the state's best resorts

that is good for golfers, couples, and families. The resort has first class amenities for kids and adults alike, including a kids' spa, a beach club, and lessons in golf, tennis and more.

For More Information

Even the worst hotels and restaurants in the Pinehurst/Southern Pines area are very nice. Unless the children play golf, a trip here isn't going to be much fun. If they are learning how to play, a trip here is a must. So for more information and a free guide, contact the **Convention and Visitors Bureau for the Village of Pinehurst/Southern Pines/ Aberdeen Area,** (910) 692-0619; www .homeofgolf.com.

Sanford

North of Pinehurst and Southern Pines, you'll find Sanford on US 1.

House in the Horseshoe (ages 5 and up)
324 Alston House Rd.; (910) 947-2051. Open 9 a.m. to 5 p.m. Tues through Sat. Free.

Built by patriot Philip Alston, the House in the Horseshoe is located about 10 miles west of Sanford in a bend in the Deep River. This cotton plantation home, built in 1772, features a gabled roof and big Flemish bond chimneys. Bullet holes in some of the walls are evidence of the Revolutionary War battles fought on the grounds. One of those battles is re-created each August.

Laurinburg

To get here, travel south on US 15/501 from the Southern Pines area or east on US 74 from Hamlet.

Indian Museum of the Carolinas (ages 5 and up)
607 Turnpike Rd.; (910) 276-5880; www.visitnc-soul.com. Open 10 a.m. to noon and 1 to 4 p.m. Wed and Thurs, and 1 to 4 p.m. Sun. Free.

The town of Laurinburg has a rich Native American heritage and offers a visit to the Indian Museum of the Carolinas. While the Lumbee Indians had the greatest impact on this region and still inhabit much of the area today, the museum features dozens of exhibits on all Carolina Native American life, including many examples of art and some 200,000 archaeological artifacts. Included are weapons, jewelry, costumes, and a dugout canoe.

Lumberton

From Laurinburg take US 74 East to Lumberton.

While Lumberton is the county seat, you won't find a lot to do here. There are some nice, affordable hotels if you're passing through and a couple of attractions that you might want to catch.

Exploration Station (ages 1 to 11)

104 N. Chestnut St.; (910) 738-1114; www.explorationkids.com. Open 10 a.m. to 5 p.m. Tues, Wed, and Fri; 10 a.m. to 8 p.m. Thurs; and 10 a.m. to 4 p.m. Sat. $

Kids play doctor in a make-believe hospital where they can examine X-rays or look after babies. They can milk a cow or watch ducks cascade down a waterfall. In all there are 11 interactive exhibit areas, including a farmhouse, bank, schoolroom, general store, the hospital, and others. The center also includes a play area designed specifically for infants. Exploration Station also presents special programs in the form of tea parties and more.

Robeson Planetarium—Science & Technology Center
(ages 5 and up)

Highway 72/711; (910) 671-6015; www.robesonsky.com. Open 8 a.m. to 5 p.m. daily. Free.

This is a small science museum that has multimedia astronomy shows and exhibits largely related to space science. When NASA telecasts from space, the center is connected. The facility is actually part of the Robeson County school system but it does offer some public programs.

Where to Eat

Fuller's Old Fashioned Barbecue. 3201 Roberts Ave.; (910) 738-8694; www.fullers bbq.com. Eat all you want off the country-style buffet here. $$

John's. 4880 Kahn Dr.; (910) 738-4709. This is a nice place for having such a simple name. John's has a good children's menu and varied American cuisine. $$

Pier 41 Seafood Restaurant. 2401 Elizabethtown Rd.; (910) 738-8555; www .pier41seafood.com. Calabash-style seafood comes out of the kitchen here. $$

Where to Stay

Since this is near the I-95 corridor, you'll find a lot of national franchise accommodations, but for local flavor try:

Sleepy Bear's Family Campground. 465 Kenric Rd.; (910) 739-4372. With a name like that, who could resist? The campground offers tent and trailer sites, a playground, a pool, and more. $

For More Information

Lumberton Area Chamber of Commerce. (800) 359-6971; www.lumberton-nc.com.

Fayetteville

With your car pointed north on I-95 out of Lumberton, travel 35 miles to reach the city of Fayetteville and Fort Bragg.

Airborne and Special Operations Museum (all ages)

100 Bragg Blvd.; (910) 483-3003; www.asomf.org. Open 10 a.m. to 5 p.m. Tues through Sat and noon to 5 p.m. Sun. Museum admission **free.** Admission to theater and simulator $–$$; children 8 and under **free** when accompanied by paying adult.

This has quickly become one of the area's premier attractions. The state-of-the-art facility houses exhibits and programs that highlight the honor, courage, duty, and heroic feats of this unique sector of our armed forces from 1940 to today. A large-screen theater features specially produced movies showing these forces in action. A 24-seat simulator allows riders to experience a helicopter attack, parachute jump, and off-road pursuit. You'll also find a memorial garden, parade area, and unit memorials.

Fascinate-U Children's Museum (all ages)

116 Green St.; (910) 829-9171; www.fascinate-u.com. Open 9 a.m. to 5 p.m. Tues, Thurs, and Fri; 9 a.m. to 7 p.m. Wed; 10 a.m. to 5 p.m. Sat; and noon to 5 p.m. Sun. $.

This is one of a growing number of centers in North Carolina that exist purely for children. The museum features a variety of interactive exhibits that let children discover the world around them. Kids can shop in the grocery and deli, hold court in a judge's robe, forecast the weather, man the emergency call center, and, of course, put on a military uniform.

First Presbyterian Church (all ages)

Located at the corner of Bow and Ann Streets; (910) 483-0121; www.firstprez.com. Open 8 a.m. to 4:30 p.m. Mon through Fri. Sun services are held at 8:30 and 10:55 a.m. **Free.**

This 1816 church is a brilliant example of Southern Colonial architecture and features a wooden truss roof. Inside you'll see lovely whale-oil chandeliers, communion silver, and handmade wrought-iron locks.

Fort Bragg Military Base (ages 5 and up)

For general information call the base at (910) 396-5401; go to www.bragg.army.mil; or visit the information center on Randolph Street and Bragg Boulevard, open 8:30 a.m. to 4:30 p.m. Mon through Fri and 9 a.m. to 4 p.m. Sat and Sun. **Free.**

More than 200 years of history are presented at Fort Bragg in Fayetteville, one of the largest military bases in the world. Home to 130,000 active military personnel and their families, including the famous 82nd Airborne Division, US Special Operations, and the US Army Parachute Team, the base is open to the public. (Nearby Pope Air Force Base

In **Memory**

While touring **Fort Bragg,** you'll come across a number of memorials to those who gave their lives in various wars. At the **JFK Chapel** you'll see stained-glass windows memorializing the Green Berets, plus a monument that the late actor John Wayne designed and donated to the base. Some of the tombstones at the **Fort Bragg Cemetery** date back to 1918.

is not open to the public.) You can tour the 200 square miles of the military reservation to see both contemporary military life and the history of the US's involvement in war. Daily parachute drops are an exciting attraction for visitors. Call (910) 396-6366 for information on drop schedules or log on to the website and click the link on the home page.

82nd Airborne Division Museum (all ages)
Building C-6841, Ardennes Road, Fort Bragg; (910) 432-3443; http://82ndairbourne divisionmuseum.com. Open 10 a.m. to 4:30 p.m. Tues through Sat. Free.

Of all the museums in Fort Bragg, this is among the most fascinating. It features thousands of artifacts from this internationally famous and historically significant division. Items on display include helmets, weapons, parachutes, aircraft, and more from World War I to Operation Enduring Freedom. A film on the division's history is also presented.

The John F. Kennedy Special Warfare Museum (all ages)
Ardennes Road and Marion Street, Fort Bragg; (910) 432-4272. Open 11 a.m. to 4 p.m. Tues through Sat. Free.

This museum features exhibits on unconventional forms of warfare, including displays on the Green Berets and Special Operations units. You'll also see military art and cultural items from around the world, mostly from the Vietnam War era.

Museum of the Cape Fear Historical Complex (ages 5 and up)
801 Arsenal Ave.; (910) 486-1330; www.museumofthecapefear.ncdcr.gov. Open 10 a.m. to 5 p.m. Tues through Sat and 1 to 5 p.m. Sun. Free.

A division of the North Carolina Museum of History, the Museum of the Cape Fear Historical Complex collects, preserves, and interprets the cultural history of southern North Carolina from prehistory to the present. It includes 3 facilities. The museum presents traditional museum exhibits that chronicle the early history of southeastern North Carolina from Native American culture and European settlement, to industrial influences, to the Civil War. Arsenal Park commemorates the day Sherman came to Fayetteville. A US Arsenal, commissioned in Fayetteville in 1836, was taken over by the Confederacy when the Civil War broke out and was seized by Sherman in March 1865. The site also includes the restored 1897 Victorian residence built by E. A. and Josephine Poe.

Where to Eat

Haymont Grill and Steakhouse. 1304 Morganton Rd.; (910) 484-0261; www .haymontgrill.com. This is a pleasant casual restaurant that serves American, Greek, and Italian dishes. $

Pierro's Italian Bistro. 217 Hay St.; (910) 678-8885; www.pierrositalianbistro.com. Pierro's serves a range of Italian dishes, including brick-oven pizzas. $$–$$$

Where to Stay

Clarion Prince Charles Hotel. 450 Hay St.; (910) 433-4444. Reminiscent of an Italian palazzo, this 1925 8-story landmark features Palladian windows and doors, marble floors and staircases, and massive columns. It's listed in Historic Hotels of America. $$$$

Deluxe Inn. 2123 Cedar Creek Rd.; (910) 484-2666. This is a good place for an overnight stop, and pets are allowed. $$

For More Information

Fayetteville Area Convention and Visitors Bureau. (800) 255-8217; www.visitfay ettevillenc.com.

History in **Fayetteville**

When you're done exploring **Fort Bragg,** you and your family will want to check out the many more attractions that await you in Fayetteville. Fayetteville has played key roles during defining moments in America's history. Named after the Revolutionary War hero Marquis de Lafayette, the legislature met here in 1789 to ratify the US Constitution. During the Civil War, General Sherman's Union troops burned the NC Arsenal, a munitions center for the Confederacy located here.

Today many structures have been painstakingly preserved in four historic districts: **Downtown Historic District, Haymount Historic District, Liberty Point National Register District,** and **Market House Square National Register,** all of which can be seen on a self-guided tour. One example of what you'll see on the tour is the **Cool Spring Tavern.** Built in 1788, it is the oldest structure in the city. The tavern housed the delegates who ratified the US Constitution. At **Liberty Point** on June 20, 1775, patriots signed a petition declaring independence from Great Britain. The building at this site is the oldest known commercial structure in Fayetteville, constructed between 1791 and 1800. The **First Presbyterian Church** was rebuilt in 1832. The building's most significant feature is a wooden truss roof, the only one of its kind in the state. If you have an appetite for history, you can get a brochure for the self-guided tour of the city's historical homes and buildings at the **Fayetteville Area Convention and Visitors Bureau,** 515 Ramsey St., (800) 255-8217; www .visitfayettevillenc.com.

Other Things to See & Do
in the Southern Piedmont

- **Adams Stage Lines.** Concord; (704) 537-5556
- **Adventure Landing.** Gastonia; (704) 866-4242; www.adventurelanding.com
- **Birkdale Village.** Huntersville; (704) 895-8744; www.birkdalevillage.net
- **Hendrick Motorsports Museum.** Harrisburg; (704) 455-3400; www.hendrick motorsports.com
- **Ice House.** Pineville; (704) 889-9000; www.pinevilleice.com
- **LaserQuest.** Charlotte; (704) 567-6707; www.laserquest.com
- **The Climbing Place.** Fayetteville; (910) 486-9638; www.theclimbingplace .com
- **Fun, Fun, Fun.** Fayetteville; (910) 864-1307
- **Jambbas Ranch.** Fayetteville; (910) 484-2798; www.jambbas.com
- **ZipQuest.** Fayetteville; (910) 488-8787; www.zipquest.com
- **Zootastic Park of Lake Norman.** Troutman; (704) 245-6446; www.zootastic park.com

Spivey's Corner

From Fayetteville, take I-95 North to US 13 East to arrive at the home of the National Hollerin' Contest.

National Hollerin' Contest (all ages)

Midway High School, 15375 Spivey's Corner Hwy.; (910) 567-2600; www.hollerincontest .com. Third Sat in June, from 11 a.m. to 7 p.m. $; preschool-age children get in free.

That's right! The best windpipes in the country show up here for this annual event, held the third Saturday of June. Since 1969 the contest has featured the lost art of hog callin'—also an early way of communicating with folk living on neighboring farms. Now the event gets national attention, with winners regularly appearing on *The Late Show With David Letterman* and other talk shows. In addition to being entertained by the champion hollerers, you'll find crafts, gospel and country music, and plenty of food. Other contests include whistlin', conch shell and fox horn blowin', junior hollerin', and ladies callin'.

The Southern Coast

Grab a blanket and the sunscreen. Plan to relax, play in the surf and sand, enjoy fresh seafood, or take a boat ride. North Carolina's Southern Coast is full of southern-facing beaches that make for calm waters and warm winds. This region is composed of the Coastal Plain, the southern tip of the Outer Banks, Cape Lookout National Seashore, and the South Brunswick Islands—a series of small barrier islands.

While many of these islands, and the communities on them, don't offer an immense number of tourist attractions, you're likely to find that they are great places to set up housekeeping at a cottage for a week and take any number of day trips.

Jim's
TopPicks on the Southern Coast

1. USS *North Carolina* battleship, Wilmington

2. Riverboat rides on Cape Fear

3. North Carolina Aquarium at Kure Beach

4. Wild ponies of Carrot Island

5. Camping at Carolina Beach State Park, Carolina Beach

6. Bald Head Island

7. Calabash restaurants

8. Southport Fourth of July Celebration

9. Museum of Coastal Carolina, Ocean Isle Beach

10. Waiting for loggerheads

THE SOUTHERN COAST

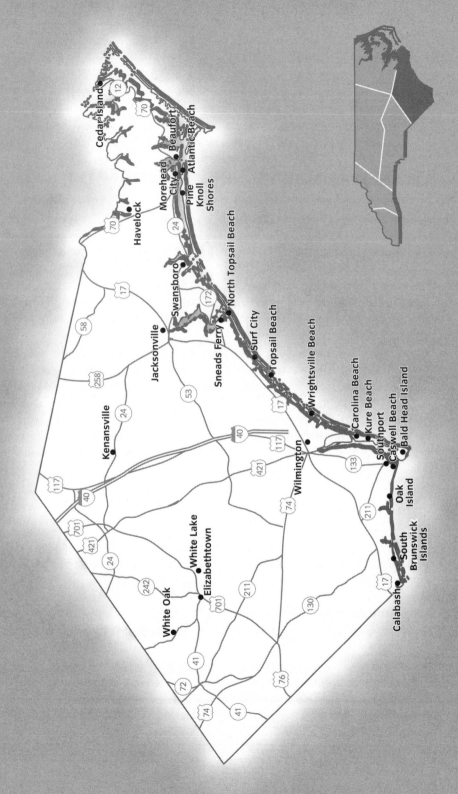

In addition, you will find some of the best golf courses in the Carolinas, a unique community that features seafood restaurants, and two of the state's educational aquariums. Here you can also learn a lot about history, from the 18th century to World War II.

Your adventure on the Southern Coast begins in the Bladen Lakes area, where you'll find a beach long before you get to the coast. The best route to take from the Charlotte area is US 74. From Raleigh I-40 is a speedy route right into Wilmington. US 17 runs the length of the coast, but it goes through many towns, so travel is generally slow. Use it to move from town to town, and stick to the major highways for longer travel.

White Oak

Located south of I-95 on SR 53, White Oak is a small rural town of only 300 residents.

Harmony Hall (ages 5 and up)
1615 River Rd.; (910) 866-4844; www.harmonyhallnc.com. Open 10 a.m. to 4 p.m. Sat and Sun, with live demonstrations of broom making, soap making, and blacksmithing from 2 until 4 p.m. Free, but donations accepted.

As you head into this area, the first stop you will want to make is at Harmony Hall, located in White Oak. Built in the 1760s, Harmony Hall is one of the oldest plantations in North Carolina and was once home to the state's first constitutionally elected governor, Richard Caswell. During the Revolutionary War, British general Charles Cornwallis commandeered the home. A period reenactment is held and wagon rides are offered during the annual **Harmony Hall Reunion Picnic** the first Saturday in May. Several other historic buildings, including a chapel, schoolhouse, and log home, have been moved to the property.

Elizabethtown

The seat of Bladen County, Elizabethtown, is south of White Oak on SR 53. Though it's the largest town around it's not a hotspot by any means. Still it's natural offerings make it worth a stop.

Tory Hole Battleground (all ages)

Located in a ravine that runs from downtown Elizabethtown to the Cape Fear River; (910) 862-2066. Free.

Historic Tory Hole Battleground includes a playground, picnic facilities, and the opportunity to learn more about the battle that took place on the grounds. In 1781, 70 patriots defeated a Tory force of more than 400 men by sending a spy, Sallie Salter, into their camp on the pretense of selling eggs. They then launched a carefully planned midnight attack.

Turnbull Creek State Forest (ages 3 and up)

4470 Sweet Home Church Rd.; (910) 588-4161; www.ncesf.org/tcesf.htm. Open 9 a.m. to 5 p.m. Mon through Fri. Free.

Turnbull Creek State Forest, located north of Elizabethtown, was founded in 1986 and is located among the mysterious Carolina Bays, whose formation is still debated by scientists. The lakes are named for the variety of bay trees found in the region. Visitors to the park can take one of several trails, including the fire control trail, where you can explore the park's firefighting equipment and scout plane. The forest caters mainly to schools in the area, but some of the educational programs may be available from the rangers at the forest office. Picnic facilities are available as well.

Jones Lake State Park (all ages)

113 Jones Lake Dr.; (910) 588-4550; www.ncparks.gov. Generally open during daylight hours. Free.

This wonderful park in Turnbull Creek State Forest offers a bounty of recreational activities within its 2,200 acres. Here you can camp, fish, hike, and swim. Interestingly, the park includes one of two natural lakes in the forest known as Carolina bays. Surprisingly, there are hundreds of thousands of these bays, named for the bay trees found growing around them, in the Southeast, but most are smaller than 500 feet in length. The Jones Lake bay, however, is approximately 8,000 feet long. The lake comprises 224 acres and nearby Salters Lake, also in the park, is 315 acres. What's more interesting is that their formation is a mystery. Scientists have long theorized about the origin of the Carolina bays. Many hypotheses have been proposed, including underground springs, wind and wave action, dissolution of subsurface minerals, and meteor showers. So far, no single explanation has gained universal acceptance. A visitor center reveals more about the Carolina bays and surrounding area.

White Lake

Take US 701 north from Elizabethtown to get here.

Before heading off to the coast, first consider this beautiful area for your family's annual vacation. Billed as "The Nation's Safest Beach," White Lake is an aging resort area that offers many of the amenities of a beach vacation, but it's not on the coast. The lake is the largest of seven lakes known as the **Bladen Lakes,** which some believe were formed by meteors that crashed into Earth more than 100,000 years ago. White Lake offers crystal-clear water with a lovely white-sand bottom, along with amusement rides, arcades, restaurants, and other commercial entertainment and activities. The cool, fresh water is safer for kids because of the absence of tides, currents, and unexpected depressions that are found at coastal beaches.

The area offers more than a dozen accommodations that include hotels, motels, cottages, and campgrounds. **Goldston's Beach,** one of the oldest recreation areas on the beach, was developed by local entrepreneurs, beginning at the turn of the 20th century. It offers accommodations in apartments, cottages, and a motel. A bathhouse is available at the beach, as is a sandwich shop for a quick lunch. The kids will probably want to head to the arcade, too, or to one of the piers to get in a little fishing. For more information call the resort at (910) 862-4578.

Where to Stay

Brisson's Cottages and Apartments. 1770 White Lake Dr.; (910) 862-2495. This company offers rooms, cottages, and efficiencies. $$$

Lasley's Motel. 1930 White Lake Dr.; (910) 862-3473. A standard motel; you'll find more of the same on the waterfront. $$$

Melwood Court. 1994 White Lake Dr.; (910) 862-2416; www.melwoodcourt.com. This establishment is a little larger than the others in the area. $$$

For More Information

Town of White Lake. (910) 862-4800; www .whitelakenc.com.

Calabash

Take US 701 south out of White Lake to Highway 130. Then take Highway 17 south to Calabash.

Now we can head to the coast. If you haven't discovered it before, a visit to Calabash, located in the southeast corner of the state on US 17, is sure to become a family tradition every time you come to this part of the coast. This small fishing community is the southernmost town in North Carolina and has become famous for the Calabash style of cooking seafood. Fish, shrimp, and other goodies are lightly breaded and deep-fried to a golden brown and are usually served with hush puppies and coleslaw. Once, more than 30 family-style restaurants lined the streets of this quaint village, where fresh local seafood is delivered daily. In 1989 Calabash merged with the Carolina Shores golfing community, which includes not only some of the best courses in the Carolinas but a wide variety of specialty shops as well. Today the number of restaurants is dwindling because of competition from other restaurants in South Carolina's bustling Myrtle Beach tourist area, but it's still a great place to get your seafood dinner.

Where to Eat

Becks, The Original Calabash Restaurant. 1014 River Rd.; (910) 579-6776; www .becksrestaurant.com. Founded in 1940 this restaurant and its recipes have been passed down from generation to generation. $$

Captain Nance's Seafood. 9939 Nance St.; (910) 579-2574. You'll be seated along with a basket of hush puppies and honey butter. $$

Coleman's Original Calabash. 9931 Nance St.; (910) 579-6875. A number of restaurants in Calabash claim to be the original. Coleman's may be. The building appears to be among the oldest on the waterfront, but it's popular. $$

Ellas of Calabash. 1148 River Rd.; (910) 579-6728. Founded in 1950, Ella's claim to fame is not as an original, but claims more fresh fish than others. $$

South Brunswick Islands

Begin your trek up the coast by heading north on US 17. Here on the South Brunswick Islands, you'll find three similar communities: Sunset Beach, Ocean Isle Beach, and Holden Beach.

SUNSET BEACH

In recent years only accessible by a unique one-lane pontoon bridge, you'll quickly learn where this laid-back island just off the coast got its name. A feeling of seclusion will quickly descend upon you as you move into one of the large cottages situated behind the tall sand dunes on Sunset Beach. This little island, only 3 miles long, is the southernmost of the three communities.

Ingram Planetarium (ages 3 and up)

7625 High Market St. in The Village at Sunset Resort; (910) 575-0031; www.museumplanetarium.org. Open 10 a.m. to 7 p.m. Mon through Fri and 10 a.m. to 5 p.m. Sat. $–$$.

Ingram Planetarium opened in summer 2002 as part of a collaboration with the nearby Museum of Coastal Carolina. It shows traditional planetarium programs on a 40-foot dome in its 90-seat theater. The center also includes a few science-related exhibits, brainteasers, puzzles, and other hands-on activities.

Where to Stay

Sea Trail Plantation & Golf Resort. 211 Clubhouse Rd.; (888) 229-5747; www.seatrail.com. This is the largest resort on Sunset Beach, offering everything from efficiencies to villas on the golf course. $$$$

Sunset Properties. 419 Sunset Blvd. South; (910) 579-9900; www.sunsetbeachnc.com. Four hundred cottages are offered by this agency. $$$

OCEAN ISLE BEACH

This island is located just north of Sunset Beach.

Ocean Isle Beach provides more surf, sand, and sunshine. Enjoy 7 miles of beaches and fish from the surf or pier. To get out on the ocean and try your fishing luck in deeper water, drop by **Ocean Isle Fishing Center on the Causeway** (910-575-3474). It offers full- and half-day fishing trips. If you'd like to try your hand at crabbing, it probably can be done just outside your back door. Everything you need is here on this island, including restaurants, specialty shops, a miniature golf course, and a waterslide.

Museum of Coastal Carolina (ages 3 and up)

21 E. 2nd St.; (910) 579-1016; www.museumplanetarium.org. Open 10 a.m. to 8 p.m. Mon, Wed, and Thurs; 10 a.m. to 5 p.m. Tues and Fri; and 10 a.m. to 1:30 p.m. Sat during summer. Hours are limited the rest of the year. $–$$.

Whether in Ocean Isle for a day or a week, make it a point to stop by the Museum of Coastal Carolina. You don't have to get wet to see the spectacular sights of local ocean life. Wall and floor murals and actual specimens from the sea in the reef room give you a feeling of actually being in the water. The museum includes shark jaws, a huge seashell collection, dioramas of coastal animal life, and Civil War artifacts. The museum also has a turtle-watch program and hosts outdoor concerts in the summer.

Where to Stay

Brick Landing Plantation. 1900 Goose Creek Rd. Southwest; (800) 438-3006. Brick Landing offers condos and villas. $$$$

Islander Inn. 57 W. 1st St.; (888) 325-4753; www.islanderinn.com. The Islander Inn offers oceanfront accommodations, featuring a heated indoor pool, Jacuzzi, and an outdoor pool overlooking the beach. A complimentary continental breakfast is included. $$$$

The Winds Resort and Beach Club. 310 E. 1st St.; (800) 334-3581; www.thewinds .com. This is a very nice resort hotel with a lovely subtropical garden. $$$$

Here's a list of Realtors who handle vacation rentals in Ocean Isle area:

Cooke Realty. 1 Causeway Dr.; (800) 622-3224; www.cookerealty.com.

Ocean Isle Beach Realty. 15 Causeway Dr.; (800) 374-7361; www.oibrealty.com.

R. H. McClure Realty, Inc. 24 Causeway Dr.; (800) 332-5476; www.rhmcclurerealty .com.

Sloane Realty. 16 Causeway Dr.; (866) 931-5201; www.sloanvacations.com.

Williamson Realty. 119 Causeway Dr.; (888) 897-5302; www.willliamsonrealty.com.

For More Information

You can call the **town of Ocean Isle Beach** at (800) 248-2504 to get information on accommodations or visit www.oceanisle beach.com.

HOLDEN BEACH

Holden Beach is easily accessible from US 74 if you're coming from the west.

If beautiful sunsets and seclusion aren't enough to keep the kids entertained, give the largest and northernmost of the Brunswick Islands a try. The 11 miles of beach have long been a favorite haunt of those who live to fish, but the area has grown to be more family oriented. It now includes a limited number of amusements, arcades, and other commercial attractions.

Festival by the Sea (all ages)

Holden Beach's biggest annual event attracts people with its arts and crafts, parade, games, and entertainment. The festival kicks off the last Friday of October with a Halloween carnival for children and continues Saturday with road races, volleyball, sand-sculpture contests, and kite-flying contests. A street dance is also traditionally held that night. Gospel singing is the center of attention on Sunday as the festival continues until dark. Call (910) 754-6644 for more information.

Where to Stay

Here's a list of Holden Beach Realtors that handle vacation rentals in Holden Beach:

Alan Holden Vacations. 128 Ocean Blvd. West; (800) 720-2200; www.holden-beach.com.

Brunswickland Realty. 123 Ocean Blvd.; (800) 842-6949; www.brunswicklandrealty.com.

Coastal Vacation Resorts. 131 Ocean Blvd. West; (800) 252-7000; www.coastalvacationresorts.com.

Craig Realty. 3262 Holden Beach Rd. Southwest; (910) 842-2628; www.craigrealty.biz.

Hobbs Realty Vacations. 114 Ocean Blvd. West; (800) 655-3367; www.hobbsrealty.com.

For More Information

Call the **town hall of Holden Beach** at (910) 842-6488 for more information.

You can call the **South Brunswick Islands Chamber of Commerce** at (800) 426-6644 for information on accommodations and golf packages.

Oak Island

Highway 211 will give you access to Oak Island.

Formerly the towns of Long Beach and Yaupon Beach, the town of Oak Island offers an unusual 65 public beach accesses (most with parking), two public boat ramps, several areas to put in canoes and kayaks, and an extensive sidewalk system for biking and walking. Here you'll find parks and playgrounds set among beautiful oak trees and even youth-friendly facilities such as a skateboard park as well as a dog park. It also includes mainland areas with a chain grocery store, department stores, and fast-food restaurants. You'll love the calm surf offered on the southern-facing islands. Here you'll be able to swim along 9 miles of beach. There is also a big arcade that includes a swimming pool as well as video games and billiard tables. The epicenter of activity is the **Oak Island Pier,** the tallest in North Carolina at a whopping 27 feet above sea level.

Oak Island Nature Center & Register Park (all ages)
End of 52nd Street; (910) 278-5518. Hours vary. Free.

Overlooking the marsh and Intracoastal Waterway, the Oak Island Nature Center offers a wide range of educational activities for children and adults alike. The Talking Trees Walking Trail introduces visitors to the dogwood, red cedar, southern magnolia, and black gum. Visitors also meet a ferret, prairie dog, hedgehog, guinea pig, rabbit, gecko, and moon crab in a small animal exhibit. The center also has a large touch tank with marine creatures native to the island community. Restrooms and picnic facilities are also located here.

Where to Stay

Blue Water Point Motel & Marina. 5710 W. 57th Place; (910) 278-1230; www.blue waterpointmotel.com. Located between the ocean and channel, this hotel caters to sailors docking at the marina. $$$$

Island Resort and Inn. 500 Ocean Dr.; (910) 278-5644; www.islandresortandinn .com. This resort has many amenities, including an oceanfront deck and a pool. $$$–$$$$

Ocean Crest Motel. 1417 E. Beach Dr.; (910) 278-3333; www.ocean-crest-motel.com. Ocean Crest is one of a few hotels located on the island. $$$

A Hoffman **Family Adventure**

For a number of years my brother and his family have rented a large house on what used to be called Long Beach on Oak Island, and they always invite an assortment of extended family members and friends to share the week with them. We've been lucky enough to make the trip for a few days on a couple of occasions.

One of the fondest memories that I have of these trips is sitting quietly in the dark on the beachfront deck waiting to spot one of the famed loggerhead turtles that visit this part of the coast during the summer. We never actually saw one of the 200- to 500-pound creatures visit, but we awoke one morning to find one had left 100 or more eggs that looked like Ping-Pong balls next to our boardwalk. These amazing creatures come from their feeding grounds hundreds of miles away, as far as Cuba or the Dominican Republic in some cases, year after year to nest. Some researchers believe the turtles return to the same place where they hatched. So far they've been able to substantiate only that the adults do return to the same beach.

Here are Oak Island's realty companies that can help you book a vacation rental:

Better Beach Rentals. 8601 E. Oak Island Dr.; (877) 441-0009; www.betterbeachrentals.com.

Coastal Vacation Resorts–Oak Island. 4434 Long Beach Rd.; (888) 703-5469; www.coastalvacationresortsoakisland.com.

Margaret Rudd & Associates. 210 Country Club Dr.; (800) 486-5441; www.rudd.com.

Oak Island Accommodations. 8901 E. Oak Island Dr.; (800) 243-8132; www.rentalsatthebeach.com.

Caswell Beach

In addition to the gentle tides along the 4 miles of beach, here you will find the **Oak Island Lighthouse,** the nation's most modern, which opened in 1958. Also located on this beach is the Oak Island Coast Guard Station and **Fort Caswell.** Built in 1826, the fort is now owned by the North Carolina Baptist Assembly. The Civil War stone-and-earthen fort was abandoned in 1865 during a violent naval bombardment north of here. Today you can tour what remains of the fort and bunkers. For more information call (910) 278-9501.

For More Information

Southport–Oak Island Chamber of Commerce. (800) 457-6964; www.oakislandnc.com.

Southport

To get to Southport, take Highway 133 north from Oak Island to Highway 211 and head east.

Southport is a picturesque old town located at the junction of the Cape Fear River, the Intracoastal Waterway, and the Atlantic Ocean. If your family enjoys sailing and deep-sea fishing, this is the place to go. But this peaceful port city, which is more than 200 years old, offers much more. You'll want to spend some time exploring the more than dozen antiques shops beneath huge old live oaks and take advantage of some of the exquisite dining available in the village. The town has become famous for the **Southport Fourth of July Celebration,** which has become one of the state's largest annual celebrations, featuring games, contests, food, and, of course, fireworks.

Amazing
North Carolina Facts

Southport was originally incorporated in 1792 as Smithville, but citizens in 1887 voted to change its name to Southport with the goal of attracting interest as a port. Their plans went awry when the larger port was established in the city of Wilmington to the north.

Brunswick Town State Historic Site (ages 5 and up)
8884 St. Phillips Rd. Southeast, Winnabow; (910) 371-6613. Open 9 a.m. to 5 p.m. Tues through Sat. **Free.**

Brunswick Town was the first capital of the colony of North Carolina and was a leading seaport during most of the 18th century. Europeans established it here in 1726 to serve as a naval port. The museum at the site allows you to examine various artifacts excavated from the remains of the original buildings, which were burned to the ground by the British in 1776. Still evident are remnants of the massive earthworks of Fort Anderson, built to help keep the Cape Fear River open for Civil War blockade runners, who shipped supplies to Confederate forces. It fell in 1865 during a fierce battle that also collapsed several other area forts. Markers have been erected to explain the history of the area.

NC Maritime Museum at Southport (all ages)
Located at Fort Johnson at the corner of Moore and Davis Streets; (910) 457-0003. Open 9 a.m. to 5 p.m. Tues through Sat. **Free.**

A branch of the NC Maritime Museum at Beaufort, this museum houses a collection of memorabilia pertaining to the vast nautical history of Southport, Lower Cape Fear, and southeastern North Carolina. It includes a 2,000-year-old 54-inch Indian canoe fragment; Civil War blockade exhibits, including a 200-pound torpedo; and an extensive collection of delicate ship models. The River Pilots, Rescues and Aids to Navigation section offers a variety of nautical instruments.

Progress Energy Visitors Center (ages 3 and up)
8520 River Rd. Southeast; (910) 457-6041. Hours vary. **Free.**

A good educational afternoon trip is only about 2 miles north of town on Highway 87. Take along a picnic lunch when you visit the Progress Energy Visitors Center. You'll want to allow about an hour to see the 30 hands-on displays on energy, electricity production, energy conservation, and nuclear power.

Where to Stay

The Captain's Bridge. 113 N. Howe St.; (910) 457-6401; www.thecaptainsbridge.com. This is one of the city's newest hotels located near the waterfront. $$$

The Inn at River Oaks. 512 N. Howe St.; (910) 457-1100; www.innatriveroaks.com. This motel will suit you if you're planning to be out and about a lot and don't want to spend a ton on lodging. $$

Riverside Motel. 103 W. Bay St.; (910) 457-6986; www.loisjanes.com. Riverside is a very small motel that is, of course, on the waterfront. $$$

For More Information

NC Brunswick Islands. (800) 795-7263; www.ncbrunswick.com.

Bald Head Island

Bald Head Island is one of North Carolina's most exclusive and beautiful vacation resorts. You won't find any cars or even a bridge to this natural and historical area. In addition to fine dining, shopping, and relaxing by the pool or on the beach, you won't have any trouble finding ways to spend your time on this island of "sea oats, sand castles, and sunsets." To get here you must take a private yacht or catch the ferry ($$–$$$) at **Deep Point Marina,** 1301 Ferry Rd. in Southport (910-457-5003). Security is provided at the 24-hour parking lot ($) at the marina. Daily trips to the island are made on the hour, 8 a.m. to 6 p.m., except noon. Return trips to the mainland are made on the half hour, 8:30 a.m. to 6:30 p.m., except 11:30 a.m. Day-trip packages that include guided tours of the Old Baldy Lighthouse and Smith Island Museum ($$$$) are also available, and some are **free** for children under 3. Call the marina for details.

Bald Head Island Club (all ages)

South Bald Head Wynd; (910) 457-7300; www.bhiclub.net. Fees vary by activity.

Most rental accommodation packages on the island include a temporary membership to the Bald Head Island Club, which offers fine dining, live entertainment, a clubhouse, and a host of recreational facilities. Here you can enjoy the swimming pool, a challenging golf course, tennis courts, and croquet greenswards. Coaching for young and old alike is available for all these activities. The club offers a range of dining experiences, including elegant evening dining, a lunch grill, a cafe for casual dining, and a poolside delicatessen.

Bald Head Island Conservancy (all ages)

7000 Federal Rd.; (910) 457-0089; www.bhic.org. Some programs require a small fee.

The conservancy sponsors workshops for young people, including canoe trips, turtle walks, beach sweeps, and conservation programs, but its biggest task is the preservation of the endangered loggerhead turtle. More than 30 percent of all the loggerhead turtle nesting sites recorded on the North Carolina coast are on this island. The Sea Turtle Nest

Protection Project is responsible for monitoring the nesting of these endangered turtles and holds special programs about them.

Old Baldy Lighthouse (all ages)

Located on Bald Head Island; (910) 457-7481; www.oldbaldy.org. Open 9 a.m. to 5 p.m. Mon through Sat and 11 a.m. to 5 p.m. Sun during summer. Hours vary at other times of the year, so call ahead or check the website. Free.

"Old Baldy," North Carolina's oldest lighthouse, built in 1817, marks the west side of Bald Head Island. Although its function was replaced by the Oak Island Lighthouse in 1935, the 110-foot tower is open for climbing. The Old Baldy Foundation, formed in 1985 and charged with maintaining the lighthouse, also operates a museum in a replica of the lighthouse keeper's cottage.

Riverside Adventure Company (ages 5 and up)

North Bald Head Wynd; (910) 457-4944; www.riversideadventure.com. Seasonal hours.

This store offers a selection of sportswear and accessories. You can also get help in planning a number of different activities, such as clamming, crabbing, cycling, and canoe trips. Equipment for these adventures—as well as beach umbrellas, chairs, or even an extra golf cart—is available for rent.

Shoals Club (all ages)

Located near Cape Fear Point; (910) 454-4888; www.shoalsclub.com. Seasonal hours. Some activities require a fee.

Just like it used to be, the Shoals Club is a place for families to enjoy seaside pastimes just as they did at the pavilions of old. The oceanfront club includes dining areas, a lounge, fitness room, shower and locker facilities, swimming pools, and direct beach access. Parents lounging on the porch can watch their children swimming in the pool below. Towel service is offered at the pool, and chairs and umbrellas are available to take to the beach as well. Regular poolside cookouts and buffets bring even more dining options, along with a chance to enjoy live music, sunsets, and socializing with fellow members and vacationers. The Shoals Club recreation department organizes a range of recreation and social

Holidays on **Bald Head**

You might want to plan your trip to Bald Head Island around one of the many special events held throughout the year, beginning with the Easter sunrise service at **"Old Baldy"** and the annual Easter egg hunt. Your family can hunt for Blackbeard's buried treasure on Memorial Day. Or you can come out for the golf cart parade, sand castle competition, and family Olympic games the weekend falling closest to July 4. Special celebrations are held on most other holidays, too.

activities for all ages that include outdoor adventures, pool games, beach volleyball, and ice-cream socials for teens. The Common at Cape Fear Station provides a place for children's day camps and teen gatherings.

Where to Stay

Accommodations on Bald Head Island include bed-and-breakfast inns, several condominiums, and vacation cottages and homes ($$$$). Whichever you choose, you'll find yourself on a vacation of luxury. Rental accommodations on the island typically come with fully equipped kitchens, washers and dryers, and a 4-passenger golf cart.

Bald Head Island Rentals. (800) 680-8322; www.baldheadislandrentals.com. $$$$

Bald Head Island Vacations. (888) 367-7091; www.baldheadislandvacations.com. $$$$

Marsh Harbour Inn. (800) 680-8322; www.marshharbourinn.com. While many of the rooms here accommodate couples, Marsh Harbour welcomes small families, too. $$$$

Sea Breeze Rentals. (910) 457-0465; www.seabreezerentals.com. $$$$

Theodosia's. (800) 656-1812; www.theodosias.com. Located on the harbor, Theodosia's also has accommodations for small families for weekend excursions. $$$$

Tiffany Rentals. (910) 457-0544; www.tiffanyrentals.com. $$$$

For More Information

Bald Head Island Information Center. (800) 234-2441; www.baldheadisland.com.

Pleasure Island

Pleasure Island is composed of the two communities of **Kure Beach** and **Carolina Beach.** Many of the accommodations on this island are older, but several have been renovated in recent years. From the north the island is accessible by car over the US 421 bridge. From the south, you'll have to take the toll ferry ($$) from Southport to Fort Fisher. Crossings begin at 8 a.m. and end at 7 p.m. year-round. They are less frequent in winter.

KURE BEACH

Kure Beach features a dozen charming hotels, motels, and inns. You can also rent one of the many available cottages. The beaches here are generally uncrowded, but several areas have lifeguards on duty. In addition, the pier, the oldest on the Atlantic coast, is conveniently located in the middle of town adjacent to a boardwalk area that becomes the bustling center of activity in the evening.

Fort Fisher State Historic Site (ages 5 and up)

1000 S. Fort Fisher Blvd.; (910) 458-5538; www.nchistoricsites.org. Open 9 a.m. to 5 p.m. Tues through Sat. Free.

Fort Fisher was one of the Confederacy's last major strongholds during the Civil War. The site includes a monument commemorating the largest land-sea battle of the war, which was fought in January 1865. Also at the earthen fort is a reconstructed gun emplacement and an interpretive history trail. The fort's museum features displays on the Confederate defense system, dioramas, an audiovisual show, and war artifacts. Picnic facilities are also available.

North Carolina Aquarium (all ages)

900 Loggerhead Rd.; (800) 832-3474; www.ncaquariums.com. Open 9 a.m. to 5 p.m. daily. $$; free for children ages 5 and under.

Arriving by ferry, the first attraction you'll come to is the North Carolina Aquarium, one of three such aquariums on the North Carolina coast. The aquarium is sure to draw your kids into the world of ocean life. Here they'll see a shark tank that includes a gigantic whale shark, where they can ask questions of one of the divers while he or she is in the tank. Visitors also get a chance to pick up a number of sea creatures at the touch pool. This aquarium also features a stingray exhibit, a turtle exhibit, a life-size whale sculpture, and an alligator pond. There are special educational programs, including films and presentations at the aquarium, in addition to special field trips.

Where to Eat

Big Daddy's. 206 K Ave.; (910) 458-8622; www.bigdaddysofkurebeach.com. Big Daddy offers steaks, seafood, and more. $$

Jack Mackerel's Island Grill. 113 K Ave.; (910) 458-7668. You'll find fun island food and decor here. $$

Where to Stay

Admiral's Quarters Motel. 129 S. Fort Fisher Blvd.; (910) 458-5050 www.admirals quartersmotel.com. This is a small motel with rooms and efficiencies near the pier by the ocean. $$

Blue Marlin Apartments and Cottages. 318 N. Fort Fisher Blvd.; (910) 458-5752; www .blue-marlin.com. The Blue Marlin is a nicely kept facility by the ocean. $$–$$$

Kure Keys Motel. 310 Fort Fisher Blvd.; (910) 458-5277; www.kurekeysmotel.com. This is a very pretty oceanfront hotel. $$$

Palm Air Cottages. 133 Fort Fisher Blvd.; (910) 458-5269; www.palmairrealty.com. Cottages have screened porches, plus there's a pool and picnic area. It is, however, 1 block from the beach. $$$

Sand Dunes Motel. 123 Fort Fisher Blvd. South; (800) 535-4984; www.thesanddunes .com. You'll find clean rooms and efficiencies here as well as an oceanfront pool, which is a nice amenity. You can use their grills for cookouts, too. $$

Seven Seas Inn. 130 Fort Fisher Blvd.; (910) 458-8122; www.sevenseasinn.com. This is a pretty motel with rooms and efficiencies, an oceanfront pool, covered gazebos, and a picnic area with grills. $$$$

For long-term rentals, try one of the following:

Beachfront Vacations, Inc. 129 Fort Fisher Blvd. South; (800) 535-4984; www.beach frontvacationsinc.com.

Island Realty. 325 Fort Fisher Blvd. North; (910) 458-8800; www.islandrealty-kurebeach .com.

For More Information

Town of Kure Beach. (910) 458-8434; www.visitkure.com.

CAROLINA BEACH

Carolina Beach is minutes north of Kure Beach on Highway 421.

Carolina Beach offers a number of amenities for a fun-filled beach vacation, and it's about a 20-minute drive south of Wilmington down Highway 421. It's full of a variety of natural areas but offers the thrill of waterslides and amusement rides along a fun-filled boardwalk area. Located at the boardwalk is **Carolina Beach Amusement Park,** which has traditional rides such as a Ferris wheel, a tilt-a-whirl, a merry-go-round, and a house of fun. After hitting the amusement park, check out the sweet treats at Brits Doughnuts. Carolina Beach Lake Park is also a popular gathering spot, with regular fireworks shows, concerts, and other events.

Carolina Beach State Park (all ages)

Located at SR 1628 and Dow Road; (910) 458-7770; www.ncparks.gov. The park is typically open during daylight hours. Visitor center hours are 9 a.m. to 5 p.m. daily. Campsite rental ($) available.

Hotels, motels, and rental cottages line blocks and blocks throughout Carolina Beach, but you can also camp at Carolina Beach State Park, located on the waterway on the west side of the island. Wet a line here, but no swimming is allowed, although public beach access is only a few minutes away. The park is one of the world's few natural habitats of the Venus flytrap, a unique carnivorous plant that traps and dissolves insects that land on its leaves. There are several nature trails in the park, and markers will help you guide your family through them. Picnic facilities are available during daylight hours. Paddleboats and kayaks are also available for rent at the park lake.

Amazing
North Carolina Facts

The rare Venus flytrap is merely the most interesting of six different species of insect-eating plants you and the kids can see at **Carolina Beach State Park.** The Venus flytrap possesses a nervous system that is similar to that of a mammal. Charles Darwin pronounced it "the most wonderful plant in the world."

Wheel Fun Rentals

107 Carolina Beach Ave. North; (910) 458-4545.

Rent a surrey bike that accommodates up to 8 people or any other kind of bike you can imagine. Boogie boards, chairs, and surfboards are also available for rent here.

Where to Eat

The Ocean Grill. 1211 S. Lake Park Blvd.; (910) 458-2000; www.oceangrilltiki.com. Once this was the Carolina Beach Pier. Now a tiki bar is located on the ocean just beyond this good restaurant. $$

Squigley's Ice Cream & Treats. 208 S. Lake Park Blvd.; (910) 458-8779. This fun ice-cream parlor serves more flavors than you can imagine. $

Where to Stay

Atlantic Towers. 1615 S. Lake Park Blvd.; (800) 232-2440; www.atlantic-towers.com. This is an 11-story tower of condos. It has a video game room and a pool. $$$$

Golden Sands Motel. 1211 S. Lake Park Blvd.; (888) 458-8334; www.goldensands carolinabeach.com. The Sands offers large oceanfront rooms in the center of town. Rates vary widely depending on the season. $–$$$

Here is a list of larger Carolina Beach Realtors that offer vacation rentals of condos and houses:

Atlantic Shores Real Estate. 9 S. Lake Park Blvd., Ste. A3; (800) 289-0028; www.atlanticshoresrealty.com.

Beach Girls Realty. 245 N. Lake Park Blvd.; (910) 458-5611; www.beachgirlsrealty.com.

Blue Water Realty. 1000 S. Lake Park Blvd.; (866) 458-3001.

Bowman & Associates Real Estate. 1420 S. Lake Park Blvd.; (866) 458-6363; www.annbowman.com.

Bryant Real Estate. 1401 N. Lake Park Blvd.; (800) 994-5222; www.bryantrealestate.com.

Cabana Suites. 222 Carolina Beach Ave. North; (800) 333-8499; www.cabanasuites.com.

Carolina Beach Realty. 1009 B-3 N. Lake Park Blvd.; (910) 458-4444; www.carolinabeachrealty.net.

North Pier Ocean Villas. 1800 Canal Dr.; (800) 476-1589; www.northpiervillas.com.

United Beach Vacations, Inc. 1001 N. Lake Park Blvd.; (910) 458-9073; www.unitedbeachvacations.com.

Walker Realty. 501 N. Lake Park Blvd.; (910) 458-3388; www.carolinabeachnc.com.

For More Information

Carolina Beach Tourism. (800) 641-7082; www.carolinabeachgetaway.com.

Wilmington

Wilmington is the largest and fastest-growing city on North Carolina's coast and offers dozens of attractions for people of all ages. From the large historic downtown district to the Intracoastal Waterway, the city is full of arts, recreation, and just plain fun, whether you are here for a day or for a week. Before you take on downtown Wilmington, you'll want to get hold of a guide map at the visitor center at the corner of Third and Princess Streets or by calling (800) 222-4757. You can either take a riverfront walking tour or see most of downtown during a driving tour in a single day. Trolley tours are available by calling (910) 763-4483. The Wilmington area has been home to many famous people, including NBA superstar Michael Jordan, television journalists David Brinkley and Charles Kuralt, singer Sammy Davis Jr., and more.

The city has come to be known as "Hollywood East." Hundreds of feature films and television shows have been made in the area, including *Firestarter, Ironweed, The Muppets Take Manhattan, I Know What You Did Last Summer, Dawson's Creek,* and *One Tree Hill.* Tours are available at the EUE/Screen Gems Studios, the largest studio east of Hollywood. And if you're lucky, you might find yourself with a chance to be an extra or to meet a star from the "other Hollywood."

Bellamy Mansion (ages 8 and up)

503 Market St.; (910) 251-3700; www.bellamymansion.org. Tours are on the hour from 10 a.m. to 5 p.m. Tues through Sat and 1 to 5 p.m. Sun. $–$$.

Bellamy is one of the most significant historic homes in North Carolina. It's an excellent example of antebellum architecture that was built by free and enslaved black artisans for John Dillard Bellamy, a 19th-century physician, planter, and business leader. After the fall of Fort Fisher in 1865, Federal troops commandeered the house as their headquarters. Today it is a museum that focuses on history and the design arts as well as historic preservation.

Burgin Wright House (ages 5 and up)

224 Market St.; (910) 762-0570. Open 10 a.m. to 4 p.m. Tues through Sat, except July 4, Thanksgiving, Christmas, and New Year's Day. $–$$.

Built in 1770, this 3-story home is an example of the gentleman's town house of the time. Its huge foundation is constructed of stone from the city's old jailhouse. As you walk through the home, you'll see a collection of lovely 18th-century furniture and decorations.

Cameron Art Museum (ages 5 and up)

3201 S. 17th St.; (910) 395-5999; www.cameronartmuseum.com. Open 10 a.m. to 5 p.m. Tues through Sun, with extended hours until 9 p.m. on Fri. $–$$; free for children ages 4 and under.

Your next stop is a cultural one, and just a few blocks down Orange Street. The Cameron Art Museum is a complex of 3 distinctive buildings dating back to the early 1800s. The museum's main attraction is a collection of 3 centuries of work by North Carolina artists. You can peruse collections of paintings, Jugtown pottery, and sculpture, all of which were created in the state. In addition, the museum attracts collections from all over the world. The joy is that you never know what you'll find here from trip to trip.

Cape Fear Museum of History and Science (ages 5 and up)

814 Market St.; (910) 341-7450; www.capefearmuseum.com. Open 9 a.m. to 5 p.m. Tues through Sat (also open Mon Memorial Day through Labor Day) and 1 to 5 p.m. Sun. $–$$; kids ages 2 and younger get in **free.**

One of Wilmington's big draws for families is the Cape Fear Museum. A 21-foot scale replica of the Wilmington waterfront and a 31-foot diorama are only two of the hundreds of exhibits at this special museum. The museum tells the story of the region from prehistoric times to the present in *Waves and Currents: The Lower Cape Fear Story,* a 600-square-foot exhibit that shows the development of this part of the coast. You'll also discover special interactive programs for children, videos, the Michael Jordan Discovery Gallery, a skeleton of a giant ground sloth, and more exhibits. Many of the programs offered at the museum change from time to time, but you can call for more information.

Cape Fear Serpentarium (all ages)

20 Orange St.; (910) 762-1669; www.capefearserpentarium.com. Open 11 a.m. to 5 p.m. Mon through Fri and 11 a.m. to 6 p.m. Sat and Sun. $$.

If you think this attraction sounds a little creepy, you're right. The Cape Fear Serpentarium houses the world's largest collection of bushmasters as well as other reptiles from all over the world. Here you'll see snakes, crocodiles, dragons, and more. It also includes the Africa Museum, which displays a fantastic collection of African tribal artifacts, including a real voodoo witch doctor's ceremonial costume, tribal swords, spears, and ritual objects.

Children's Museum of Wilmington (ages 1 to 11)

116 Orange St.; (910) 254-3534; www.playwilmington.org. Open 9 a.m. to 5 p.m. Mon through Sat and 1 to 5 p.m. Sun. $; **free** for infants under age 1.

This hands-on play space features state-of-the art exhibit areas themed on a three-ring circus, a pirate ship and port area, and an international diner and grocery. Other features include a toddler area, animal adventures, an art room, and a science lab.

Cotton Exchange (all ages)

321 N. Front St.; (910) 343-9896; www.shopthecottonexchange.com. Most shops are open 10 a.m. to 5:30 p.m. Mon through Sat and 1 to 5 p.m. Sun.

Park at the waterfront and take the short walk down Front Street to the Cotton Exchange, which features more than 30 unique restaurants and shops in well-preserved, century-old buildings. The shops once served as warehouses for the former cotton company, but now you'll find specialty shops, clothing stores, and antiques.

EUE/Screen Gems Studios (all ages)

1223 N. 23rd St.; (910) 343-3500; www.screengemsstudio.com. Tours offered on weekends noon to 2 p.m. $$$.

Rides on **the River**

Captain J. N. Maffitt Cruises, located at **Riverfront Park** at the corner of Market and Water Streets, offers taxi rides to the USS *North Carolina* memorial ($). Rides run every half hour, except 11:30 a.m. and 3:30 p.m. You can also catch a boat there for an informative sightseeing cruise on the **Cape Fear River.** *Henrietta III* cruises depart from Water and Dock Streets April through December. This narrated tour ($–$$) takes you about 8 miles down the river. It's a good way to get a look at the historic buildings and learn about the importance of the port town. Tours are offered at noon Tuesday through Saturday. An additional 2:30 p.m. cruise is offered April through October. Call **Cape Fear Riverboats** at (800) 676-0162 or visit www.cfrboats .com for more information.

Take a tour of the largest full-service motion-picture facility in the US east of California. Since 1984 EUE/Screen Gems Studios has turned out hundreds of films, television shows, and commercials. Nine sound stages and support services can accommodate virtually any imaginable production. The tour on foot includes a visit to the former *Dawson's Creek* and *One Tree Hill* sets.

Ghost Walk of Old Wilmington (ages 6 and up)
Riverfront at Market and Water Streets; (910) 794-1866; www.hauntedwilmington.com. Offered at 8:30 p.m. nightly during daylight saving time; 6:30 p.m. Tues through Sat in Nov and Mar; and 6:30 p.m. Thurs through Sat in Dec, Jan, and Feb. $$$.

Offered by actors who fancy themselves ghost hunters, the ghost walk takes participants on a journey into the depths of Old Wilmington. From creepy alleyways to the windy riverfront, you'll hear tales of pirates and cutthroats who once terrorized this port city. Homes and landmarks, beneath centuries-old live oaks with Spanish moss dangling from their limbs, bring dismal accounts of poor lost souls. The same group offers a Hollywood location walk.

Greenfield Park and Gardens (ages 5 and up)
1510 3rd St.; (910) 341-7855. The park generally is open daily during daylight hours. Free.

If you make it to Wilmington in the spring or summer, take the 5-mile scenic drive around Greenfield Park and Gardens, located south of the USS *North Carolina* on US 421. Greenfield Lake is the recreational center of the 180-acre park, but spend a little time cruising through the cypress and dogwood trees. In the spring the park comes alive with color as azaleas and roses begin to bloom. At the lake you can bring along a picnic lunch, rent a canoe or paddleboat, or take a hike down the 4-mile walking trail.

Moores Creek National Battlefield (ages 5 and up)

200 Moores Creek Rd.; (910) 283-5591; www.nps.gov/mocr. Open 9 a.m. to 5 p.m. daily. **Free.**

Another educational afternoon trip to take if you're staying in Wilmington is to the Moores Creek National Battlefield, a 30-minute drive north on Highway 210, off US 421. This site commemorates the dramatic Revolutionary War battle fought to end British rule in North Carolina in February 1776. Markers and monuments lead you through a self-guiding trail and help explain the battle. A visitor center includes a small museum with photos, an audiovisual program, and war memorabilia. The site is also a nice place for a picnic.

Tregembo Animal Park (all ages)

5811 Carolina Beach Rd.; (910) 392-3604; www.tregemboanimalpark.com. Open 10 a.m. to 5 p.m. daily. $–$$; children under 2 are admitted **free.**

About 10 miles north of Carolina Beach you can treat your kids to a trip to the Tregembo Animal Park. The zoo includes more than 70 different animals in 5 acres of forest-like surroundings. You'll see zebras, baboons, monkeys, exotic birds, a Siberian tiger, and a camel. The zoo has a gift shop and plenty of concessions as well. Two small museums feature mounted animals, fossils, arrowheads, and World War II memorabilia.

USS *North Carolina* (ages 3 and up)

Located at US 17/74 and 76/421; (910) 251-5797; www.battleshipnc.com. Open daily 8 a.m. to 8 p.m. mid-May through mid-Sept and 8 a.m. to 5 p.m. the rest of the year. $$–$$$; **free** for ages 5 and under.

One of the most popular tourist attractions in Wilmington is the USS *North Carolina*, located across the Cape Fear River just west of downtown. Known as "The Showboat," the battleship was commissioned in 1941, served in all 12 major Pacific naval campaigns in World War II, and earned 15 battle stars. It was the most powerful battleship in the world at the time. In 1961 the ship was carefully restored, and today it stands majestically as a memorial in honor of the nearly 10,000 North Carolinians who gave their lives during the war. Plan to spend at least 2 hours exploring the ship's 9 decks, including the mess deck and galley, sick bay, and engine room. The kids will be amazed at the size of the 16-inch guns that trim the deck. They certainly will want to take a peek through the captain's periscope for a view of downtown. A look at the barbershop and living quarters provides an interesting perspective on military life in the 1940s. Signs, pictures, and push-button tapes will guide you through the ship. A picnic area and snack bar are located nearby.

Wilmington Railroad Museum (ages 5 and up)

501 Nutt St.; (910) 763-2634; www.wilmingtonrailroadmuseum.org. Open 10 a.m. to 5 p.m. Mon through Sat and 1 to 5 p.m. Sun, Apr through Oct. Open 10 a.m. to 4 p.m. Mon through Sat the rest of the year. $–$$; **free** for children under age 2.

All aboard for the Wilmington Railroad Museum, where you'll find that the railroad is almost as important as the river is in this port town. The museum features dozens of exhibits from the railroads, dating back to 1840, and model railroad displays. You can board a steam locomotive and a caboose outside the museum. There's also an interactive children's Thomas the Tank Engine play area.

The Zebulon Latimer House (ages 5 and up)

126 S. 3rd St.; (910) 762-0492. Open 10 a.m. to 4 p.m. Mon through Fri and noon to 5 p.m. Sat. $; **free** for ages 5 and under.

The furniture in this 1852 home is the original furniture that belonged to this prominent merchant and his family. While it isn't the oldest home in the area, it is unique because of its Italianate Revival construction. The house is headquarters for the Lower Cape Fear Historical Society, which conducts tours of the homes in the historic district.

Where to Eat

Chris's Restaurant. 853 S. 17th St.; (910) 763-1791. Greek and Italian are on the menu here. $$

Elijah's. Located in Chandler's Wharf at 2 Ann St.; (910) 343-1448. This is one of Wilmington's better casual restaurants, featuring seafood and more standard American cuisine. $$

Paddy's Hollow. Located in the Cotton Exchange at 321 N. Front St.; (910) 762-4354; www.paddyshollow.com. With its cobblestone walk and antique brick, this friendly restaurant has more turn-of-the-20th-century atmosphere than you can imagine. $$

The Pilot House. Located in Chandler's Wharf at 2 Ann St.; (910) 343-0200; www.pilothouserest.com. This is another casual restaurant overlooking the Cape Fear River. It serves good Southern-style food. $$

Riverboat Landing. 2 Market St.; (910) 763-7227; www.riverboatlanding.com. Low-country and coastal cuisine are the specialties of the house. $$$$

The Salt Works. 6301 Oleander Dr.; (910) 350-0018. Burgers and great onion rings are popular mainstays here, but breakfast is pretty good, too. Cash only. $$

Where to Stay

You might find deciding where to stay in Wilmington a little more difficult than it is for the rest of the coast. There are simply a lot of choices. But skipping the chain hotels, here are a few possibilities:

The Carolinian Inn. 2916 Market St.; (800) 528-1234; www.thecarolinianinn.com. Featuring 60 rooms, this inn will provide a comfortable stay. $$$

Graystone Inn. 100 S. 3rd St.; (910) 763-2000; www.graystoneinn.com. One of the most highly recommended B&Bs in the city, the four-star inn welcomes children over the age of 12. $$$$

Hotel Tarrymore. 102 S. 2nd St.; (910) 763-3806. A boutique hotel, the Tarrymore offer suites in the heart of Wilmington's historic downtown. $$$$

River Suites. 224 S. Water St.; (910) 458-4297. Luxury condos are offered on the waterfront. $$$

For More Information

Wilmington/Cape Fear Coast Convention and Visitors Bureau. 505 Nutt St.; (877) 406-2356; www.capefearcoast.com.

Wrightsville Beach

Wrightsville Beach is a family community that has become a popular meeting place for reunions or extended-family vacations. It's quieter than most area beaches, and a beautiful 5-mile stretch of white beach has been well preserved. The area offers fine hotels, motels, apartments, and cottages. The village also offers a number of delightful restaurants and shops. Johnny Mercer's Pier and several marinas will give you the opportunity for fishing, but if you come here you'll probably be charmed into just relaxing.

Airlie Gardens (ages 5 and up)

300 Airlie Rd.; (910) 798-7700; www.airliegardens.org. Open 9 a.m. to 5 p.m. daily, with some extended hours for events and peak seasons. $; children ages 5 and younger get in free.

If you're heading from Wilmington to Wrightsville Beach, take an hour or so to visit Airlie Gardens, located just off US 74/76. The 5-mile scenic drive features extensive azalea and camellia plantings, truly a sight to behold during the month of April. It has a collection of more than 100,000 azaleas. The century-old garden features a variety of rare evergreen trees, stately live oaks, well-kept lawns, and lakes as you make your journey through the park. Formal gardens, sculptures, nature trails, and more await the visitor.

Where to Eat

Blockade Runner. 275 Waynick Blvd.; (910) 256-2251; www.blockade-runner.com. You can order off the menu, but the Blockade Runner is known for its buffets. $$

The Oceanic Restaurant. 703 S. Lumina Ave.; (910) 256-5551; www.oceanicrestaurant.com. Great views are afforded at this oceanfront restaurant. Prime rib and seafood are the specialties. $$

South Beach Grill. 100 S. Lumina Ave.; (910) 256-4646; www.southbeachgrillwb.com. Enjoy a great burger on the patio for lunch or visit in the evening for unique, eclectic, regional cuisine for dinner. $–$$

Where to Stay

Back on the beach in Wrightsville, your accommodation choice should probably be a cottage from one of the local Realtors:

Bryant Real Estate. 1001 Lumina Ave.; (910) 256-3764; www.bryantrealestate.com.

Holiday Vacations. 2002 Eastwood Rd.; (910) 256-2911; www.holidayvacations.com.

Intracoastal Realty. 605 Causeway Dr.; (800) 822-4588; www.intracoastalrealty.com.

Here are some other choices if you choose not to rent a cottage:

Blockade Runner Resort. 275 Waynick Blvd.; (800) 541-1161; www.blockade-runner.com. This popular resort has all waterfront rooms and several water activities on-site. $$$$

The Harbor Inn. 701 Causeway Dr.; (888) 507-9402; www.harborinnwb.com. Although it's not on the beach, this is a nice place with a pool, access to the beach, and a short dock for fishing or watching the boats come in. $$$

One South Lumina. 1 S. Lumina Ave.; (800) 421-3255; www.onesouthlumina.info. This beachfront hotel is within walking distance to stores and other amenities and offers large rooms and suites. $$$–$$$$

Station 1. 95 S. Lumina Ave.; (800) 635-1408; www.station1condos.com. Leasing a condo or town house here gives you access to tennis and basketball courts, a pool, and a barbecue pit. $$–$$$

Surf Suites. 711 S. Lumina Ave.; (910) 256-2275; www.surfsuites.com. All 46 rooms here have kitchens, and it's AAA approved. $$$$

Waterway Lodge. 7246 Wrightsville Ave.; (800) 677-3771; www.waterwaylodge .com. Bike rentals are available from this pet-friendly lodge. Rooms and condos are offered, and kids under 12 stay **free.** $$$$

For More Information

Wilmington/Cape Fear Coast Convention and Visitors Bureau. (800) 222-4757; www.capefearcoast.com.

Topsail Island

From Wilmington take US 17 north to Highway 50 to reach Topsail Island.

You'll find that the beaches on Topsail Island are still largely uncrowded, but you'll also discover many other fun things to do on this island, located midway between Jacksonville and Wilmington. The island got its name from merchant sailors who frequently saw pirates hiding in the marshes on the west side of the island. Tall foliage hid the ships, but the sailors could see the tops of the sails, hence the name Topsail (pronounced topsil) Island.

SURF CITY

Surf City is the commercial center of Topsail Island, but the beauty of the beaches has been well preserved. One of the last old-fashioned swing bridges in North Carolina will take you across the Intracoastal Waterway. Concerns about the bridge's safety have spurned talks of a new bridge in recent years.

The *Belle of Topsail* (all ages)
111 N. New River Dr.; (910) 328-1621. $$$–$$$$.

While the *Belle,* a replica of a 1880s riverboat, does dinner and sightseeing cruises, families will want to take the pirate cruise. Passengers aboard the *Belle* are headed out for a nice, quiet trip when they are met by mischievous swashbucklers aboard a pirate vessel. Older children have the option of heading out ahead of Mom and Dad on the pirate ship if they dare.

The Gift Basket

201 New River Dr.; (910) 328-1905.

Find an interesting blend of gifts, beach supplies, and other goodies here. You'll want to try one of the more than 30 flavors of fudge and a big glass of freshly squeezed lemonade. The shop also stocks a healthy supply of North Carolina–made products, from crafts to confections.

Where to Eat

Island Delights. 316 N. New River Dr.; (910) 328-1868; www.islanddelightssurfcity.com. Hamburgers, steaks, pitas, and a whole host of other dishes are offered here. $–$$$

Max's Pizza. 602 Roland Ave., #A; (910) 328-2158; www.maxspizza.com. We list Max's because it's usually easy to get everybody to go along with having pizza. $

Mollie's Casual Dining. 107 N. Shore Dr.; (910) 328-0505. For a casual dinner, breakfast, or lunch, head to Mollie's. $

Where to Stay

Here is a list of Surf City Realtors offering condo and cottage vacation rentals:

A Beach Place Realty. 203 S. Topsail Dr.; (910) 328-2522; www.abeachplace.com.

Bryson and Associates. 809 Roland Ave.; (800) 326-0747; www.brysontopsail.com.

Island Real Estate. 405 Roland Ave.; (800) 622-6886; www.topsailvacation.com.

Topsail Realty, Inc. 712 S. Anderson Blvd., Topsail Beach; (910) 328-5241; www.topsail realty.com.

Treasure Realty. 1950 Highway 172; (910) 327-4444; www.treasurerealty.com.

United Beach Rentals. 326 N. New River Dr.; (910) 328-6732; www.unitedbeachvaca tions.com.

TOPSAIL BEACH

Topsail Beach is the southernmost community on Topsail Island. It's accessible only from the north via Highway 50.

Topsail Beach is the least crowded area on the island, but there are two fishing piers and a quaint shopping district. Stop in at **Island Treasures,** a different sort of souvenir shop in a rustic building on the south end. It's a good place to browse for gifts or for the kids to pick up a game or water toy. The shop also features a Christmas corner and North Carolina art, pottery, and porcelain.

Karen Beasley Sea Turtle Rescue and Rehabilitation Center
(all ages)

822 Carolina Ave.; (910) 328-3377; www.seaturtlehospital.org. Open for visitors 2 to 4 p.m. Mon, Tues, and Thurs through Sat. **Free.** Donations are accepted, and the center conducts a turtle adoption program to raise funds.

While the mission of this rescue center and sea turtle hospital is to conserve and protect marine turtles by rescuing, rehabilitating, and releasing them back into the wild, part of that goal is public education about the endangered species. Visitors can see injured turtles and view occasional releases.

Topsail Island Missiles and More Museum (all ages)

720 Channel Blvd.; (910) 328-1038. Open 2 to 4 p.m. Tues and Thurs through Sat, Apr through Oct. **Free.**

In the community center you can visit the Topsail Island Museum where Operation Bumblebee, a US missile project from the 1940s, and the history of the island are explained.

Amazing
North Carolina Facts

In the 1940s Topsail Beach played a significant role in the origin of the US space program. Tall, white concrete structures, used as observation towers during Operation Bumblebee, still stand. Operation Bumblebee was a secret US Navy project that resulted in the development of the ramjet and technology that allowed human beings to break the sound barrier. These findings also led to the development of the US space program and other advances in technology. The former test launchpad has been converted into a patio, and in 1993 the building where the test rockets were assembled was converted into the town's community center and a museum.

Videotapes, operation displays, and World War II artifacts help depict this island's history, including Native American and pirate occupations.

Topsail Island Tours (all ages)
720 Channel Blvd.; (910) 546-8687; www.fishtopsail.com. $$$.

A Bubba Gump Kids Shrimp Tour, sightseeing cruises, and a buccaneer cruise all depart from here. Swimwear is suggested for the buccaneer cruise, since splashing water is part of the act.

Where to Eat

The Beach Shop and Grill. 701 S. Anderson Ave.; (910) 328-6501. This popular gathering spot is a great place to get a burger, hot dog, and orangeade to wash it all down. $

Breezeway Restaurant. 636 Channel Blvd.; (910) 328-7751; www.breezewaymotel.com. Breezeway offers mainly seafood but has other items as well. Check out the seafood lasagna. $$

Where to Stay

Breezeway Motel and Restaurant. 636 Channel Blvd.; (910) 328-7751; www.breezewaymotel.com. This is the home of the famous restaurant by the same name. $$

Sea Path Realty. 920 S. Anderson Ave.; (910) 328-4201; www.topsailcottages.com. Sea Path offers cottages and houses on the beach and canal. $$$$

Sea Vista Motel. 1521 Ocean Blvd.; (800) 732-8478; www.seavistamotel.com. Basic rooms and efficiencies are offered on the beach. $$$$

NORTH TOPSAIL BEACH

Head north from Surf City on Highway 210, and you'll find North Topsail Beach.

This community is noted for natural diversity. It was once a separate island, but time slowly turned the sea into land. Now you'll find picturesque marshes home to egrets, herons, and other graceful creatures, against a backdrop of dense maritime forests. Just minutes away are beautiful sand dunes and roomy beaches.

Where to Stay

Villa Capriani. 790 New River Inlet Rd.; (800) 934-2400. This is a picturesque facility, offering villas with an array of amenities. Several pools and tennis courts are on the premises. $$$$

For More Information

The Greater Topsail Area Chamber of Commerce & Tourism. (800) 626-2780; www.topsailcoc.com.

Pender United Tourism. (800) 626-2780; www.visitpender.com.

Jacksonville

From Sneads Ferry take Highway 172 north to Highway 24.

Bear Island and Hammocks Beach State Park
(ages 3 and up)

1572 Hammocks Beach Rd.; (910) 326-4881; www.ncparks.gov. Access via ferry from the dock off Highway 24, about 20 miles south of Jacksonville. Ferry leaves every half hour from 9:30 a.m. to 5:30 p.m. daily. $.

A short drive and ferry ride from Camp Lejeune is Bear Island and Hammocks Beach State Park. This isn't an expedition for softies. Bear Island's 892 acres constitute a naturally preserved area with huge shifting sand dunes, a maritime forest, and marshlands. A primitive family camping area is available, or you can bring supplies for a picnic and take a swim from the unspoiled beaches. If you want to take in the natural beauty of the island, the interpretive displays at the ferry dock will get you started on one of the nature trails.

Shrimp **Festival**

The town of Sneads Ferry, located on the mainland on Highway 172, is home to the annual **Sneads Ferry Shrimp Festival.** Since 1971 the community has sponsored this two-day event, usually held the second weekend in August. Here the whole family will enjoy a parade, carnival, arts and crafts, historical displays, and, of course, lots of fresh shrimp. Call (910) 327-4911 or log on to www.sneadsferryshrimpfestival.com for more information.

Camp Lejeune (all ages)

Jacksonville is home to Camp Lejeune, a 110,000-acre US Marine Corps base. There aren't any formal tourist attractions on the base, but you can get a glimpse of how the marines live and work by visiting the site. You'll need to present a valid driver's license, automobile registration, and proof of insurance at the information center on Highway 24 to be admitted onto the base. Make sure you take the kids to the **Beirut Memorial,** located just east of the camp on US 17. The large granite memorial was built in honor of the 273 American marines, sailors, and soldiers who were killed in the 1983 attack on the US barracks in Lebanon. Along Lejeune Boulevard, each Bradford pear tree represents the loss of one life from US involvement in Lebanon and in the 1983 US-led invasion of Grenada. Other points of interest are the **Onslow Vietnam Veterans Memorial** and the **Montford Point Marine Museum.** For more information about the base's self-guided tour, call (910) 451-7426.

Where to Stay

The Liberty Inn. 1723 Lejeune Blvd.; (910) 353-3336; www.libertyinnlejeune.com. This is a pretty inn and surprisingly inexpensive, with rooms and efficiencies plus the added bonus of a game room. $$

For More Information

Onslow County Tourism. (800) 932-2144; www.onslowcountytourism.com.

Pine Knoll Shores

Continue on Highway 24 to Highway 58 and cross Bogue Sound. This route delivers the family to another barrier island.

North Carolina Aquarium (all ages)

1 Roosevelt Dr.; (252) 247-4003; www.ncaquariums.com. **Open 9 a.m. to 5 p.m. daily; closed Thanksgiving, Christmas, and New Year's Day. $$; free for children under 6.**

At the aquarium you'll dive deep into a sea of exhibits, programs, and a live, hands-on display. Exhibits take guests through an exhibit storyline that begins in the mountains and ends in the open ocean. This aquarium features live loggerhead turtles, colorful fish tanks, and an open tank where the kids can pick up crabs and other sea creatures. It's okay— they won't hurt you. The aquarium also sponsors presentations on-site and at various locations throughout the area. In the *Living Shipwreck* exhibit, divers answer questions. Visitors get a chance to meet ocean creatures, alligators, and others face to face. Outside, the aquarium has 2 nature trails, a marsh overlook where you can bird-watch, a fossil hunt, a beautiful bronze sculpture, and a reflecting pool.

Theodore Roosevelt Natural Area (ages 3 and up)

1 Roosevelt Dr. **Open 9 a.m. to 5 p.m. Mon through Sat and 1 to 5 p.m. Sun. Free.**

This small community, a long slender island, is home to the Theodore Roosevelt Natural Area and the North Carolina Aquarium, one of three located along North Carolina's coast. The area is dedicated primarily to preservation, but you'll also find a hiking trail and observation towers.

Where to Stay

Atlantis Lodge. 123 Salter Path Rd.; (800) 682-7057; www.atlantislodge.com. Oceanfront suites with efficiency kitchens are offered at the pet-friendly location. It includes a waterfall pool and lounge with pool and table tennis. $$

Atlantic Beach

From Pine Knoll Shores take Highway 58 to Atlantic Beach.

Atlantic Beach is a little more popular than some of the other beach communities on the Southern Coast. It's a good central location for active families looking to fill their vacation with day trips and other adventures. Atlantic Beach is host to a sand-sculpture contest, usually held the first weekend in May, and the Carolina Kite Fest in October.

Fort Macon State Park (ages 3 and up)

Located at the east end of Highway 58; (252) 726-3775; www.ncparks.gov. The park, including picnic facilities and bathhouse, is open generally during daylight hours. Free.

Fort Macon State Park is one of the most popular attractions here. The fort is a massive, 5-sided fortress constructed in 1826 to protect the region against foreign attacks. It was seized from Union forces at the start of the Civil War and changed hands several times over the course of the war. Fort Macon served as a federal prison for nearly a decade after the Civil War and was garrisoned for use during World War II. Rangers present programs on a daily basis during vacation seasons, including a deafening musket-firing demonstration. They also conduct tours of the fort, or you can tour it yourself with the help of push-button tapes and mannequin displays. Some parts of the fort, including the commandant's quarters, have been restored to their wartime condition.

Where to Stay

Here are Atlantic Beach's larger realty companies:

Atlantic Beach Realty/Ocean Resorts. 407 Causeway Rd.; (877) 733-9570; www .atlanticbeachrealty.net.

Atlantic Sun Properties. 205 Atlantic Beach Causeway; (252) 808-2786; www .atlanticsunproperties.com.

Beach Vacation Properties. 301 Commerce Way; (800) 334-2667; www.beach vacationproperties.com.

Bluewater GMAC Vacation Rentals. 610 Atlantic Beach Causeway; (866) 348-8975; www.bluewater.com.

Cannon & Gruber Realtors. 509 Atlantic Beach Causeway; (800) 317-2866; www.cannongruber.com.

Coldwell-Banker Spectrum Properties. 555 Atlantic Beach Causeway; (800) 334-6390; www.spectrumproperties.com.

Realty World First Coast Realty. 407 Atlantic Beach Causeway; (800) 972-8899; www.realtyworldfirstcoast.com.

Sufside Realty. 204 Sandpiper Dr.; (252) 726-0950; www.surfsiderealty.com.

Your other choices, if you choose not to rent, include:

Atlantic Beach Villas. 715 W. Fort Macon Rd.; (800) 438-6493. One- to three-bedroom condos with both indoor and outdoor pools, a private boardwalk to the beach, and recreation room are offered here. $$$

Bogue Shores Suites. 1918 W. Fort Macon Rd.; (800) 613-5043. Bogue Shores Suites is located soundside and will accommodate small families. $$$

Oceanana Family Resort. 700 E. Fort Macon Rd.; (252) 726-4111; www.oceana-resort.com. More homey than fancy, the resort features two- and three-bedroom apartments, a **free** breakfast of fruit and pastries served by the pool daily, and occasional watermelon parties. You can relax on the oceanfront lawn while the kids play on the playground. $$$

Seahawk Motor Lodge. 105 Salter Path Rd.; (800) 682-6898; www.seahawk-villas.com. This is a small, very nice facility with rooms, cottages, and horseback-riding packages. $$$

Morehead City

Just north of Atlantic Beach, across the bridge on US 70 on the mainland, is Morehead City, a beautiful coastal town with ample dining and shopping offerings.

The History Place (ages 5 and up)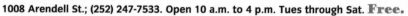
1008 Arendell St.; (252) 247-7533. Open 10 a.m. to 4 p.m. Tues through Sat. Free.

The museum is a potpourri of changing exhibits, ranging from native artifacts to vintage clothing to war items to shells. Most of its collections deal with Native Americans who once lived here and the area's connection to the Civil War.

The Morehead Center for Performing Arts (all ages)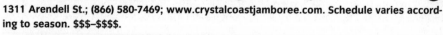
1311 Arendell St.; (866) 580-7469; www.crystalcoastjamboree.com. Schedule varies according to season. $$$–$$$$.

This theater presents a variety of fun, with Vegas-style variety shows appropriate for the entire family. Song, dance, and performance from various eras and genres create a show and atmosphere that's fun for everyone. There's even a weekly magic show and regular laser light shows.

Seafood **Galore**

The lovely waterfront community of Morehead City is the host of the **North Carolina Seafood Festival,** held the first weekend in October. Here you'll be treated to seafood galore and can enjoy the flounder-flinging contest, as well as live entertainment and plenty of games and activities for the kids. Activities are held mainly on the waterfront, but the county abounds with events, including sailboat and road races, and tennis and golf tournaments. Call (252) 726-6273 or log on to www.ncseafoodfestival.org for more information.

Where to Eat

Mrs. Willis' Restaurant and Lounge. 3002 Bridges St.; (252) 726-3741. This is an old local favorite, with lots of homemade specialties served in a rustic atmosphere. $

Sanitary Fish Market and Restaurant. 501 Evans St.; (252) 247-3111; www.sanitaryfishmarket.com. Not all seafood places serve it as fresh as they do at this outstanding establishment that is famous for its hush puppies. $$$

Where to Stay

Morehead City is a great town for day trips while staying on the nearby coast.

Accommodations at Atlantic Beach are more likely to suit families, but if you prefer more picturesque, quiet surroundings, try:

Buccaneer Inn. 2806 Arendell St.; (800) 682-4982. The Buccaneer has simple but well-kept accommodations that are more affordable than many properties in the area.

For More Information

Carteret County Tourism Authority. (800) 786-6962; www.crystalcoastnc.org.

Beaufort

US 70 crosses the Beaufort Inlet from Morehead City to Beaufort, one of North Carolina's oldest towns, dating back to the late 1600s.

Beaufort Historic Site (all ages)
138 Turner St.; (252) 728-5225; www.beauforthistoricsite.org. Guided tours are held at 10 and 11:30 a.m. and at 1 and 3 p.m. Mon through Sat. $–$$; children under 6 are free.

If you can't catch a bus tour, guided tours and living-history demonstrations are offered at the Beaufort Historic Site. You'll see weavers working on antique looms and more. The site includes 4 homes built around the turn of the 19th century: The courthouse was built in 1796; the county jail was built in 1829; and the apothecary and doctor's office were built about 1859 and remained in use until as late as 1933. About 100 buildings in a 12-block area have been totally restored, and you'll see many authentic pieces of furniture and tools used at the time.

Carrot Island Ferry Adventures (ages 5 and up)

Located on Orange Street; (252) 728-7555. Ferries leave every 30 minutes from 9 a.m. to 5 p.m. daily. $–$$.

Sometimes you can see the wild ponies of Carrot Island and Shackelford Banks grazing the shoreline from the Beaufort waterfront, but for a better look and to learn more, you'll want to catch the ferry from Harpoon Willie's on Orange Street. Not only will you see the ponies, but you can also swim in the crystal-clear waters and hunt for shells along the white, sandy beach. The Rachel Carson Estuarine Reserve, which spans this chain of islands, offers occasional 2.5-hour guided tours, including a Kid's Island Adventure. These point out various aspects of nature and maritime heritage and are conducted in addition to the ferry trips.

Historic Beaufort (ages 5 and up)

Bus trips depart from Beaufort Historic Site, 138 Turner St.; (252) 728-5225; www.historic beaufort.com. Tours are at 11 a.m. and 1:30 p.m. Mon, Wed, and Fri and 11 a.m. Sat, Apr through Oct. $$.

You'll want to spend some leisurely hours strolling the boardwalk in this picturesque waterfront town, or catch the big red double-decker bus for a tour of Historic Beaufort-by-the-Sea. Historic Beaufort Bus Tours will take you on a 1-hour tour of North Carolina's third-oldest town, narrated by a guide dressed in 18th-century clothes.

North Carolina Maritime Museum (ages 3 and up)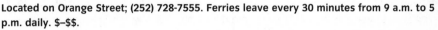

315 Front St.; (252) 728-7317; www.ncmartimemuseums.com. Open 9 a.m. to 5 p.m. Mon through Fri, 10 a.m. to 5 p.m. Sat, and 1 to 5 p.m. Sun; closed New Year's Day, Thanksgiving, and Christmas. Free.

The skills of the seafarers of yesteryear come alive at the North Carolina Maritime Museum. The museum features full-size watercraft and displays that help you discover many of the mysteries of the sea. The museum is a repository for the *Queen Anne's Revenge,* which scientists have confirmed was the ship of the famed Blackbeard, who ran aground here in 1718. Artifacts, recovered from 25 feet of water by state underwater archaeologists with the aid of the museum, are being housed and conserved and prepared for exhibit here. At the **Harvey W. Watercraft Center,** located across the street, you can see how these wooden boats were made as skilled craftspeople construct them in front of you. The museum also sponsors special programs throughout the year, including the *Strange Seafood* exhibition and trips on a research vessel, where you can actually help collect and identify marine life. No admission is charged to the museum, but call ahead for information on special events and trips.

Cedar Island

The ferry to the Outer Banks leaves from the town of Cedar Island on the island of the same name. (It's about a 45-minute drive from Beaufort to Cedar Island. Take US 70 north to Highway 12, which crosses a bridge onto the island.) You'll want to be sure to call ahead and make reservations for this and all other toll ferries you plan to use. Reservations can be made up to 30 days in advance. For a complete ferry schedule or to make reservations, call (800) 773-1094. If you don't make reservations, the wait can be hours long. The trip to the Outer Banks is more than two hours, so be sure to have something for the kids to do.

Outer Banks/Cedar Island Stables (all ages)
120 Driftwood Dr.; (252) 225-1185. $$$$.

If you have some time before you hop the ferry, you can spend it on horseback before you leave. The Outer Banks/Cedar Island Stables offer horseback rides for children and adults, both experts and novices. Experienced parents can lead their children on a half-hour beach ride.

Havelock

Heading back to the west from Beaufort on Highway 101, you come to Havelock.

Croatan National Forest (ages 5 and up)
Off US 70; (252) 638-5628; www.fs.usda.gov. Sites and trails in the forest are generally open during daylight hours Apr through Oct. All facilities are free except camping sites ($).

Havelock is home to Cherry Point Marine Corps Air Station and is largely a retirement community. But you'll also find the 157,000-acre national forest bordering the Neuse River, which is home to deer, black bears, eagles, the endangered red-cockaded woodpecker, and a host of other creatures. The forest has a nice family campground, and you can hike, fish, and swim here. It's also home to the carnivorous Venus flytrap and several other rare plants.

Kenansville

Traveling from Havelock to Kenansville takes about two hours via US 17 from either Highway 58 or US 70. Take US 17 to Jacksonville and then US 258 to Highway 24 and head west.

Kenansville is located west of the Croatan National Forest in North Carolina's heartland, which includes more farmland than anything else.

Other Things to See & Do
on the Southern Coast

- **Blackbeard's Lair.** Surf City; (252) 328-4200
- **Carolina Beach Jungle Mini-Golf and Batting Cages.** Carolina Beach; (910) 458-8888
- **Eternal Riverview Stables.** Morehead City; (252) 726-8513
- **Jungle Rapids.** Wrightsville Beach; (910) 791-0666; www.junglerapids.com
- **Lynnwood Park Zoo.** Jacksonville; (910) 938-5848; www.lynwoodparkzoo .com
- **Patio Playground.** Topsail Island; (910) 328-6491
- **Professor Hackers Lost Treasure Golf & Raceway.** Atlantic Beach; (252) 247-3024; www.losttreasuregolf.com
- **Climb On.** Wilmington; (910) 612-5352
- **Springbrook Farms Trolley and Carriage Tours.** Wilmington; (910) 251-8889; www.horsedrawntours.com
- **Thailan Hall.** Wilmington; (910) 343-3664; www.thailanhall.org
- **Wilmington Ice House.** Wilmington; (910) 686-1987; www.wilmingtonice.com

Cowan Museum (ages 5 and up)

411 S. Main St.; (910) 296-2149; www.cowanmuseum.com. Open 10 a.m. to 4 p.m. Tues through Sat and 2 to 4 p.m. Sun. **Free.**

You won't find a lot to do between Havelock and the small town of Kenansville, but the Cowan Museum makes for a good stop while you're on the road. Built in 1848, the museum offers an interesting perspective on early American life. Hundreds of items, from tools to sewing machines, fill the museum's displays. Also on the grounds are a classic one-room schoolhouse and a blacksmith's shop.

Liberty Hall (ages 5 and up)

409 S. Main St.; (910) 296-2175. Interpreters provide guided tours of the grounds 10 a.m. to 4 p.m. Tues through Sat and 2 to 4 p.m. Sun. $; children age 5 and under get in **free.**

Also on Highway 24 you'll find Liberty Hall, a plantation built for the Kenan family in the early 1800s. Here you can explore the main house, a restored example of antebellum architecture, where you will see 2 dining rooms (one for winter, one for summer), a wine cellar, and bedrooms, all of which have been fully furnished. You can also see the attached kitchen, carriage house, and smokehouse.

The Northern Coast

N orth Carolina's Northern Coast offers much more than the thrill of riding waves in the surf, an abundance of sunshine, and all the other amenities that come with a beach vacation. Here you'll also find rich history, intertwined with the present. The inland towns offer tours of majestic old homes and museums, while area islands offer evidence of the early settlers' trials as they first began to settle the mysterious New World. At the turn of the 20th century, coastal winds lured two brothers from Ohio to learn to fly. They are memorialized in Hatteras.

Jim's TopPicks on the Northern Coast

1. Cape Hatteras Lighthouse, Buxton

2. Wright Brothers National Memorial, Kill Devil Hills

3. Jockey's Ridge State Park, Nags Head

4. *The Lost Colony,* Manteo

5. *Elizabeth II* State Historic Site, Manteo

6. Wild mustangs of Corolla

7. North Carolina Aquarium on Roanoke Island

8. Ferry rides

9. Nags Head Pier fishing

10. Cruising Highway 12

THE NORTHERN COAST

But don't forget to take advantage of the area's natural offerings. In the Outer Banks the land works in fragile balance with the sea. That sometimes angry sea once threatened America's tallest lighthouse in this land of lighthouses. There is also much to learn about the ocean and the creatures that live in and around it. You'll find ample opportunity to observe nature and interact with it through fishing and the educational programs available along the coast.

From Raleigh, US 64 is the easiest and most direct route to the Manteo and Nags Head areas. US 264 presents a little different picture from the car window and is a more direct route to the Ocracoke area. Once here, navigation won't likely be much of a problem. US 17 runs the length of the coastal plain inland. Highway 12 runs through the 75 miles of Cape Hatteras National Seashore, which includes Ocracoke, Hatteras, and Bodie Islands.

Kinston

Starting in the southern part of the Northern Coast region, at the intersection of US 17 and US 258, find the city of Kinston, on the banks of the Neuse River, the longest river contained entirely in the state of North Carolina.

Caswell No. 1 Fire Station Museum (all ages)

118 S. Queen St.; (252) 522-4676. Open 10 a.m. to 4 p.m. Tues, Thurs, and Sat. Free.

In 1895 a fire nearly destroyed downtown Kinston, so the city responded by building this fire station. It's now a museum that includes a 1922 American LeFrance Pumper and a collection of helmets, nozzles, ladders, fire extinguishers, and other memorabilia. The station is the oldest brick building in Kinston.

CSS *Neuse* State Historic Site (ages 3 and up)

2612 W. Vernon Ave. (US 70 Business); (252) 522-2091; www.nchistoricsites.com. Open 9 a.m. to 5 p.m. Tues through Sat. Free.

Part of North Carolina's Civil War heritage is told in Kinston, even though it's less than a heroic epic. In Kinston you will find the CSS *Neuse* State Historic Site. The *Neuse,* known as "the gunboat," is a 158-foot ironclad ship that looks somewhat like a river barge. The Confederate Navy began construction of the boat in 1862, but it would never be completed. In March 1865 the Confederacy launched the boat in a hasty attempt to improve its faltering chances in the Civil War, but on March 12 the crew set fire to the ship and sank it to keep it from being captured by the enemy. A museum has been created on the grounds where the boat rests to tell about its history and the role this river town played in the Civil War. The museum includes a slide show and artifacts from the vessel.

Also on the site is the **Governor Caswell Memorial,** dedicated to Richard Caswell, the first governor of the independent state of North Carolina. He served in that post for six years and headed the committee that wrote the state constitution. You can see a sound and light show depicting the governor's life and visit his grave at the site.

CSS *Neuse II* (all ages)

Corner of Heritage and Gordon Streets; (252) 560-2150; www.cssneusefoundation.com. Open 9 a.m. to 2 p.m. Mon through Fri, 9 a.m. to 5 p.m. Sat, and 1 to 5 p.m. Sun. Free.

The CSS *Neuse* Foundation built this replica of the *Neuse* to illustrate what a sailor's life was like during the Civil War. It rests on a grassy lawn near downtown. The foundation representatives who led fund-raising efforts to build it say it is the only full-sized Civil War ironclad replica in the country.

The Exchange Nature Center (all ages)

401 W. Caswell St.; (252) 939-3367; www.neusewaypark.com. Open 9:30 a.m. to 5 p.m. Tues through Sat and 1 to 5 p.m. Sun. Free.

In addition to wildlife exhibits, this facility includes a fishing pond with piers and canoe rentals. There's also a campground with RV and tent sites. It's also part of Neuseway Park.

Health & Science Museum (all ages)

403 W. Caswell St.; (252) 939-3302; www.neusewaypark.com. Open 9:30 a.m. to 5 p.m. Tues through Sat and 1 to 5 p.m. Sun. Free.

Kinston's Health & Science Museum at Neuseway Park includes a small planetarium as well as science exhibits. A giant Operation game (you remember the guy with the red lightbulb nose, don't you?), a kid-size replica of Lenoir Memorial Hospital, and giant replicas of the mouth, stomach, and intestines, big enough to crawl through, aim to teach kids about health. Other exhibits such as a bubble machine and giant pendulum give insight into physics.

Where to Eat

Kings Restaurant. 405 E. New Bern Rd.; (252) 527-2101; www.kingsbbq.com. Kings is one of the oldest and arguably one of the best barbecue places in the state. $

Where to Stay

West Parke Inn & Suites. 4774 US 70 West; (252) 527-1500. The West Parke has a heated pool and offers a continental breakfast. $$$

For More Information

Kinston Convention and Visitors Bureau. (800) 869-0032; www.visitkinston .com.

Kinston-Lenoir County Chamber of Commerce. (252) 527-1131; www.kinston chamber.com.

New Bern

East of Kinston on US 70 at the junction with US 17 is where you'll find New Bern.

New Bern is the picture of Southern hospitality, located on the scenic Trent and Neuse Rivers. Settled in 1710 by German and Swiss colonists, it is North Carolina's second-oldest city and the state's first capital.

A Day at the Farm (all ages)

183 Woodrow McCoy Rd., Cove City; (252) 514-9494; www.adayatthefarm.com. Open seasonally. Fees charged for various activities.

This historic dairy farm comes complete with old dairy barns, milking equipment, and period antiques. If it's fall, check out the pumpkin patch. Other times of the year, visit the peanut patch, fish and duck pond, farm animals, and the playground, or take a hayride.

Firemen's Museum (ages 5 and up)

410 Hancock St.; (252) 636-4087. Open 10 a.m. to 4 p.m. Mon through Sat. $.

The Firemen's Museum features Civil War relics in addition to an extensive collection of early firefighting equipment. Original photographs have been preserved for the museum's displays, and you also will be able to view old steam pumpers and other firefighting equipment used in the 19th century.

Tryon Palace Historic Site and Gardens (ages 5 and up)

610 Pollock St.; (800) 767-1560; www.tryonpalace.org. Open 9 a.m. to 5 p.m. Mon through Sat and 1 to 5 p.m. Sun. Two-and-a-half-hour tours begin every half hour. $$–$$$.

The city of New Bern features more than 150 historic landmarks, including Tryon Palace Historic Site and Gardens. Guided tours of the luxurious restored home of British Royal Governor William Tryon, built in 1770, are available from costumed guides. The palace you see today is a replica of the original, which burned in 1798. You and your children not only will see the antiques and furniture that adorn the home but also will enjoy the demonstrations of cloth making, candle making, blacksmithing, and more.

Also part of the complex is the **Dixon-Stevenson House,** built in 1828 and decorated with furniture and antiques from the Federal and Empire periods. The **John Wright Stanly House,** built in 1783, also is part of the complex. The home has been furnished with pieces from that period, and the gardens have been designed like 18th-century English

Amazing
North Carolina Facts

Caleb Bradham invented Pepsi-Cola in 1898 at his pharmacy located at 256 Middle St. in New Bern. The pharmacy has been turned into a museum of sorts, with a video about the history of Pepsi and memorabilia. You can also purchase Pepsi collectibles here. For more information call (252) 636-5898 or log on to www.pepsistore.com.

gardens. The **NC History Center at Tryon Palace** includes interactive experiences and rotating exhibits. This innovative experience transports visitors to the 19th century, where they can sail a ship or distill turpentine. Take a trolley tour ($$–$$$) of New Bern's Historic District from Tryon Palace for an additional fee, or you can get a **free** walking map here and continue to explore the city on your own.

Where to Eat

The Chelsea Restaurant. 335 Middle St.; (252) 637-5469; www.thechelsea.com. The Chelsea building was initially used by Caleb Bradham, inventor of Pepsi-Cola, as his second drugstore. $$

Cow Cafe. 319 Middle St.; (252) 672-9269; www.cowcafe.com. Ice cream is made on the premises, plus the kids can play in the barnyard and meet MooAnnie, who plays the keyboard. $

Where to Stay

Many of the accommodations in New Bern are B&Bs geared toward couples. You'll also find a few chain franchises, and a couple other choices.

BridgePointe Hotel & Marina. 101 Howell Rd.; (877) 283-7713; www.bridgepointehotel.com. Located on the Neuse and Trent Rivers across from Historic Downtown New Bern, the BridgePointe is near all the local attractions. $$$

Vacation Resorts International. 1141 Broad Creek Rd.; (800) 625-4874; www.vrivacations.com. This organization offers 120 waterfront condos with a lot of amenities, such as golf and tennis privileges, bike rentals, and a playground on premises. $$$$

Aurora

From New Bern take Highway 55 east to Highway 306 and head north to the small town of Aurora.

Aurora Fossil Museum (ages 3 and up)

400 Main St.; (252) 322-4238; www.aurorafossilmuseum.com. Summer hours are 9 a.m. to 4:30 p.m. Mon through Sat and 1:30 to 4:30 p.m. Sun. Free.

This museum tells the story of the coastal plain from the birth of the Atlantic Ocean to the present and features an unusual exhibit of life in the ocean 15 million years ago. Here you can view dozens of fossils from the Miocene and Pliocene epochs and even give fossil finding a shot yourself at a mound across the street at the Pit of the Pungo. It's restocked periodically with donated soil that contains real fossils.

For More Information

Craven County Convention & Visitors Bureau. (800) 437-5767; www.visitnewbern.com.

Greenville

At Aurora, Highway 306 merges with Highway 33, which will take you west to Greenville, one of the largest cities in the coastal region.

Here you will find plenty to do, whether your family is into the arts, history, or the outdoors. In Pitt County, discover more than 20 parks, 6 art galleries, a number of museums, and dozens of points of historical interest. Greenville is also the home of **East Carolina University,** one of the state's larger universities, that includes a spectacular historic district and typical college town offerings.

Greenville Museum of Art (ages 5 and up)

802 S. Evans St.; (252) 758-1946; www.gmoa.org. Open 10 a.m. to 4:30 p.m. Tues through Fri and 1 to 4 p.m. Sat and Sun. Free.

The Greenville Museum of Art holds permanent collections and maintains space for traveling exhibitions. The Commons Gallery features works of North Carolina artists, which make up about half of the museum's collection. The Francis Speight and Sarah Blakeslee Gallery is a permanent exhibition of works by the two who called Greenville home. In the Look & Learn Gallery, two- and three-dimensional art from the museum's Education Collection engage young visitors in various activities.

River Park North (all ages)

1000 Mumford Rd.; (252) 329-5461; www.greenville.nc.gov. Generally open during daylight hours. Free.

The city of Greenville's River Park North on the Tar River is one of the nicest facilities of its kind. Here you can fish, hike, and picnic year-round, and paddleboats are available on Saturday and Sunday when the weather is nice. You can also borrow a rod and reel here.

The Walter L. Stasavich Science and Nature Center (all ages)

1000 Mumford Rd.; (252) 329-4560. Open 9:30 a.m. to 5 p.m. Tues through Sat and 1 to 5 p.m. Sun. $.

River Park North is also home to another museum, the Walter L. Stasavich Science and Nature Center. Here the kids will love looking at the displays of African animals, colorful butterflies, and huge mammals. The live reptile display and turtle touch tank are also big draws.

Where to Eat

B's Barbecue. 751 B's Barbecue Rd. This restaurant near the university is so popular, so well known, so extraordinary, it doesn't even have a website or published phone number. $

Chico's Mexican Restaurant. 521 Cotanche St.; (252) 757-1666; www.chicos restaurant.com. This is a fun Mexican restaurant near East Carolina University. There is great selection on both the adult and children's menus. $

Trio. 22 N. Main St.; (864) 467-1000; www
.triocafe.com. Brick-oven pizzas and other
Italian fare are served at Trio. $$

Where to Stay

If you aren't headed to the beach, Greenville
is a good central location from which to
explore this area, especially the aspects that
relate to history. Here are a couple choices
for accommodations; unfortunately, neither
has a pool, which you have to go to the larger
places to find.

City Hotel and Bistro. 203 SW Greenville
Blvd.; (252) 355-8300; www.cityhoteland

bistro.com. This beautiful, well-appointed
hotel is located close to Eastern Carolina Uni-
versity. $$$

East Carolina Inn. 3900 Stantonsburg Rd.;
(252) 752-2122; www.eastcarolinainn.net.
This inn offers nice accommodations but limited amenities. $

For More Information

**Greenville–Pitt County Convention &
Visitors Bureau.** (800) 537-5564; www.visit
greenvillenc.com.

Washington

From Greenville catch US 264 east to the city of Washington.

"The Original Washington," named in 1775 for the George who would become the first
president of the US in 1789, might prove the perfect quiet stopping point before or after a
trip to the beach. Many of the buildings on the waterfront have been renovated but aren't
open to the public. A number of them have been converted into shops and restaurants
if you're interested in a quiet day of shopping. The city of Washington provides a map of
its historic district for walking tours. Pick one up at the visitor center, 138 S. Market St.
(252-948-9415).

North Carolina Estuarium (all ages)

223 E. Water St.; (252) 948-0000; www.partnershipforthesounds.org. **Open 10 a.m. to 4 p.m.
Tues through Sat. $.**

Hundreds of artifacts, dioramas, artwork, and historical and audiovisual displays tell the
story of the estuaries and detail some of the threats to coastal waterways and surrounding land. Aquariums and terrariums include live specimens. A short pontoon boat tour is
also available.

Whichard's Beach Marina Campground (all ages)

3660 Whichard Beach Rd.; (252) 946-0011.

While many of the bed-and-breakfast inns here have minimum age requirements for
children, Whichard's Beach Marina Campground offers adventure for the whole family.
Located a mile south of town on US 17 along the Pamlico River, the campground offers
beaches, a marina, a game room, a waterslide, and more. $

Where to Eat

Pia's of Washington. 156 W. Main St.;
(252) 940-0600; www.chefpias.com. Mediterranean cuisine tops the menu here. There
are plenty of choices for kids on and off the
children's menu. $$$

Where to Stay

**Tranters Creek Resort and Camp-
ground.** 6573 Clarks Neck Rd.; (252)
948-0850; www.tranterscreekresort.com.
Located on the waterfront, Tranters offers
campsites, creekside cabins, and lots of
family-oriented amenities. $–$$

For More Information

Washington Visitor Center. 138 S. Market
St.; (800) 546-0162; www.visitwashingtonnc
.com.

Bath

Bath is just a few miles east of Washington on Highway 92.

Goose Creek State Park (all ages)

2190 Camp Leach Rd.; (252) 923-2191; www.ncparks.gov. **Typically open during daylight
hours.** Free; **fees charged for primitive campsites.**

Giant oak trees draped in Spanish moss stand in blackwater marshes of the Pamlico River
at Goose Creek State Park. Bald cypress and ash grow up to 90 feet in this pristine part of
the region. It's a fantastic place to explore nature, discover wildlife, and learn about the
swamp. A sandy beach is located on the river where swimming is permitted. There are no
boat rentals here, but the area is a popular place to paddle. Two boardwalks let you actually walk out into the swamp and marsh.

Historic Bath (ages 5 and up)

207 Carteret St.; (252) 923-3971; www.nchistoricsites.org. **Open 9 a.m. to 5 p.m. Tues
through Sat. $.**

If you tell the kids Blackbeard once lived here, you probably won't have a problem getting them to Bath. This is North Carolina's first town, settled in the late 17th century and
incorporated in 1705. Here you can tour the **Palmer-Marsh House,** which features one
of Santa Claus's favorite stopping points—a 17-foot-wide chimney. The **Van Der Veer
House,** built in 1795, features a gambrel roof and houses trinkets and other items that
highlight the town's three centuries of history. **Saint Thomas Church,** the oldest church
in North Carolina, is also part of the historic district. It has walls that are more than 2
feet thick. A nice place for a picnic is on the waterfront, located nearby on Front Street.
The **Bonner House**—nestled among elm, walnut, cedar, and dogwood trees—is one of
the best remaining examples of early 19th-century Carolina architecture and is available
to tour. From the front of this home is a view of Plum Point, where the notorious pirate
Edward Teach, known better as Blackbeard, lived.

Belhaven

To reach Belhaven from Bath, head east on Highway 99.

Belhaven Memorial Museum (ages 3 and up)
211 E. Main St.; (252) 943-2357. Open 1 to 5 p.m. daily except Wed. **Free.**

Do your kids collect things? If they do, they will get a kick out of the Belhaven Memorial Museum. Located in Belhaven city hall, this museum grew out of a collection begun by Mrs. Eva Blount Way at the turn of the 20th century. It started with her collection of 30,000 buttons but has grown to include wonderful and whimsical coins, shells, war memorabilia, tools, and more. There is also a handful of bizarre items on display, including mummified and preserved animals.

Where to Eat

Back Bay Cafe. 413 Pamlico St.; (252) 944-2870. Back Bay serves salads, sandwiches, and soups with a European twist. $

Swan Quarter

Continuing east from Belhaven on US 264 takes you to Swan Quarter.

Swan Quarter Wildlife Refuge (all ages)
38 Mattamuskeet Rd., Highway 94; (252) 926-4021; www.fws.gov/swanquarter. Open year-round during daylight hours. **Free.**

This refuge consists of 16,500 acres of salt marsh and woodlands bordering Pamlico Sound. Fishing is allowed at Bell Island from a 1,100-foot pier, but you and the kids might be more interested in just sitting back and watching. The refuge is host to a number of migratory birds, including terns, black ducks, brown pelicans, and loons.

Mattamuskeet National Wildlife Refuge (all ages)
Highway 94, Swan Quarter; (252) 926-4021; www.fws.gov/mattamuskeet. Generally open during daylight hours. **Free.**

A more popular stopping point is the Mattamuskeet National Wildlife Refuge, farther east on US 264 near Engelhard. The 50,000-acre refuge includes **Lake Mattamuskeet,** the largest natural lake in North Carolina. It is 18 miles long and 5 to 6 miles wide but averages only 2 feet (a swan's neck) in depth. The refuge provides protection for migratory birds, such as ducks, geese, tundra swans, and occasionally a bald eagle. Fishing and crabbing are allowed at the lake and adjacent canals during the spring, summer, and fall. During the winter the refuge is home to birds that migrate from as far away as Canada.

Ocracoke

Now we'll jump across Pamlico Sound to the Outer Banks, starting with **Ocracoke Island.**

You can get to the village of Ocracoke by ferry from Swan Quarter or Cedar Island. The crossing time is more than two hours, and the cost is $10 for the average vehicle. Reservations are highly recommended; without them waits can be very long.

At Ocracoke, Highway 12 runs up the length of the island. Although it is quiet in Ocracoke, your family will love this charming village on the southern tip of the island. The island, 16 miles long, is home to just 700 people, many of whom still carry an Elizabethan accent, in terms like "hoigh toid" for "high tide." It is so charming here, in fact, it barely seems to change from visit to visit. Ocracoke has been named America's Best Beach in the annual survey by Dr. Beach.

By the time you get to **Ocracoke Village,** you'll find the narrow streets—lined with countless shops, ice-cream stands, restaurants, and inns—fairly crowded during the summer months. But don't worry about the crowds; you'll find plenty of room to stretch out north of the village. Before arriving in Ocracoke, get a walking map, available on the ferries and at the **National Park Service Visitor Centers** located at the ferry docks. Find a place to park and start exploring. Staying longer than a day, you'll find more than a dozen hotels, several bed-and-breakfast inns, and rental cottages that are available.

Banker Ponies (all ages)

North of Ocracoke Village on Highway 12 are the Banker Ponies. These small horses ran wild on the island until the late 1950s, when they were penned at their current home. The ponies are descendants of horses brought to the New World by Spanish explorers as early as the 16th century and can be viewed and photographed from an observation deck just off the highway.

Ferries

Reservations for toll ferries are recommended and can be made up to 30 days in advance. For a complete ferry schedule or to make reservations, call (800) 773-1094. Also find details at www.ncdot.gov. The ferries on longer routes such as these are fairly comfortable and include air-conditioned lounges, complete with snack machines. The kids will probably want to spend some time on the sundeck to take in spectacular views of the islands and the shrimpers who will be hard at work.

Bikes, Tours & **More**

A fun way to see the village and most of the island is by bicycle. **The Slushy Stand** (252-928-1878), on the corner of Highway 12 and Silver Lake Road, provides more than just a quick snack. Here you can rent bikes for adults and children ($–$$$). If you're ready to hit the beach, you can also rent umbrellas, chairs, and boogie boards. You can also call **Ride the Wind Surf Shop** (252-928-6311; www.surfocracoke.com) or **Restless Native Boat Rentals** (252-928-1421). **Austin Boat Tours** (252-928-4361) can help you plan your trip. It provides family activities, guided tours, and more. Active families will find a lot to do on Ocracoke Island. **Schooner Windfall Sailing Tours** (252-928-7245; www.schoonerwindfall.com) is ready to get you out on the water. If wetting a line is more your pace, here are the local fishing charters: **Anchorage Marina** (252-928-6661), **Capt. David Nagel, "Drum Stick"** (800-825-5351), **"Miss Kathleen"** (252-928-4841; www.ocracokesportfishing.com), **"Rascal" Sportfishing** (252-928-6111), and **Tarheel Charters** (252-928-9966).

Ocracoke Lighthouse (all ages)
Lighthouse Road; (252) 928-4531; www.ocracokepreservation.org. Free.

If you don't plan to spend some time taking in the history of this island, you'll miss a lot of the charm it has to offer. The white stucco Ocracoke Lighthouse is located west of the village. Hike if the weather is nice because parking is extremely limited on the small street. Built in 1823, the lighthouse is the state's oldest still in operation. Its beam that shines at night can be seen from 14 miles away, but it's not open for climbing. A nearby historic home has been moved to this location and converted to a museum with antiques, tools, and Civil War artifacts.

Teach's Hole (all ages)
West end of Highway 12; (252) 928-1718; www.teachshole.com. Open 10 a.m. to 5 p.m. daily. Free.

Teach's Hole is a pirate specialty shop that includes an exhibit about one of the island's most famous visitors—Edward Teach, also known as Blackbeard the Pirate. A self-guided tour depicts the escapades of the swashbuckler and his companions.

Where to Eat

Because of the tourist nature of the area, even the pubs in Ocracoke are kid-friendly, so while it may look like a place for adults to party, most pubs treat children well.

Amazing
North Carolina Facts

Blackbeard was killed in a battle near Ocracoke by the British Royal Navy in 1718. Some say his treasure is still buried on the coast. Expeditions to find this treasure have even been conducted as far south as Topsail Island.

Back Porch. 110 Back Rd.; (252) 928-6401; www.backporchocracoke.com. This is one of the better seafood places on the island. It has a children's menu and basket-size portions in case there are any other light eaters in the family. $$–$$$

Captain Ben's Restaurant. Highway 12; (252) 928-4741. Captain Ben's offers a more budget-minded selection of seafood, plus other American dishes. $–$$

Howard's Pub and Raw Bar. Highway 12; (252) 928-4441; www.howardspub.com. This is one of the kid-friendlier places, offering an array of burgers, chicken, and pizza as well as oysters and the best onion rings. It has checkers, mind benders, and other assorted games for you to play while waiting for your meal. $

Pony Island Restaurant. Highway 12; (252) 928-5701. This is one of the few restaurants on the island that tend to be family-style in both price and atmosphere. $$

Where to Stay

In case I haven't made it clear, you're not going to find a lot of places to stay along the Northern Coast, at least not until you get to Ocracoke. Then the decision gets difficult.

Anchorage Inn & Marina. Highway 12; (252) 928-1101; www.theanchorageinn.com. Located on Silver Lake, this is a pet-friendly place with rooms and some efficiencies. There is a small cafe, too. $$–$$$

Beachcomber Campground. Highway 12; reservations for this oceanfront campground, 3 miles from the village, can be made by calling (252) 928-4031. The campground gets you away from the hustle and bustle of tourists and is very scenic and nicely kept. $

Blackbeard's Lodge. 111 Back Rd.; (800) 892-5314; www.blackbeardslodge.com. This is Ocracoke's oldest hotel, with 38 rooms and apartments. $$$

Bluff Shoal Motel. Highway 12; (252) 928-4301; www.bluffshoal.com. This is a small motel located on the harbor with very reasonable prices but few amenities. $$–$$$

The Castle on Silver Lake. Silver Lake Road; (800) 471-8848; www.thecastlebb.com. Very nice rooms and condos with piers are waiting here at this inn that offers bikes and a game room. $$$$

Edward's of Ocracoke. SR 1343; (252) 928-4801; www.edwardsofocracoke.com. Edward's is a small, homey facility. It has bikes for rent on-site. $$–$$$

Harborside Motel and Shop. Highway 12; (252) 928-3111. As the name indicates, this motel is indeed on the harbor. It, too, is a small facility, with just 14 rooms and 4 efficiencies. $$$

Ocracoke Island Realty. Highway 12; (252) 928-6261; www.ocracokeislandrealty.com. This is one of three large realty companies that handle rental of a number of cottages on the island, as well as several condos.

For More Information

Ocracoke Civic and Business Association. (252) 928-6711; www.ocracokevillage .com.

Hatteras

The **free** Ocracoke ferry will deliver you and your vehicle across Ocracoke Inlet to Hatteras Island, the central island in the Outer Banks. Highway 12 continues up the length of the island.

By the time you get to the northern portion of Ocracoke Island, where the **Cape Hatteras National Seashore** begins, you'll find that the major attractions here are the sun, sand, and unspoiled beauty. You will also find an ample supply of shops where you can buy a cheap T-shirt or grab a snack. The seashore is more undeveloped than any other portion of the Atlantic Coast, but a visit to any one of the villages here provides ample opportunity for educational and adventurous day trips. **Hatteras Village,** the southernmost community on Hatteras Island, is home to a renowned charter fishing fleet and the **Graveyard of the Atlantic Museum,** where the remnants of the original Fresnel lens that once shone bright atop the Cape Hatteras Lighthouse is now displayed.

Camping

Four camping areas are available along the **Cape Hatteras National Seashore** on a first-come, first-served basis, except for the one on Ocracoke, where reservations are recommended. Make reservations by calling (877) 444-6777 or log on to www.recreation.gov. All of these National Park Service facilities have showers, restrooms, tables, drinking water, and grills, but no utility hookups. Campgrounds are located at Oregon Inlet, Cape Point in Buxton, Frisco, and on Ocracoke Island. Get more information on the entire Cape Hatteras National Seashore by calling (252) 473-2111. Fees are $20 per night.

Where to Eat

Breakwater Restaurant. 57896 Highway 12, Oden's Dock; (252) 986-2733; www.break waterhatteras.com. Open for dinner only, this is a nice restaurant that features unusual seafood dishes, beef, and other American cuisine. $$$

Dinky's. Highway 12, Hatteras Village; (252) 986-2020. More upscale dining with crab cakes and prime rib comes to the table at Dinky's. $$$

Hatterasman Drive-In. Highway 12; (252) 986-1001; www.thehatterasman.com. Come here for a change of pace. Fish tacos, burgers, sushi, burritos, seafood, smoothies, and desserts are offered. $

Sonny's Waterfront Restaurant. Highway 12; (252) 986-2922. Like many restaurants in the area, seafood is the specialty, especially the buffet, but Sonny's serves pasta, steak, and chicken, too. $$

Teach's Island Bar and Grill. Teach's Lair Marina, Highway 12; (252) 986-2460; www .teachslair.com. The marina location brings this restaurant a lot of atmosphere and good food, with a range of selections from burgers to fish. $$

Where to Stay

Breakwater Inn. 57896 Highway 12; (252) 986-2565. Pets are permitted here, and the motel has a pool and efficiencies. $$–$$$

Hatteras Marlin Motel. 57753 Highway 12; (252) 986-2141. A wide selection of rooms, suites, and efficiencies is available here. $$–$$$$

Hatteras Realty. Highway 12 South; (252) 995-5466. You'll have to rent by the week here, but the facilities are very nice and affordable when making arrangements that way. $$$

Sea Gull Motel. Highway 12; (252) 986-2550. This waterfront motel has a pool and efficiencies, rooms, and cottages. $$$

Here is a list of companies that have rental locations here and other places on the Outer Banks:

Colony Realty Corp. (800) 962-5256; www .hatterasvacations.com.

Dolphin Realty Inc. (800) 338-4775; www .dolphin-realty.com.

Midgett Realty. (800) 527-2903; www .midgettrealty.com.

Outer Beaches Realty, Inc. (800) 627-1850; www.outerbeaches.com.

Sun Realty. (800) 334-4745; www.sunrealty nc.com.

Surf or Sound Realty. (800) 237-1138; www.surforsound.com/obvb.

Vacation Traditions. (866) 935-8844; www .vacationtraditions.com.

Graveyard of **the Atlantic**

Off the coast of Hatteras Island are the dangerous Diamond Shoals, a bank of shifting sand ridges beneath the sea. They have been blamed for helping to sink more than 600 ships in the area, earning Hatteras the nickname "Graveyard of the Atlantic." Some of the sunken ships are visible from shore, depending on tides and the shifting sand. Much of Hatteras Island is untamed and uncrowded. Take some time for a quiet walk on the beach or just take in the scenery.

Fishing

With the Gulf Stream only about 30 miles from the islands, fishing is ideal offshore from Hatteras, a quiet community on the southern tip of Hatteras Island. Fishing charters are available from a number of fishing centers in the area. Charters are only for experienced anglers as they go for yellowfin tuna, dolphin, and king mackerel on offshore tours. By chartering a small boat in the sound and hiring a guide, you can go for trout, flounder, and striped bass in one of the sounds. Or try your luck fishing from the pier located a few miles north of the village or at one of the other six piers located along the Hatteras seashore. Trout, blues, mullet, and flounder are just a few of the possibilities when fishing from a pier in Hatteras.

Call the North Carolina Division of Marine Fisheries at (800) 682-2632 or log on to www.ncfisheries.net for information on regulations.

Frisco

Push on north up Highway 12 just a little farther, and find another of the island's tiny villages, Frisco.

Frisco Native American Museum and Natural History Center
(ages 3 and up)

Highway 12; (252) 995-4440; www.nativeamericanmuseum.org. Open 11 a.m. to 5 p.m. Tues through Sun. $.

The museum features authentic collections of ancient artifacts from the island's original inhabitants, and the center features a nature trail, exhibits, a pavilion, and a picnic area. Many of the artifacts, including a dugout canoe, come from an archaeological excavation site at Buxton Village.

Where to Eat

Gingerbread House Bakery. Highway 12; (252) 995-5204; www.gbhbakery.com. It's not all about the treats at the Gingerbread House; it's also about great pizza. $

Where to Stay

The same rental companies that offer accommodations at Hatteras Village offer rentals at Frisco, too.

Frisco Woods Campground. Highway 12; (800) 948-3942. Located on Pamlico Bay, this campground is very comfortable, with hot and cold water, a pool, playground, and more. It offers tent and RV sites. $

Buxton

Now get ready to climb. Buxton, farther north on Highway 12, is the home of the tallest lighthouse in the US.

Cape Hatteras Lighthouse (ages 4 and up)

Highway 12; (252) 473-2111; www.nps.gov/caha/index.htm. Open daily 9 a.m. to 5:30 p.m. in summer and until 4:30 p.m. the rest of the year. $–$$ to climb.

At 208 feet, the Cape Hatteras Lighthouse is an international symbol for the North Carolina coast and has gained more national attention over the past decade. Erosion from the treacherous sea began to threaten the 100-year-old lighthouse, and plans were undertaken to save it. As a result, in 2000 the lighthouse was moved about 1 mile inland. You can still climb the 248 steps to the top of the lighthouse and get a spectacular view of the surrounding area from the outside. Children must be old enough to make the climb on their own and be at least 42 inches tall. On the grounds of the lighthouse is the Cape Hatteras Visitors Center and Museum.

Where to Eat

Angelo's Pizzeria. Highway 12; (252) 995-6364. Specializing in Italian cuisine, featuring pizza and calzones, Angelo's also has a game room. $

Buxton Munch Company. Osprey Shopping Center, Highway 12; (252) 995-5502; www.buxtonmunch.com. Salads, melts, burgers, quesadillas, subs, wraps, fried chicken, and vegetarian selections are on the menu here. $

The Captain's Table. Highway 12; (252) 995-3117. Across from the lighthouse entrance, the captain serves baby back ribs, local seafood, soup, pasta, salads, homemade desserts, and milk shakes. It has a kids' menu. $$

Diamond Shoals Restaurant. Highway 12; (252) 995-5217; www.diamondshoals.net. Diamond Shoals serves local seafood and it's open for breakfast. $

Finnegan's Dining Haul. Highway 12; (252) 995-3060. Hot submarine sandwiches, hamburgers, hot dogs, pizza, seafood, and chicken are offered here. $

The Fish House Restaurant. Highway 12, soundfront; (252) 995-5151. Fresh local seafood, pork, steaks, and pasta are all on the menu. $$

Island Perks Diner. Milepost 61, Highway 12; (252) 986-1111. Breakfast and desserts are popular offerings here, but Island Perks also serves burgers, tuna salad, soups, and other traditional diner offerings. $

Orange Blossom Bakery & Cafe. Highway 12; (252) 995-4109; www.orangeblossom bakery.com. Breakfast, including fresh baked goods and gourmet coffee, is the specialty here. Try the Apple Ugglies. It's also open for lunch and dinner. $

Rusty's Surf and Turf. Highway 12; (252) 995-4184; www.rustyssurfnturf.com. This steak and scallop–type place might be more for Mom and Dad, but the kids will find a thing or two on the menu as well. $$$

Where to Stay

Buxton Beach Motel. 46211 Old Light-house Rd.; (252) 995-5972; www.buxton beachmotel.com. Rooms, efficiencies, apart-ments, and cottages are offered here. $$$

Cape Hatteras Motel. Highway 12; (800) 995-0711; www.capehatterasmotel.com. You'll find rooms, efficiencies, and apart-ments at this waterfront motel. $$$$

Cape Pines Motel. Highway 12; (252) 995-5666; www.capepinesmotel.com. This is a small motel, but it does have a pool and bar-becue area. $$$

Lighthouse View Motel. Highway 12; (252) 995-5680; www.lighthouseview.com. This is one of the larger and nicer accommodations in Buxton. $$

Tower Circle. 46423 Old Lighthouse Rd.; (252) 995-5353. Rooms and efficiencies are offered here. It also has a small playground. $$$

Rodanthe

Leaving Buxton and pointing your car north takes you through the small fishing village of Avon, gaining popularity among kiteboarders. A few restaurants and motels operate here but not much else. From there you drive about 15 more miles to the communities of Salvo, Waves, and Rodanthe, which seemingly blend into one. The entire northern end of Hat-teras Island was once known as Chicamacomico (pronounced chik-a-ma-COM-i-co), but in 1874 the US Postal Service changed the name to Rodanthe.

Chicamacomico US Lifesaving Service Station (all ages)

Highway 12; (252) 987-1552; www.chicamacomico.net. Open 10 a.m. to 5 p.m. Mon through Fri, mid-Apr through Nov. $–$$.

The Chicamacomico US Lifesaving Service Station, established in 1874, is one of North Carolina's oldest lifesaving stations. It includes 2 stations and 5 outbuildings, making it the largest lifesaving station in the country. The original buildings are also on the National Reg-ister of Historic Places. The villagers who have volunteered here have been credited with saving the lives of hundreds of sailors who found themselves caught in fierce winter and tropical storms. Reenactments of such rescues are performed weekly at the station during summer months.

Pea Island National Wildlife Refuge (all ages)

708 N. Highway 64; (252) 987-2394; www.fws.gov/peaisland. Open 9 a.m. to 4 p.m. daily Apr through Nov and weekends the rest of the year. Free.

Just north of Rodanthe begins the 5,915-acre Pea Island National Wildlife Refuge and part of the Charles Kuralt Trail, a series of refuges in coastal Virginia and North Carolina. Use the observation platforms that expand across brackish water, salt flats, and marshes throughout the area to view hundreds of species of local birds and any number of birds

Laura Barnes **Shipwreck**

From Highway 12 you can see the *Laura Barnes* shipwreck of 1921. It is one of the few shipwrecks that are usually visible, depending on the shifting sands. The 120-foot ship, one of the last sailing schooners built in America, ran aground during a storm, her crew saved by the US Coast Guard. A swimming area and a picnic area are available nearby.

migrating to and from the refuge. The refuge also has a visitor center and nature trail, and bird walks and children's programs are held during the summer and fall.

Waterfall Action Park (all ages)

On Highway 12 north of Rodanthe; (252) 987-2213; www.waterfallactionpark.com. Open noon to 10 p.m. daily May through Sept. Prices vary by attraction.

If the kids are ready for a little bit of modern adventure, try Waterfall Action Park. It's one of the area's largest fun parks and includes waterslides, racecars, kiddie cars, miniature golf, bumper boats, bungee jumping, and more. This is the largest such park on the Outer Banks.

Where to Eat

Boardwok South Restaurant. 24267 Highway 12; (252) 987-1080. Asian, American, and seafood are offered for lunch and dinner. $$

Lisa's Pizzeria. Highway 12; (252) 987-2525. Pizzas, subs, and calzones are here. $

Uncle Pauly's Restaurant. Milepost 40, Highway 12; (252) 987-1623. Uncle Pauly has as much variety as any place in the area. $$

Where to Stay

Salvo Inn Motel. Highway 12 (oceanside), Salvo; (252) 987-2240. Efficiencies and cottages are available here. $$$

Sea Sound Motel. 24224 Sea Sound Rd., Rodanthe; (252) 987-2224; www.seasound motelobx.com. This is a very small hotel, but it has a pool, basketball courts, and a picnic area. $$–$$$$

Coquina Beach

After you cross the bridge over Oregon Inlet, still on Highway 12, you move out of the largely unpopulated areas and into a more traditional tourist area.

Bodie Island Lighthouse (all ages)

Highway 12, 8 miles south of juncture of US 158/64; (252) 441-5711. Free.

Bodie Island begins in the south at Coquina Beach, home of the Bodie Island Lighthouse. A visitor center, exhibits, and nature trail are open during daylight hours from May through September, but the lighthouse, built in 1872, is not open to climb. In 2009 the National Park Service began the first major renovation of the lighthouse since it was built. The project will also enhance the surrounding, already picturesque area, too.

Manteo

At Whalebone, Highway 12 encounters US 64, which crosses Roanoke Sound west onto Roanoke Island.

You may want to take this 20-minute side trip into the late 16th century before continuing north to the popular Nags Head resort area, or plan on it as a day trip during your vacation. In Manteo there is plenty to fill a day and evening, or even several days and evenings. Roanoke Island is the site of the earliest English settlements sent by Sir Walter Raleigh beginning in 1584. Many sites and attractions here depict the lives of those settlers and others who helped shape the New World.

Barrier Island Aviation (all ages)
Dare County Airport; (252) 473-4247; www.barrierislandaviation.com. $$$$.

This company offers 30-minute scenic air tours of the Outer Banks, with seating for up to 3 passengers. Tours fly over Wright Brothers National Memorial, Jockey's Ridge State Park, and lighthouses.

Elizabeth II State Historic Site
and Roanoke Island Festival Park (all ages)

Highway 64, across from the Manteo waterfront; (252) 475-1506; www.roanokeisland.com. Open 9 a.m. to 5 p.m. daily Mar through Dec. $$; free for children 5 and under. Admission tickets are valid for 2 consecutive days.

Coming from Highway 64, your first stop might be the *Elizabeth II* State Historic Site and Roanoke Island Festival Park. The *Elizabeth II* is a replica of the 16th-century sailing ship that brought some of the first settlers to America. Your kids will love striking up conversations with the interpretive guides dressed as sailors who work for Queen Elizabeth. They stay in character for the year 1585, so comments about television or cars won't be understood. The kids might even get an opportunity to help hoist the sails.

After you tour the small vessel, you'll want to see the living-history camp a short walk away. It's 1585 here, too, folks. You might find the queen's sailors whipping up a meal, crafting tools, or preparing food for winter storage. Also at the park is an **American Indian Town** that details the Algonquin Indian history and culture through a re-creation of the homes, agricultural sites, and other areas that the early settlers encountered when they first arrived in the New World. Finally, visitors can dress up and play the part of settlers at the **Roanoke Adventure Museum.** In addition, the museum presents audiovisual displays on the history of the island. Picnic facilities and snacks are available on-site, and the museum hosts temporary art exhibits and live performances at a variety of spaces inside the park.

Elizabethan Gardens (all ages)

1411 US 64/264; (252) 473-3234; www.elizabethangardens.org. Open daily 9 a.m. to about an hour before dusk. $–$$; children through age 5 are admitted free.

Plan to spend an hour or so wandering through the Elizabethan Gardens, located at the Fort Raleigh National Historic Site. Visitors entering the well-manicured gardens through a replica of a Tudor gatehouse are led past myriad herbs, flowers, shrubs, water fountains, sculptures, and trees.

Fort Raleigh National Historic Site (all ages)

US 64; (252) 473-5772; www.nps.gov/fora. Open year-round during daylight hours. Free.

Fort Raleigh National Historic Site, where remains of the first European settlements dating back to the mid-16th century are preserved, is open for tours. The site includes a visitor center with exhibits of artifacts from the original site constructed in 1585. The center features the Elizabethan Room, adorned with the paneling and fireplace from a 16th-century home. At the center you can also see a film on the attempts to establish the colonies and displays on colonial life. In addition, in 1950 the National Park Service reconstructed the small earthen fort here at the same location where it was originally built in 1585. Many of the artifacts, including a wrought-iron sickle and a Native American pipe excavated from the site, are on display at the center. Park interpreters present programs and special events at various locations of the site throughout the year.

The Lost Colony (all ages—look for an appropriate presentation)

1409 US 64/264; (252) 473-3414; www.thelostcolony.org. The 2-hour production is presented early June through late Aug at 8:30 p.m. nightly, except Sat. $$–$$$.

Your trip to Manteo won't be complete without seeing *The Lost Colony* outdoor drama, which plays on the waterfront on the grounds of Fort Raleigh. Children and adults alike will be enthralled as the 150-member cast re-creates through drama, song, and dance the events leading to the mysterious disappearance of the men, women, and children who came here from England in 1587. Written by Pulitzer Prize–winner Paul Greene, *The Lost Colony* opened in 1940 and has been playing ever since. The play also commemorates the birth of Virginia Dare, the first European child born in the New World, who disappeared along with the other colonists. Exactly what happened to them remains a mystery. Weather changes rapidly on the waterfront, so bring along a jacket as well as bug repellent to keep the mosquitoes away.

The Lost Colony Children's Theater also presents other special productions for children who might not be able to make it through the evening show. These are performed at various locations on the Outer Banks throughout the season. Call the Lost Colony Box Office for times, locations, and ticket prices.

Amazing
North Carolina Facts

At an incredible 5.2 miles, the **Virginia Dare Bridge,** named for the first English child born in North America, is the longest bridge in the state. Opened in 2002, it takes motorists over Croatan Sound, connecting Mann's Harbor and Manteo.

North Carolina Aquarium (ages 3 and up)

SR 1116, also known as Airport Road; (252) 473-3493; www.ncaquariums.com. Open 9 a.m. to 5 p.m. daily; closed Thanksgiving, Christmas, and New Year's Day. $$; **free** for children ages 2 and under.

Take a jaunt on Airport Road, 3 miles north of US 64, to the North Carolina Aquarium. It's one of three such aquariums on the coast, but here visitors can touch an alligator, feed a stingray, or meet Opal the Octopus.

In addition to the displays of fresh- and saltwater habitats and a touch tank, the aquarium offers special programs and educational films throughout the year. At this aquarium you'll see sharks in a 285,000-gallon tank and a variety of coastal environmental displays, including one on Outer Banks hurricanes.

Outer Banks Air Charters (all ages)

Dare County Airport; (252) 256-2322; www.outerbanksaircharters.com. $$$$.

Shipwrecks are a cool addition to these tours that also fly over all of the sights. This operator also flies over Bodie Island Lighthouse.

Waterfront Shops

207 Queen Elizabeth Ave.

After your visit to the *Elizabeth II,* journey through the quaint waterfront village on Roanoke Sound. At the Waterfront Shops take your time and explore the many unusual shops and restaurants, where you can find lunch or dinner. At the **Candle Factory** (252-473-3813) you can watch craftspeople produce candles in the shape of seashells, lighthouses, and more. Many more shops in the village will take you back in time. **Manteo Blacksmith Shop,** 408 Queen Elizabeth Ave. (252-473-1709), is a working blacksmith shop offering live demonstrations of this age-old craft. **My Secret Garden,** 101 Sir Walter Raleigh St. (252-473-6880), is a fun gift shop full of eclectic treasures. You'll also find a comfortable bookstore, jewelry, and more in the Waterfront Shops.

Where to Eat

Big Al's Soda Fountain and Grill. 716 US 64/264; (252) 473-5570; www.bigalsobx.com. You can probably guess what kind of food you'll get here, so we'll skip it and say we just like the name. Try the homemade ice cream, though. $

Darrell's Seafood Restaurant. US 64/264; (252) 473-5366; www.darrellsseafood.com. If the old real estate adage "location, location, location" is true, Darrell's will be in business for a long time. Darrell's specialty is grilled marinated tuna, but the menu also includes a healthy portion of local catches, a good children's menu, and baskets for light eaters. $$

1587 Restaurant. 405 Queen Elizabeth St.; (252) 473-1587; www.1587.com. This is a sort of casual, five-star restaurant on the waterfront. Great gourmet food is served in an elegant, yet comfortable, setting. $$$

Where to Stay

Dare Haven Motel. 819 N. Main Hwy.; (252) 473-2322; www.darehaven.com. This hotel has 24 rooms and is nice, but there's no pool. $$–$$$

Duke of Dare Motor Lodge. 100 S. Virginia Dare Rd.; (252) 473-2175. This is a AAA-approved facility with 57 rooms. $$

Elizabethan Inn. 814 US 64; (800) 346-2466; www.elizabethaninn.com. This is a nice period-themed inn with mainly standard rooms. $$–$$$$

For vacation rentals, try these:

Pirate's Cove Vacation Rentals. 1 Sailfish Dr.; (888) 314-5799; www.pirates-cove.com.

Strawser Vacation Rentals. (252) 473-0815; www.cheapobxvacations.com.

Nags Head

A little farther north from Whalebone, where you sidetracked to Manteo, on Highway 12 is Nags Head.

Here you'll find more of what you expect from a standard tourist center. It's not exactly crowded, but hotels, vacation cottages, and condominiums line the strip between the beach and Highway 12. You will find plenty of attractions, amusements, and eateries to choose from here. Until you get to Nags Head, the islands often aren't wide enough to accommodate much more than the highway, but this broader area has an array of services, including major retail chain and outlet stores. Here you also get a fair share of water parks, waterslides, miniature golf courses, and gift shops. Nags Head is a good central location if you are planning to stay a week or more in the area. Not only can you enjoy the sand, sun, and surf, but there's also simply a lot to do, rain or shine.

Jennette's Pier (all ages)

Milepost 16.5; (252) 255-1501; www.jennettespier.net. $.

Originally built in 1939, this was one of the first piers on the Outer Banks. Battered by storms many times over the years, it was knocked down by Hurricane Isabel in 2003. It was purchased by the NC Aquarium Society and rebuilt as a different kind of educational pier operated by the state's aquariums. Fishing is still the main activity at Jennette's, but the state presents a variety of programs and exhibits on ocean wildlife, alternative energy, and more.

Jockey's Ridge State Park (all ages)

West Carolista Drive; (252) 441-7132; www.jockeysridgestatepark.com. Open during daylight hours. **Free.**

If hang gliding is a little too adventurous for your family, it's almost as much fun to sit back and watch it being done at Jockey's Ridge State Park. This is the site of the largest sand dune on the East Coast, located on US 158. Most people come here to climb the 140-foot dune, while others come to fly kites in the wide-open, 414-acre park. Walking across the vast white sand almost makes you feel like you're walking across the desert. Unlike desert wilderness areas, it has picnic facilities available.

Kitty Hawk Kites (ages 5 and up)

Several locations throughout the Outer Banks; (877) 359-8447; www.kittyhawk.com. **Prices vary by activity.**

For the ultimate family adventure, check in with Kitty Hawk Kites, just off Highway 12 on US 158, across the street from Jockey's Ridge State Park (it also has outlets at Avon, Duck, and Corolla). Kitty Hawk Kites offers lessons in kayaking, sailboarding, kiteboarding, and hang gliding and sells kites and kite supplies. Even young children can be accommodated in kayaking tours, but you must weigh at least 80 pounds to take hang-gliding lessons. Regardless of what kind of adventure the family is into, this is the place to stop for all those needs.

Nags Head Pier (all ages)

Milepost 11, Beach Road; (252) 441-5141; www.nagsheadpier.com.

Any time is a good time to try your fishing luck on the Nags Head Pier, one of the oldest and longest on the Outer Banks. Tackle is available for rent, as is a cleaning station. The pier is open 24 hours a day in spring, summer, and fall. The Pier House Restaurant located here will even clean and cook your catch.

Where to Eat

The Dunes Restaurant. Milepost 16.5, Highway 12; (252) 441-1600; www.thedunes restaurant.com. This family restaurant will offer more children's selections than most. $$

A Fishy **Tale**

Even though the following story might not be completely true, it's not a lie. It's a fishing story.

I took the kids to **Nags Head Pier** to get in a little fishing early one morning. I had given up on doing any serious fishing since I started taking the kids, but I was having just as much fun helping bait the hooks, untangling lines, and occasionally untangling my kids. We had spent about three hours catching small sea trout and other species, with even the seasoned anglers on the pier around us doing the same. Then, suddenly, the big one hit. My daughter's pole bent to nearly breaking, the 8-year-old pulling back with all her might, and I sprung into action, saying, "Reel it in, Jessie, reel it in." After hours (well, OK, minutes) of fighting the blue at the end of the line, a crowd (well, OK, five people) gathered around us. "It's a blue," a shirtless boy said, examining the razor-sharp teeth in the fish's mouth. "What'd ya catch 'em with?" "Uh, Dad?" my daughter asked. "Calamari," I whispered. "Calamari," Jessie said, turning to the boy with an air of confidence. She immediately turned back to me and asked, "Dad, what's calamari?"

Jockey's Ribs. Milepost 13, Beach Road; (252) 441-1141. Cute name for a cute barbecue restaurant. $

New York Pizza Pub. Milepost 10, 158 Bypass; (252) 441-2660. This place is unique in that the kids can get pizza and Mom and Dad can get steak. $–$$

The Pier House Restaurant. Milepost 11, Beach Road; (252) 441-4200; www.nags headpier.com. Treat the family to tasty local seafood in a casual dining atmosphere with an oceanfront view here on the Nags Head Pier. $$–$$$

Scoops Ice Cream Parlor. Milepost 12.5 on Highway 12.; (252) 441-4485. Get homemade ice cream, smoothies, and shakes in addition to sandwiches. $

Yellow Submarine. 5000 S. Croatan Hwy.; (252) 441-3511; www.yellowsubmarineobx .com. The owners probably aren't the first out of the '60s to think of the name, but you can probably guess what they serve. $

Where to Stay

We won't even attempt to list all the places you can find to stay in the Nags Head area, but here are just a few:

Beacon Motor Lodge. 2617 S. Virginia Dare Trail; (800) 441-4804; www.beacon motorlodge.com. This AAA-approved facility has rooms, suites, and efficiencies. The kids will love the game room as much as the pool. $$$$

Blue Heron Motel. 6811 Virginia Dare Trail; (252) 441-7447; www.blueheronnc.com. The Blue Heron offers rooms and efficiencies on the ocean. $$$$

The Dolphin Motel. 8017 Old Oregon Inlet Rd.; (252) 441-7488; www.dolphinmotel.net. You might find this motel a little more affordable. $$$

Nags Head Inn. 4701 S. Virginia Dare Trail; (800) 327-8881; www.nagsheadinn.com. This inn is one of the larger ones in the area, with 100 rooms. $$$$

Among the largest realty companies are the following:

Cove Realty. 105 E. Dunn St.; (800) 635-7007; www.obxcola.com.

Nags Head Realty. 2300 S. Croatan Hwy.; (800) 222-1531; www.nagsheadrealty.com.

Prudential Resort Realty. 2229 S. Croatan Hwy.; (800) 458-3830; www.resortrealty.com.

Stan White Realty. 2506 S. Croatan Hwy.; (800) 338-3233; www.outerbanksrentals.com.

Village Realty. 5301 S. Croatan Hwy.; (800) 548-9688; www.villagerealtyobx.com.

Kill Devil Hills

Kill Devil Hills is just minutes from Nags Head. In fact, Nags Head, Kill Devil Hills, and Kitty Hawk all seem to blend into one vacation resort.

Kitty Hawk Aero Tours (all ages)
First Flight Airport, 171 Bay Dr.; (252) 441-8687. $$$–$$$$.

Offered in conjunction with Kitty Hawk Kites, Kitty Hawk Aero Tours offers a chance to take a flight from the same place the Wright brothers made so many attempts in their quest to fly. The tour flies over Oregon Inlet to observe the ocean life that includes sharks, porpoises, and sea turtles. You'll also be flown over the Bodie Island Lighthouse and Jockey's Ridge. Open cockpit planes are available, too. Call for reservations.

Nags Head Wood Ecological Preserve (all ages)
701 W. Ocean Acres Dr., off US 158; (252) 441-2525; www.nature.org. Admission to the preserve is free, but some programs may require a fee. Generally open during daylight hours.

Now it's off to learn a little bit about one of nature's more unusual offerings at Nags Head Wood Ecological Preserve, where freshwater pools have bubbled up to create this 1,100-acre protected wetland. Owned by the Nature Conservancy, walking trails and displays provide an interesting look at one of the last and most diverse forests on the islands. The woodlands include dunes adjacent to a majestic hardwood forest. The staff presents guided tours and educational programs throughout the year that explain the diversity of the area.

Wright Brothers National Memorial (all ages)
Milepost 8, US 158; (252) 441-7430; www.nps.gov/wrbr. Open 9 a.m. to 5 p.m. daily; closed Christmas Day. $.

This is where human beings learned to fly. On December 17, 1903, two bicycle shop owners from Dayton, Ohio, named Orville and Wilbur Wright took the first powered flying machine on a sustained flight. After several attempts that day, they kept the machine aloft for 59 seconds and traveled 852 feet. Today the Wright Brothers National Memorial, on US 158 north of Kill Devil Hills, stands on the same spot as a tribute to their accomplishment. It includes a museum on the history of flight and a demonstration of the principles they used, which are still instrumental to modern flight. Reproductions of the brothers' glider and the 1903 airplane are on display, and you will want to check out the reproduction of their camp workshop and hangar.

Other Amusements (all ages)

The Kitty Hawk/Kill Devil Hills area offers plenty of history, but don't forget about traditional family fun. You won't have any trouble finding these, but here is a short list of locations on the north end of the Croatan Highway: **Colington Speedway** (252-480-9144) has 3 tracks available to please kids of most every age; **Professor Hacker's Lost Treasure Golf** (252-480-0142) has 36 holes complemented with waterfalls, dinosaur footprints, lost treasure, and a mining train that takes you to the first hole; **Wet 'n Wild Bumper Boats** (I don't think we need to say anything more).

Where to Eat

Bob's Grill. 1203 S. Croatan Hwy.; (252) 441-0707. Bob's serves breakfast, lunch, and dinner and is open all night on weekends. $

Chili Peppers. Milepost 5.5, US 158 Bypass; (252) 441-8081; www.chilli-peppers.com. Funky selections with a Southwestern flair are offered along with burgers and seafood. $$

Colington Cafe. 1029 Colington Rd.; (252) 480-1123; www.colingtoncafe.com. You'll have to make reservations well in advance to eat here. This is one of the nicest restaurants in the area, serving mainly French cuisine. $$$

Jolly Roger. Milepost 6.75, Beach Road; (252) 441-6530; www.jollyrogerobx.com. Homemade Italian cuisine, seafood, steaks, and prime rib offer something for everyone. $$$

Kelly's Outer Banks Restaurant & Tavern. Milepost 10.5, US 158 Bypass; (252) 441-4116; www.kellysrestaurant.com. Southeastern seafood, beef, and pasta are offered in a fine-dining atmosphere in which children are welcome. $$$$

Miller's Restaurant. Milepost 9.5, Beach Road; (252) 441-7674; www.millerseafood.com. Seafood is the specialty here. $$

Where to Stay

Cavalier Motel. Milepost 8.5 Highway 12; (252) 441-5584; www.cavaliermotel.net. Rooms, efficiencies, and cottages make this a great place no matter what you're looking for. As a bonus, the Cavalier has a large swimming pool for adults, a small one for the kiddies, and a large play area equipped with swings, shuffleboard, horseshoes, and volleyball courts. $$$

Ocean House Motel. Milepost 9.5, Oceanfront Road; (866) 536-1790; www.oceanhousemotel.com. Standard rooms are offered at Ocean House. $$$

Outer Banks Motor Lodge. 1509 Virginia Dare Trail; (877) 625-6343; www.obxmotorlodge.com. Rooms and efficiencies are offered here. $$–$$$$

Kitty Hawk

Kitty Hawk is just to the north of Kill Devil Hills.

Children at Play Museum (ages 1 to 8)

Milepost 4.5; (252) 261-0290; www.childrenatplayobx.com. Open 10 a.m. to 5 p.m. Tues through Sat. $.

Appropriately themed on the Outer Banks, this children's museum offers interactive experiences to help little ones learn about fishing, flying, lighthouses, and lifesaving. Through fun, colorful exhibits on which children climb and play, they learn motor skills and facts about various parts of the coast, including science and history.

Kitty Hawk Kayaks—Kayak and Surf School (ages 5 and up)

6150 N. Croatan Hwy.; (866) 702-5061; www.khkss.com. $$$$.

Kitty Hawk Kayaks offers over a dozen guided tours, rental kayaks, and self-guided tours. Coastal studies field trips and overnight trips are also available. They also offer a 1-day surf school and a 3-day surf camp.

The Promenade (all ages)

Barlow Road near the Wright Brothers Memorial Bridge. For information on golf attractions, call (252) 261-4900; for information on water sports, call (252) 261-4900; www.promenadeobx.com. Fees vary by activity.

With dozens of activities for the entire family, The Promenade is a 30-acre entertainment park that offers everything from golf to water sports. Yet it isn't a traditional entertainment center because the fun takes place in more peaceful surroundings with abundant wildlife. The eatery includes a coffee and draft house as well as ice cream and other snacks. You'll find a driving range, grass putting greens, a playground, and opportunities for kayaking and other water sports.

Where to Eat

Jimmy's Seafood Buffet. 4117 N. Croatan Hwy.; (252) 261-4973; www.jimmysobxbuffet.com. It's noisy at Jimmy's, but that might work well with children. The food is good, but a little expensive for buffet-only. $$$$

John's Drive-In. 3716 N. Virginia Dare Trail; (252) 261-6227. The milk shakes are why people go to John's, but you can get sandwiches here, too. $

Where to Stay

Atlantic Realty. 4729 N. Croatan Hwy.; (800) 334-8401; www.atlanticrealty-nc.com.

Beach Haven. 4104 Virginia Dare Trail; (252) 261-4785; www.beachhavenmotel.com. This is one of the prettier hotels among the northern beaches. It's AAA approved, has a putting green and bikes, and other beach items are available for a fee. $$$$

For vacation rentals, here are a couple options:

Kitty Dunes Realty & Rentals. (888) 860-3863; www.kittydunes.com.

Southern Shores Realty Services. (800) 334-1000; www.southernshores.com.

For More Information

Dare County Tourist Bureau. (800) 629-4386; www.outerbanks.org.

Corolla

It's a little out of the way, but a drive up Highway 12 to this northernmost point on the North Carolina coast may prove very relaxing. At the Virginia state line are wild horses believed to be descendants of Spanish mustangs abandoned here centuries ago. You will travel through the communities of Southern Shores and Duck before leaving Dare County.

Back Country Outfitters & Guides (all ages)

107-C Corolla Light Town Center; (252) 453-0877; www.outerbankstours.com. By appointment only. $$$$.

Backcountry Outfitters offers wild horse safaris in addition to other ecotours. The wild horse safari is a 2-hour journey to see the wild mustangs left behind by early explorers almost 500 years ago. Naturalist guides take guests over 30 miles of backcountry, beach dunes, and off-road residential areas where the powerful horses roam free.

Corolla Wild Horse Museum (all ages)

1126 School House Ln.; (252) 453-8002; www.corollawildhorses.com. Open 11 a.m. to 4 p.m. Mon through Thurs. **Free.**

This museum, dedicated to the preservation of the local wild horse population, is located in the Old Corolla Schoolhouse, in the heart of historic Corolla Village. Visitors see interactive displays and learn about local history and the story of the horses that inhabit this area. Kids' programs are held on Tuesday and Thursday from 11 a.m. to 2 p.m.

Amazing
North Carolina Facts

The wild Spanish mustang was named the official horse of the state of North Carolina in 2010.

Amazing
North Carolina Facts

From one of the northernmost points in North Carolina, where Highway 12 ends at Corolla, to the Virginia border, roam descendents of Spanish mustangs that apparently survived early 16th-century shipwrecks. Other theories suggest the horses survived as the Spanish settlers fell ill. You can still see them roaming the beaches in some protected areas, but development is forcing them into tourist and residential areas. In 1926 a *National Geographic* article estimated that there were as many as 6,000 horses roaming the land. Today, because some have been systematically removed and others killed, there may be as few as 100 roaming the nearly 15,000 acres.

Currituck Beach Lighthouse (all ages)

Highway 12 at Corolla Village Road; (252) 453-8152; www.currituckbeachlight.com. Open daily Easter through Thanksgiving 9 a.m. to 5 p.m. (until 8 p.m. on Thurs). $.

The Corolla area is one of the narrowest points on the barrier islands. Bordered by Currituck Sound on the west and the Atlantic Ocean on the east, sand frequently blows onto the highway from the dunes that line it here and at other narrow points on the island. Highway 12 ends at the Currituck Beach Lighthouse, a redbrick tower built in 1875. Its 214 steps are open for climbing thanks to the renovation efforts of the Outer Banks Conservationists over the past two decades.

The Whalehead Club at Currituck Heritage Park (ages 5 and up)

1100 Club Rd.; (252) 453-9040; www.whaleheadclub.com. Open 9 a.m. to 5 p.m. daily. Some tours require advance registration. $–$$.

Built in the mid-1920s to satisfy industrialist Edward Collings Knight Jr.'s passion for hunting waterfowl, the Whalehead Club is a spectacular landmark on the Currituck Outer Banks. Knight and his wife used the Corolla home as their winter residence from 1925 to 1934. It still boasts Tiffany lamps, cork-tiled floors, and brass duck head and water lily hardware. A Children's Tour and Treasure Hunt is offered for children ages 6 to 12 ($). This tour teaches participants about the history and art of the home and gives them a greater appreciation for the environment and geography of the area as well as giving them some navigational skills. A ghost tour ($) is recommended for guests age 6 and older.

Where to Eat

Spanky's Grille & Pizza. Milepost 3.5 Highway 12; (252) 261-1917; www.spankysnc .com. Spanky's is a great place for breakfast or a midday meal. $

Creswell

It's hard to get the kids to leave the beach, but now that we've explored the length of the Outer Banks, let's head back inland. US 64 is the quickest and easiest route out of the centrally located Manteo area. We will first head through the Alligator River National Wildlife Refuge.

Alligator River National Wildlife Refuge (all ages)

Located about 4 miles west of the US 64/264 split, traveling west from Manteo; (252) 473-1131; www.fws.gov/alligatorriver. Generally open during daylight hours. Fees charged for some activities.

The Alligator River National Wildlife Refuge is one of the most spectacular unspoiled areas in the state. It has great paddling trails, a wildlife drive, hiking trails, and a variety of wildlife and habitats. Bogs, freshwater and brackish water marshes, hardwood swamps, and Atlantic white cedar swamps comprise the area. Plant species include pitcher plants and sundews, cranberries, bays, white cedar, pond pine, gums, red maple, and a wide variety of herbaceous and shrub species. The refuge is one of the last remaining native homes of black bear on the Eastern Seaboard and includes concentrations of ducks, geese, and swans. Other wildlife you might see here include wading birds, shorebirds, American woodcocks, raptors, white-tailed deer, raccoons, rabbits, quail, river otters, and, of course, American alligators. The area is also part of a red wolf repopulation project.

Pettigrew State Park (all ages)

2252 Lake Shore Rd.; (252) 797-4475; www.ncparks.gov. Open during daylight hours. Free.

About 60 miles west of Manteo is Pettigrew State Park on crystal-clear Phelps Lake and the Scuppernong River. Majestic cypress trees, tulip poplars, and swamp chestnut oaks create a spectacularly unique environment in addition to food and shelter for migrating birds. The park includes 17,000 acres and plenty of room for camping, hiking, fishing, and picnicking on your way off the coast.

Somerset Place Historic Site (ages 5 and up)

Pettigrew State Park, 2572 Lake Shore Rd.; (252) 797-4560; www.nchistoricsites.org. Open 9 a.m. to 5 p.m. Mon through Sat and 1 to 5 p.m. Sun, Apr through Oct, and 10 a.m. to 4 p.m. Mon through Sat and 1 to 4 p.m. Sun, Nov through Mar. Free.

The plantation at what is now Pettigrew State Park was one of the largest plantations in the South and operated for some 80 years. Somerset is a 14-room manor built in the 1830s for Josiah Collins III, who was from Somerset, England. The rice plantation and Greek Revival mansion became a popular gathering place for the upper class of the time and served as an example of the South's slave-supported economy. Somerset, which houses an extensive collection of slave records, is the site of a homecoming for descendants of slaves and slaveholders. In recent years a number of Native American artifacts have been pulled from the lake. Two dugout canoes, possibly 4,000 years old, are on display year-round, but more of the artifacts and history are presented during **Indian Heritage Week,** held at Pettigrew the third week in September. Weekdays schoolchildren from the area visit to learn about the history of the Algonquin Indians, who were wiped out by European-imported disease.

Williamston

Staying on US 64 brings you west to this agriculturally based town.

Fort Branch (ages 3 and up)
Located on SR 1416, 12 miles north of Williamston on Highway 125; (800) 776-8566; www .fortbranchcivilwarsite.com. Open 1:30 to 5:30 p.m. Sat and Sun, Apr through the first weekend in Nov. Free.

Most people who visit this part of the state come to see Fort Branch, an earthen Civil War fort. On display are 8 of the fort's original 12 cannons, which Confederate soldiers pushed into the Roanoke River after General Lee surrendered at Appomattox in 1865. The Fort Branch Civil War Reenactment is held the first weekend in November, and the Fort Branch Spring Living History Program is another intriguing event this site offers.

Where to Stay

Green Acres Family Camping Resort. 1679 Green Acres Rd.; (252) 792-3939; www .greenacresnc.com. A stay at this campground comes with a lot of extras, including a pool, a playground, a volleyball court, horseshoes, a miniature golf course, and scheduled activities. $

Robersonville

Back on US 64, heading west from Williamston, you can really pick up the pace if stock car racing is your thing.

East Carolina Motor Speedway (ages 3 and up)
4918 US 64; (252) 795-3968; www.ecmotorspeedway.com. Races begin at 7:30 p.m. Sat, Apr through Oct. $–$$$.

This is a hard-surface racetrack, featuring late-model stock cars and sportsman-class racing.

Tarboro

Tarboro, west from Robersonville on US 64 at the junction with US 258, is another town with its roots grounded deeply in the history of the 18th century.

Historic District Recreation Trail (ages 5 and up)

Tour headquarters located at Blunt Bridgers House,130 Bridgers St.; (252) 823-4159. Open 10 a.m. to 4 p.m. Mon through Fri and 2 to 4 p.m. Sat, Apr through Nov. $.

This is a prime location to study the architecture of the period, both in the charming downtown area and on the historic walking tour. The 16-acre Town Common includes an 1860 cotton press, herb garden, and nature trail. The **Blount-Bridgers House** ($; **free** for children ages 11 and under) features the work of artist Hobson Pittman (1899–1972), whose works are in collections at the Metropolitan Museum of Art in New York as well as the Corcoran Gallery in Washington, DC.

Rocky Mount

The city of Rocky Mount is a great stopping point on the way to or from the beach. Get here from Tarboro via US 64, heading west. From the north or south, I-95 crosses the city's western edge. Numerous other roads also converge here.

Children's Museum and Science Center (up to age 10)

Imperial Centre for Arts and Sciences, 270 Gay St.; (252) 972-1167; www.museum.imperial centre.org. Open 10 a.m. to 5 p.m. Tues, Wed, and Sat; 10 a.m. to 9 p.m. Thurs and Fri; and 1 to 5 p.m. Sun. $; free for children under 3.

The Children's Museum and Science Center, located at the Imperial Centre for the Arts and Sciences includes interactive science exhibits, a digital planetarium, and other pro-gramming. Exhibits include *Extreme Deep,* which brings the sea floor to the surface in dramatic fashion, giving guests the chance to walk on the ocean floor. Other exhibits, including a live animal gallery, introduce visitors to a variety of scientific concepts.

Sunset Park (all ages)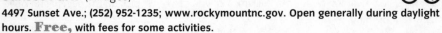

4497 Sunset Ave.; (252) 952-1235; www.rockymountnc.gov. Open generally during daylight hours. Free, with fees for some activities.

Stop at Sunset Park, where you can take a break from driving and have a picnic. You'll also find a miniature train here as well as a merry-go-round, a skate park, and a spray park.

Where to Eat

Gardner's Barbecue. 1331 N. Wesleyan Blvd., (252) 442-0531; 841 Fairview Rd., (252) 442-5522; and Westridge Shopping Center, (252) 443-3996; www.gardnersfoods.com. This is eastern barbecue country and Gard-ner's has built a reputation. $

For More Information

Nash County Travel & Tourism. (800) 849-6825; www.rockymounttravel.com.

Wilson

Head south on US 301 to the town of Wilson, one of the state's premier barbecue locales.

Imagination Station (all ages)

224 E. Nash St.; (252) 291-5113; www.imaginescience.org. **Open 9 a.m. to 5 p.m. Mon through Sat. $; free for children under age 4.**

After grabbing a bite at one of the several restaurants recognized far and wide for quality barbecue beef, pork, and chicken, head to this unusual science center, which has exhibits that will make your hair stand on end. Included are daily science demonstrations on everything from chemistry to electricity, a state-of-the-art computer lab, and dozens of hands-on exhibits. Learn about the human body; see spiders, snakes, and turtles; and discover how strong simple machines make us.

Where to Eat

Parker's Barbecue. US 301 and I-95; (252) 237-0972. Parker's has been in business since 1946. That has to mean something. $

Vollis Simpson's **Whirligigs**

Local farm equipment repairman Vollis Simpson has garnered quite a reputation for himself. The Wilson native began building his extravagant collection of what have been named *whirligigs* at his farm 8 miles south of Wilson nearly 30 years ago. Since then they have been exhibited at the North Carolina Museum of Art, at museums in Boston, at the 1996 Olympics in Atlanta, and in stores in Manhattan. The pieces made of found objects stand as high as 30 feet. Some have reflectors; some make noise; all of them move. Some are simple windmills, while others take the shape of a guitar, a horse, or a man. The address of this display is 7219 Oscar Loop Rd. in Lucama. It's located off Wiggins Mill Road. Stop and ask for directions if you need to!

Windsor

If you choose to head north instead of west from Williamston, you can take US 17 to reach Windsor.

Historic Hope Plantation (ages 5 and up)

132 Hope House Rd.; (252) 794-3140; www.hopeplantation.org. Open 10 a.m. to 3:30 p.m. Mon through Fri, 10 a.m. to 4:30 p.m. Sat, and 2 to 4:30 p.m. Sun. $–$$.

Travel east on Highway 308 from SR 17and you'll find the Historic Hope Plantation. This site includes the circa 1803 home of David Stone, one of North Carolina's governors, and features an extensive library and a fabulous collection of 18th- and 19th-century furniture. Also at the site is the **King-Bazemore House,** built in 1763.

Livermon Recreation Park and Mini-Zoo (all ages)

103 N. York St.; (252) 794-5553. Open 8 a.m. to 8 p.m. Mon through Fri and 9 a.m. to 8 p.m. Sat and Sun during summer, and 8 a.m. to 5 p.m. daily the rest of the year. Free.

Livermon Recreation Park and Mini-Zoo is a great place to stop if you're on the road. Take along the makings for a picnic (grills are available if you want to cook hot dogs or hamburgers) and let the kids run off some steam on the playground equipment. They can also tour the little zoo and see the 30 different varieties of animals, including birds, goats, and a llama. The zoo offers an opportunity to see the animals up close and even pet some of them. Canoes are also available for use at the on-site lake for no charge.

Peanuts! Get your peanuts here!

Peanuts might be more synonymous with the state of Georgia than they are with North Carolina, but they've been cranking out peanuts here for four generations. **Bertie County Peanuts,** 217 US 213, Windsor; (800) 457-0005; www .pnuts.net, began cooking their nuts in a popcorn popper. Now they cook a half-dozen different kinds of peanuts, plus peanut candy and more.

Gatesville

Merchant Millpond State Park (all ages)

SR 1403; (252) 357-1191; www.ncparks.gov. Open during daylight hours. Free, but a fee is charged for camping and canoes.

Sans Soucie **Ferry**

If you've taken a ferry on your trip to the Outer Banks or you're getting ready to, drop by and see the **Sans Soucie Ferry** on the Cashie River. The ferry isn't marked on state maps, but you can find it by taking Highway 308 east from Windsor. Go about 10 miles and take a right onto SR 1500. The ferry is one of three surviving two-car inland river cable ferries in North Carolina. It's open daily, and crossing is **free.**

If you and your family love nature, you'll want to stop at Merchant Millpond State Park near Gatesville. This enchanting park is accessible via US 158 and Highways 32 and 37, but you rarely find big crowds here. With more than 2,900 acres, there is more than enough elbow room. The main feature is a millpond created when the gristmill and dam were constructed in 1811. Here is a chance to canoe through some of North Carolina's oldest cypress trees, some of which may be more than 1,000 years old, with massive trunks rising out of the swamp's blackwater. Canoes are available for rent by the hour, day, or overnight—if you are ready to rough it in the park's canoe-in campground. You can also fish and hike, or you can enjoy one of the interpretive nature programs offered by the park. The park is brimming with wildlife, including turtles, woodpeckers, owls, and other birds, and even two primitive species of fish.

Edenton

To continue your trip, take Highway 37 to Highway 32 south to Edenton.

Historic Edenton (ages 5 and up)

Visitor center located at 108 N. Broad St.; (252) 482-2637. Open 9 a.m. to 5 p.m. Mon through Sat and 1 to 4 p.m. Sun. Admission is free.

Located at the head of Albemarle Sound, this place has been called one of the prettiest towns in the South, and as soon as you drive in, you'll see why. History abounds here, as it does in many of the coastal communities. Today Edenton is largely a retirement community, and many of the inns won't accommodate younger children. The scenery and history, however, make it worth the stop. On the tour you will see the 1782 home of Penelope Barker, who organized the Edenton Tea Party, in which 51 local women showed their support for banning consumption of British tea. It was considered one of the first occasions when women took part in a political act. In addition, the tour will show you the **Chowan County Courthouse** (circa 1767), a very distinguished building from the time; the **James Iredell House** (circa 1773), the residence of one member of the first US Supreme Court; and the **Cupola House** (circa 1758), the state's oldest remaining wooden structure.

For More Information

Chowan County Tourism Development Authority. (800) 775-0111; www.visiteden ton.com.

Hertford

US 17 takes you to SR 1336 and to Hertford.

Newbold-White House (ages 5 and up)

151 Newbold White Rd.; (252) 426-7567. Open 10 a.m. to 4 p.m. Thurs through Sat, April through Oct. $.

Newbold-White House, the oldest brick house in North Carolina, was built on this site, settled in 1685. Did you get that? 1685! That's old! The home has been restored to mint condition and is decorated with 17th-century furnishings.

Elizabeth City

On US 17 you can head east to Elizabeth City. The chamber of commerce (252-335-4365) can provide you with a map for a historic walking tour as well as information on the Albemarle Sound area.

Great Dismal Swamp State Park (ages 5 and up)

2294 US 17 North; (252) 771-6593; www.ncparks.gov. Open 8 a.m. to 5 p.m. daily. Fee for some activities. Admission is free with a fee for some activities.

OK, so this park doesn't have the most inviting name, but it is one of the most spectacular environmental wonders in the state. Running through four counties in northeastern North Carolina and into Virginia's Chesapeake, the largest swamp in the eastern US and its adjacent canal were ravaged by two centuries of logging. So in 1973 the federal government made it a national wildlife refuge and the state of North Carolina created a park on 22 square miles here to further protect the ecology. Here visitors can hike, bike, and explore

S-Shaped **Bridge**

As you travel farther east on US 17, you come to a rather obscure attraction. The S-Shaped Bridge is the only bridge of its kind in the country. Built in 1929, it was constructed to replace a floating bridge that historians have dated to 1798.

Other Things to See & Do
on the Northern Coast

- **Swing Zone.** New Bern; (252) 634-4263; www.swingzone.net
- **Greenville Fun Park.** Greenville; (252) 757-1800
- **Inner Banks Artisan Center.** Washington; (252) 975-2223
- **Portsmouth Island ATV Excursions.** Ocracoke; (252) 928-4484; www.ports mouthislandatvs.com
- **Equine Adventures.** Frisco; (252) 995-4897; www.equineadventures.com
- **Ghost Tours of the Outer Banks.** Manteo; (252) 573-1450; www.ghosttours oftheobx.com
- **Pirate Adventures of The Outer Banks.** Manteo; (252) 489-4881; www .piratesobx.com
- **Blackbeard's Miniature Golf Park.** Nags Head; (252) 441-4541
- **Galaxy Golf.** Nags Head; (252) 441-5875
- **Nags Head Dolphin Watch.** Nags Head; (252) 449-8999; www.nagshead dolphinwatch.com
- **Outer Banks Bear Factory.** Nags Head; (252) 441-1212
- **Outer Banks Standup Paddle.** Duck; (252) 305-3639; www.outerbankssup.com
- **Nags Head Raceway.** Corolla; (252) 480-4639

the swamp in a rented canoe. A visitor center details the history of the swamp, including its role in the Underground Railroad.

Museum of the Albemarle (all ages)

501 S. Water St.; (252) 335-1453; www.museumofthealbemarle.com. Open 10 a.m. to 4 p.m. Tues through Sat. Free.

If you do nothing else in Elizabeth City, see this museum. This branch of the North Carolina Museum of History provides a fine overview, from prehistoric times to the present, of the all-important waterway and the 10 counties that surround it. Here you will see Native American relics and other artifacts from the region. *Crafted from Silver* features an array of tea services, flatware, and other items. From a 1690 tablespoon to 1947 jewelry, the exhibit includes pieces made or owned by North Carolinians. Among those objects are spoons and sugar tongs produced by Edenton silversmiths during the 18th and 19th centuries. In addition, the museum offers a wide array of programs and special events throughout the year. The brightly colored Discovery Room includes periodically changing themes to help tell the story of this region's history to young children.

Appendix:
Events & Celebrations

With glorious weather most of the year, the Tar Heel State has no shortage of fun festivals year-round. From mountain Christmases to fun-filled Fourths at the beach, from coon dogs to wooly worms, you'll find plenty to suit your family. To get more information call (800) VISITNC or check out www.visitnc.com.

We've already covered some of the events North Carolina has offered for years, but here are some additional events that are the state's biggest and most unusual month by month:

JANUARY

American Kennel Club Dog Agility Trial. Fletcher; (828) 687-1414

Kwanzaafest. Durham; (919) 683-1709

Winterfest. Blowing Rock; (877) 295-7801; www.blowingrockwinterfest.com

FEBRUARY

Anniversary at Moores Creek Battlefield. Currie; (910) 283-5591

Annual Model Train Show. Kinston; (252) 527-2517

Carolina Jazz Festival. Chapel Hill; (919) 962-1449

Civil War Living History Day. Elizabeth City; (252) 335-1453; www.elizabethcityhasit.com

Fort Anderson Living History Civil War Reencampment. Wilmington; (910) 371-6613

Kinston Bluegrass Festival. Kinston; (252) 522-5923; www.kinstonwinterbluegrass.com

Southern Spring Show. Charlotte; (800) 849-0248; www.southernshows.com

Sugar Bear's Birthday Celebration. Sugar Mountain; (800) 784-2768; www.skisugar.com

MARCH

Anniversary of the Battle at Guilford Courthouse. Greensboro; (336) 288-1776

NC Renaissance Faire. Raleigh; (866) 468-7630; www.ncrenfaire.com

Pig Pickin' Contest. Newport; (919) 223-7447; www.newportpigcooking.com

St. Patrick's Festival. Emerald Isle; (919) 354-6350

APRIL

Blockhouse Steeplechase. Tryon; (800) 438-3681; www.blockhouseraces.com

Blowing Rock Trout Derby. Blowing Rock; (828) 295-7851; www.blowingrock.com

The Dogwood Festival. Fayetteville; (910) 323-1934; www.faydogwoodfestival.com

Festival of Flowers. Asheville; (877) 245-8667; www.biltmore.com

Food Lion AutoFair. Concord; (800) 455-3267; www.charlottemotorspeedway.com

Merlefest. Wilkesboro; (800) 343-7857; www.merlefest.org

National Whistling Championship. Louisburg; (919) 496-4771; www.whistlingiwc.com

NC Gold Festival. Marion; (800) 959-9033; www.ncgold.org

North Carolina Azalea Festival. Wilmington; (910) 794-4650; www.ncazaleafestival.org

North Carolina Pickle Festival. Mount Olive; (919) 658-3113; www.ncpicklefest.org

Queens Cup Steeplechase. Waxhaw; (704) 843-7070

Topsail Island Spring Fling. Surf City; (910) 328-4722

MAY

Buggy Festival. Carthage; (910) 947-2331; www.thebuggyfestival.com

Chicken Festival. Siler City; (919) 742-3333

Day Out with Thomas the Tank Engine. Blowing Rock; (800) 526-5740

Engelhard Seafood Festival. Engelhard; (252) 542-0419; www.englehardseafoodfestival.com

Flat Rock Music Festival. Flat Rock; (828) 692-2005; www.flatrockmusicfestival.com

Food Lion Speed Street. Charlotte; (704) 455-6814; www.600festival.com

Ham and Yam Festival. Smithfield; (919) 934-0887; www.hamandyam.com

Hang Gliding Spectacular. Nags Head; (877) 359-8447; www.hangglidingspectacular.com

North Carolina Potato Festival. Elizabeth City; (252) 338-4104; www.ncpotatofestival.com

Ramp Festival. Waynesville; (828) 456-8691

White Squirrel Festival. Brevard; (828) 884-3278; www.whitesquirrelfestival.com

JUNE
Gates County Swampfest. Gatesville; (252) 357-0677

Hillsborough Hog Day. Hillsborough; (919) 732-8156; www.hillsboroughchamber.com

North Carolina Rhododendron Festival. Bakersville; (800) 227-3912; www.bakersville.com

Wright Kite Festival. Kill Devil Hills; (877) 359-8447; www.kittyhawk.com

JULY
Bele Chere. Asheville; (828) 259-5800; www.belecherefestival.com

Brevard Music Festival. Brevard; (828) 259-5800

Coon Dog Day. Saluda; (704) 749-2581; www.saluda.com

Day Out with Thomas the Tank Engine. Dillsboro; (800) 872-4681; www.gsmr.com

Eastern Music Festival. Greensboro; (336) 333-7450; www.easternmusicfestival.org

AUGUST
American Legion World Series. Shelby; (704) 466-3847; www.clevelandcountybaseball.com

Annual Sourwood Festival. Black Mountain; (828) 669-2300; www.blackmountain.org

Lazy Daze Arts and Crafts Festival. Cary; (919) 469-4000; www.townofcary.org

Mountain Heritage Day. Mount Mitchell; (828) 675-4611; www.ncparks.gov

NC Mineral and Gem Festival. Spruce Pine; (828) 765-9033; www.ncgemfest.com

Pirate Invasion. Beaufort; (252) 728-5225; www.beaufortpirateinvasion.com

Smokey Bear's Birthday Party. Brevard; (704) 877-3130; www.cradleofforestry.com

Sneads Ferry Shrimp Festival. Sneads Ferry; (910) 327-0432; www.sneadsferryshrimpfestival.com

Virginia Dare's Birthday Celebration. Manteo; (252) 473-3414; www.outerbanks.org

Waldensian Festival. Valedese; (828) 879-2126; www.visitvaldese.com

SEPTEMBER
Ayden Collard Festival. Ayden; (252) 746-7080; www.aydencollardfestival.com

Benson Mule Days. Benson; (919) 894-3825; www.bensonmuledays.com

Carousel Festival. Burlington; (336) 222-5030

A Day Out with Thomas the Tank Engine. Spencer; (704) 636-2889; www.nctrans.org

Festival in the Park. Charlotte; (704) 338-1060; www.festivalinthepark.org

North Carolina Shakespeare Festival. High Point; (336) 841-2273; www.ncshakes.org

OCTOBER
Albemarle Craftsman's Fair. Elizabeth City; (252) 338-3954; www.albemarlecraftsmansfair.com

Cherokee Indian Fair. Cherokee; (800) 438-1601; www.cherokee-nc.com

NC Barbecue Festival. Lexington; www.barbecuefestival.com

North Carolina Chili Festival. Havelock; (252) 447-1101; www.havelockchamber.org

Wooly Worm Festival. Banner Elk; (828) 898-5605; www.woolyworm.com

NOVEMBER
Carolinas Carousel Parade. Charlotte; (704) 525-0250; www.carouselparade.org

Fall Living History Encampment. Kinston; (252) 522-4676

Hog Happenin'. Shelby; (704) 739-7760; www.hoghappenin.com

Holly Festival. Holly Ridge; (910) 329-7081

Southern Christmas Show. Charlotte; (704) 347-8787; www.southernshows.com

DECEMBER
Crystal Coast Christmas Flotilla. Morehead City; (800) 786-6962; www.crystalcoastnc.org

A Dickens Christmas in the Village. Asheville; (888) 561-5437; www.biltmorevillage.com

First Flight Anniversary Celebration. Kill Devil Hills; (252) 441-7430; www.firstflight.org

Holiday Lights at the Garden. Belmont; (704) 825-4490; www.dsbg.org

Santa Express. Dillsboro; (800) 872-4681; www.gsmr.com

Santa Train. Spencer; (704) 636-2889; www.nctrans.org

Tanglewood Festival of Lights. Clemmons; (336) 778-6300; www.tanglewoodpark.org

General Index

Activities Index